UNCITRAL

THE UNITED NATIONS
COMMISSION ON
INTERNATIONAL TRADE LAW

UNCITRAL

THE UNITED NATIONS COMMISSION ON INTERNATIONAL TRADE LAW

UNITED NATIONS

New York, 1986

UNITED NATIONS PUBLICATION
Sales No. E.86.V.8
ISBN 92-1-133284-2
01500 P

Foreword

The object of this book is to acquaint the reader with the United Nations Commission on International Trade Law (UNCITRAL) and its work towards the harmonization and unification of the law of international trade. Its intended audience are persons with an interest in international trade law who wish to learn about the background, organization and functioning of UNCITRAL and about the activities of the Commission in this field, as well as those seeking detailed information about particular texts emanating from the work of the Commission. Persons with interests in the structure and functioning of international organizations and in the role of such organizations in the international harmonization and unification of law should also find it of value.

The book is designed to be of use to scholars, practitioners and researchers, as well as to those with more general interests. Part one of the book gives an account of the origin and mandate of the Commission and describes its organization. It also discusses the Commission's work programme, its methods of work, and its activities other than substantive work on topics within its work programme.

The substantive work of the Commission on topics within its programme of work is described in part two. This part also provides information on actions taken by the General Assembly with respect to projects completed by the Commission, and on diplomatic conferences convened by the General Assembly that have adopted conventions based upon draft texts prepared by the Commission.

The textual material in parts one and two contains liberal references to basic documents and other source material in order to assist researchers and others seeking further information about the subjects discussed. Unless otherwise indicated, documents referred to by document numbers are documents of the United Nations. Where relevant, references are given to the volumes of the *Yearbook of the United Nations Commission on International Trade Law*, which contain reproductions of documents. References to the *Yearbook* are given in brackets as [*Yearbook 19. .*].

The annexes contain legal texts and other material emanating from the work of UNCITRAL, including texts that have been adopted in final form by the Commission and conventions adopted by diplomatic conferences on the basis of draft texts prepared by the Commission. Also reproduced in the annexes is material related to the Commission's work, such as the resolution of the General Assembly that established the Commission and set forth its mandate, and other relevant resolutions of the General Assembly.

The three appendices to the book contain, respectively, lists of Chairmen of the Commission, Chairmen of UNCITRAL working groups and Secretaries of the Commission.

The information in the book is current as at August 1985.

UNCITRAL secretariat
Vienna International Centre
P.O. Box 500
A-1400 Vienna, Austria

CONTENTS

Part One

Introduction to the Commission and its work

I. Origin, mandate and organization of the Commission

A. Origin of the Commission

1. The United Nations Commission on International Trade Law (UNCITRAL) was created by the General Assembly in 1966[1] in order to enable the United Nations to play a more active role in reducing or removing legal obstacles to the flow of international trade. In establishing UNCITRAL, the General Assembly recognized that conflicts and divergencies arising from the laws of different States in matters relating to international trade constitute an obstacle to the development of world trade. The General Assembly considered it desirable that the process of harmonization and unification of the law of international trade be substantially co-ordinated, systematized and accelerated and that a broader participation by States be secured.

2. The events leading to the establishment of the Commission began with the placement of an item entitled "Consideration of steps to be taken for progressive development in the field of private international law with a particular view to promoting international trade" on the agenda of the twentieth session (1965) of the General Assembly, as a result of an initiative taken by the Government of Hungary.[2] In connection with this agenda item, the United Nations Secretariat prepared a preliminary survey on the unification of the law of international trade for the Sixth Committee of the General Assembly.[3] The survey referred to the difficulties faced by parties engaging in international commercial transactions as a result of the multiplicity of and divergencies in national laws, and contained a review of some of the methods by which unification in the field of international trade law might be achieved. On the basis of a recommendation contained in that survey, the General Assembly[4] requested the Secretariat to prepare a comprehensive report on the progressive development of the law of international trade.

3. The Secretariat commissioned Professor Clive Schmitthoff of the City of London College to prepare a preliminary study of the subject as the basis for its report, and consulted with the secretariats of relevant United Nations organs and regional economic commissions, specialized agencies and other inter-

---

[1]General Assembly resolution 2205 (XXI) [*Yearbook 1968-1970*, part one, chap. II, sect. E]. See annex I, below.

[2]*Official Records of the General Assembly, Nineteenth Session, Annex No. 2*, document A/5728 [*Yearbook 1968-1970*, part one, chap. I, sect. A].

[3]"Unification of the law of international trade: note by the Secretariat", *Official Records of the General Assembly, Twentieth Session, Annexes*, agenda item 92, document A/C.6/L.572 [*Yearbook 1968-1970*, part one, chap. I, sect. C].

[4]General Assembly resolution 2102 (XX) [*Yearbook 1968-1970*, part one, chap. II, sect. A].

national governmental and non-governmental organizations. The report noted that some progress had been achieved towards unification and harmonization in certain areas of international trade law, but it also described certain short-comings. Firstly, progress had been slow in relation to the time and effort expended. Secondly, developing countries that had recently obtained independence had only had the opportunity to participate in those efforts to a small degree. Thirdly, none of the agencies that were active in the field had a membership that represented all of the principal geographic regions or all of the principal economic systems in the world. Fourthly, there had been insufficient co-ordination and co-operation among the agencies active in that field.[5] The report proposed the creation by the General Assembly of a new United Nations organ to systematize and accelerate the process of harmonization and unification of the law of international trade and to remedy the shortcomings that had characterized the process.[6]

4.   The report was considered by the Sixth Committee during the twenty-first session (1966) of the General Assembly.[7] On the basis of the deliberations and recommendation of the Sixth Committee, the General Assembly adopted the resolution establishing the Commission.[8]

B.   Mandate of the Commission

5.   The mandate given by the General Assembly to UNCITRAL, as the "core legal body within the United Nations system in the field of international trade law",[9] was to further the progressive harmonization and unification of the law of international trade by:

(a)   Co-ordinating the work of organizations active in this field and encouraging co-operation among them;

(b)   Promoting wider participation in existing international conventions and wider acceptance of existing model and uniform laws;

(c)   Preparing or promoting the adoption of new international conventions, model laws and uniform laws and promoting the codification and wider acceptance of international trade terms, provisions, customs and practices, in collaboration, where appropriate, with the organizations operating in this field;

(d)   Promoting ways and means of ensuring a uniform interpretation and application of international conventions and uniform laws in the field of the law of international trade;

---

[5]"Progressive development of the law of international trade: report of the Secretary-General", *Official Records of the General Assembly, Twenty-first Session, Annexes,* agenda item 88, documents A/6396 and Add.1 and 2 [*Yearbook 1968-1970,* part one, chap. II, sect. B].

[6]*Ibid.,* documents A/6396 and Add.1 and 2, paras. 211-234 [*Yearbook 1968-1970,* part one, chap. II, sect. B].

[7]*Official Records of the General Assembly, Twenty-first Session, Annexes,* agenda item 88, document A/6594 [*Yearbook 1968-1970,* part one, chap. II, sect. D]. The summary records of the proceedings of the Sixth Committee on this item are contained in *Official Records of the General Assembly, Twenty-first Session, Sixth Committee,* 947th-955th meetings [excerpts appear in *Yearbook 1968-1970,* part one, chap. II, sect. C].

[8]General Assembly resolution 2205 (XXI) [*Yearbook 1968-1970,* part one, chap. II, sect. E]. See annex I, below.

[9]See, for example, General Assembly resolution 37/106, para. 7 [*Yearbook 1982,* part one, sect. D].

(e) Collecting and disseminating information on national legislation and modern legal developments, including case law, in the field of the law of international trade;

(f) Establishing and maintaining a close collaboration with the United Nations Conference on Trade and Development;

(g) Maintaining liaison with other United Nations organs and specialized agencies concerned with international trade;

(h) Taking any other action it may deem useful to fulfil its functions.[10]

C. Composition, officers and organization of the Commission

6. The Commission was originally composed of 29 States;[11] its membership was expanded in 1973 to 36 States.[12] Membership is structured so as to be representative of the various geographic regions and the principal economic and legal systems of the world. Thus, nine members are African States, seven are Asian States, five are East European States, six are Latin American States, and nine are West European and other States.[13] Members of the Commission are elected by the General Assembly for terms of six years, the terms of half of the members expiring every three years.[14]

7. At each of its annual sessions,[15] the Commission elects a chairman (appendix I), three vice-chairmen and a rapporteur. These officers constitute the bureau of the Commission. In accordance with a decision taken by the Commission at its first session (1968),[16] the election of the officers is such that each of the five regions mentioned in paragraph 6, above, is represented on the bureau.

8. Much of the preparatory work of the Commission is carried out within working groups and by the UNCITRAL Study Group on International Payments (see chapter II and appendix II). These groups are discussed below.

D. Secretariat of the Commission

9. The International Trade Law Branch of the United Nations Office of Legal Affairs serves as the substantive as well as the administrative secretariat of the Commission. The professional members of the Branch are all trained

---

[10]General Assembly resolution 2205 (XXI), sect. II, para. 8 [*Yearbook 1968-1970*, part one, chap. II, sect. E]. See annex I, below.

[11]*Ibid.*, para. 1 [*Yearbook 1968-1970*, part one, chap. II, sect. E].

[12]General Assembly resolution 3108 (XXVIII), para. 8 [*Yearbook 1974*, part one, chap. I, sect. C].

[13]General Assembly resolution 2205 (XXI), sect. II, para. 1 [*Yearbook 1968-1970*, part one, chap. II, sect. E]; General Assembly resolution 3108 (XXVIII), para. 8 [*Yearbook 1974*, part one, chap. I, sect. C].

[14]General Assembly resolution 2205 (XXI) [*Yearbook 1968-1970*, part one, chap. II, sect. E]; General Assembly resolution 3108 (XXVIII) [*Yearbook 1974*, part one, chap. I, sect. C].

[15]See chapter II, section B.1.

[16]*Official Records of the General Assembly, Twenty-third Session, Supplement No. 16* (A/7216), para. 14 [*Yearbook 1968-1970*, part two, chap. I, sect. A].

lawyers. The UNCITRAL secretariat carries out legal research on subject-matters within the programme of work of UNCITRAL and prepares reports, preliminary draft texts and commentaries on draft legal texts. These documents serve as a basis for the work of the Commission and of its working groups and groups of experts.[17] The UNCITRAL secretariat also prepares the draft reports of sessions of the Commission and its working groups. Thus, it performs functions for the Commission that in some other organs are performed by recognized legal scholars engaged to serve as special rapporteurs in connection with particular topics. The UNCITRAL secretariat also provides or organizes administrative services for meetings of the Commission and of its working groups and groups of experts. Originally located in New York, the International Trade Law Branch was transferred to Vienna in September 1979, after the opening of the Vienna International Centre.

10.   The Chief of the International Trade Law Branch serves as the Secretary of the Commission (appendix III). Each UNCITRAL working group is also served by a Secretary, who is selected by the Chief of the International Trade Law Branch from among the professional members of the Branch. The Secretary of a working group is responsible for and co-ordinates the substantive and administrative services provided by the secretariat to the working group.

---

[17]See chapter II, section B.

II. Programme and methods of work

A. Programme of work

1. *Initial programme of work*

11.   When UNCITRAL was established by the General Assembly in 1966, the Assembly did not assign it specific topics upon which to work. Rather, the Commission itself decided upon the topics that it would take up. At its first session (1968), after considering a number of suggestions by member States, the Commission adopted nine topics as the basis of its future work programme: international sale of goods, international commercial arbitration, transportation, insurance, international payments, intellectual property, elimination of discrimination in laws affecting international trade, agency, and legalization of documents.[1] Priority status was accorded to international sale of goods, international commercial arbitration and international payments. The Commission then chose particular items within each topic to consider separately and in depth.[2] Additional topics, including international legislation on shipping and liability for damage caused by products intended for or involved in international trade, were subsequently added to the Commission's initial programme of work.[3]

2. *Current long-term programme of work*

12.   The Commission established the foundation for its current long-term programme of work at its eleventh session (1978), on the basis of topics suggested by the Secretariat after considering proposals made by Governments and after consulting with various international organizations.[4] The Commission considered that its new work programme should be composed of topics that

---

[1] *Official Records of the General Assembly, Twenty-third Session, Supplement No. 16* (A/7216), paras. 40 and 48 [*Yearbook 1968-1970*, part two, chap. I, sect. A].

[2] *Ibid.*, para. 48 [*Yearbook 1968-1970*, part two, chap. I, sect. A].

[3] See chapter VII, section A and chapter XII.

[4] *Official Records of the General Assembly, Thirty-third Session, Supplement No. 17* (A/33/17), paras. 37-71 [*Yearbook 1978*, part one, chap. II, sect. A]; *ibid., Thirty-first Session, Supplement No. 17* (A/31/17), paras. 65 and 66 [*Yearbook 1976*, part one, chap. II, sect. A]; "Programme of work of the Commission: report of the Secretary-General" (A/CN.9/149 and Corr.1 and 2 and Add.1-3) [*Yearbook 1978*, part two, chap. IV, sect. A]; "Co-ordination of work between the Commission and other international organizations: note by the Secretary-General" (A/CN.9/154); "Programme of work of the Commission: recommendations of the Asian-African Legal Consultative Committee: note by the Secretary-General" (A/CN.9/155) [*Yearbook 1978*, part two, chap. IV, sect. B, pp. 195-196]; and "Programme of work of the Commission: proposal by France: note by the Secretary-General" (A/CN.9/156) [*Yearbook 1978*, part two, chap. IV, sect. C].

had global significance and should include topics of special interest to developing countries.[5] Accordingly, it selected a number of topics, which were accorded priority.[6] Additional topics have been added to the Commission's programme of work, subsequent to its eleventh session, on the basis of proposals arising from within the Commission[7] as well as from the international community.[8]

B. Methods of work

1. *The Commission*

13.   The Commission carries out its work at its annual sessions, which are held alternately in New York at the United Nations Headquarters and in Vienna, the seat of the UNCITRAL secretariat.[9]

14.   The Commission reports to the General Assembly on the work done at each of its annual sessions. These reports are also submitted to the Trade and Development Board of the United Nations Conference on Trade and Development (UNCTAD) for its comments.[10]

2. *Working groups and study group*

15.   The substantive preparatory work on topics within the Commission's programme of work is usually assigned by the Commission to one of its working groups.[11] There are currently three UNCITRAL working groups, whose membership varies according to the subject-matter to be dealt with,

---

[5]*Official Records of the General Assembly, Thirty-third Session, Supplement No. 17* (A/33/17), para. 43 [*Yearbook 1978,* part one, chap. II, sect. A].

[6]*Ibid.,* paras. 67-69 [*Yearbook 1978,* part one, chap. II, sect. A].

[7]For example, as a result of the Commission's work on international contracts for the construction of industrial works (see chapter VIII); see *Official Records of the General Assembly, Thirty-third Session, Supplement No. 17* (A/33/17), para. 71 [*Yearbook 1978,* part one, chap. II, sect. A]; *ibid., Thirty-fourth Session, Supplement No. 17* (A/34/17), paras. 89-100 [*Yearbook 1979,* part one, chap. II, sect. A]; *ibid., Thirty-fifth Session, Supplement No. 17* (A/35/17), paras. 118-143 [*Yearbook 1980,* part one, chap. II, sect. A]; *ibid., Thirty-sixth Session, Supplement No. 17* (A/36/17), paras. 71-84 [*Yearbook 1981,* part one, sect. A]. Similarly, topics arose from the Commission's work on legal aspects of automatic data processing (see chapter XI), *Official Records of the General Assembly, Thirty-ninth Session, Supplement No. 17* (A/39/17), paras. 133-136 [*Yearbook 1984,* part one, sect. A].

[8]For example, the topic of liability of operators of transport terminals (see chapter VII, section B); see also *Official Records of the General Assembly, Thirty-eighth Session, Supplement No. 17* (A/38/17), paras. 109-115 [*Yearbook 1983,* part one, sect. A]; *ibid., Thirty-ninth session, Supplement No. 17* (A/39/17), paras. 105-113 [*Yearbook 1984,* part one, sect. A].

[9]Report of the Committee on Conferences, *Official Records of the General Assembly, Thirty-fourth Session, Supplement No. 32* (A/34/32), para. 32 *(e)* (iii). Prior to the transfer of the UNCITRAL secretariat from New York to Vienna, sessions of the Commission alternated between New York and Geneva; see General Assembly resolution 2205 (XXI), section II, para. 6 [*Yearbook 1968-1970,* part one, chap. II, sect. E]; General Assembly resolution 31/140, sect. I, para. 4 *(c).*

[10]See General Assembly resolution 2205 (XXI), section II, para. 10 [*Yearbook 1968-1970,* part one, chap. II, sect. E]. See annex I, below.

[11]Exceptions to this practice were the drafting of the UNCITRAL Arbitration Rules (see chapter VI, section A.1) and the Legal Guide on Electronic Funds Transfers (see chapter XI, section A).

which is assigned by the Commission. At present, two working groups, the Working Group on the New International Economic Order and the Working Group on International Contract Practices, are composed of all member States of the Commission. Each working group typically holds one or two sessions a year, depending on the subject-matter to be covered; these sessions also alternate between New York and Vienna. A chairman is elected at each session of a working group to preside over the session (appendix II). At the end of each session, the working group prepares a report to the Commission on the work carried out at the session.

16.   At its eleventh session, the Commission adopted the following general policy concerning the referral of a topic to a working group:

"As a general rule, the Commission should not refer subject-matters to a working group until after preparatory studies had been made by the Secretariat and the consideration of these studies by the Commission had indicated not only that the subject-matter was a suitable one in the context of the unification and harmonization of a law, but that the preparatory work was sufficiently advanced for a working group to commence work in a profitable manner."[12]

Furthermore, the Commission has adopted a policy of refraining from dealing with a subject-matter while it is being dealt with in a working group.[13]

17.   For most sessions of an UNCITRAL working group, the Secretariat prepares background research studies analysing various aspects of the subject under consideration by the working group. Such studies examine the existing law at both the national and international levels, highlight problems and difficulties in the application and interpretation of existing law and suggest possible approaches or solutions. If work on a topic is directed towards the formulation of legal rules, the Secretariat prepares drafts of the rules, and sometimes commentaries on draft rules, to serve as a basis for the deliberations of the working group. The preparation of the Legal Guide on drawing up International Contracts for the Construction of Industrial Works[14] was carried out by the Working Group on the New International Economic Order on the basis of draft chapters of the Legal Guide prepared by the Secretariat.

18.   The UNCITRAL Study Group on International Payments is composed of experts from international organizations and banking and trade institutions. It has been involved in work on such matters as the draft conventions on international negotiable instruments,[15] the Legal Guide on Electronic Funds Transfers,[16] and the provisions for a universal unit of account of constant value for use in international transport and liability conventions.[17]

---

[12] *Official Records of the General Assembly, Thirty-third Session, Supplement No. 17* (A/33/17), paras. 67 and 68 [*Yearbook 1978,* part one, chap. II, sect. A]. This general policy was departed from with respect to the work of the Commission in the area of international contracts for the construction of industrial works (see chapter VIII).

[13] *Official Records of the General Assembly, Thirty-sixth Session, Supplement No. 17* (A/36/17), para. 92 (1) *(c)* [*Yearbook 1971,* part one, chap. II, sect. A].

[14] See chapter VIII.

[15] See chapter V.

[16] See chapter XI, section A.

[17] See chapter X.

3. Participation at sessions of the Commission and its working groups

19.   Member States are encouraged to send representatives that are expert in the fields to be dealt with to sessions of the Commission and its working groups. Because of the importance of having all interested parties participate in the development of a text for the unification of law, from its early stages to its final form, all States that are not members of the Commission, as well as interested international organizations, are invited to attend sessions of the Commission and its working groups as observers.[18] States Members of the Commission that are not members of a particular working group may, of course, also attend sessions of the working group as observers. Observers are permitted to participate in discussions in the Commission and working groups to the same extent as members. By tradition, decisions in sessions of the Commission and its working groups are taken by consensus.[19]

4. Group of Experts

20.   The Secretariat has consulted an *Ad Hoc* Group of Experts in the New International Economic Order in connection with the preparation of draft chapters of the Legal Guide on drawing up International Contracts for the Construction of Industrial Works.[20] This group is composed of individual practising lawyers as well as representatives of certain organizations with expertise in the field of industrial works contracts.

5. Finalization and adoption of uniform legal rules

21.   After a working group has prepared a draft text of a convention or model law, the Commission sometimes requests the Secretariat to prepare an explanatory commentary on the draft text in order to assist the Commission or Governments and international organizations in considering the draft text. In most cases, the text drafted by the working group, together with the commentary, if any, is circulated to Governments and interested international organizations for their comments. The Secretariat prepares an analysis of the comments received and the draft text is then revised, either by the working group or by the Commission itself. After the revision, the text is finalized and adopted by the Commission.

22.   In the case of a draft convention adopted by the Commission, the practice of the Commission has been to recommend that the General Assembly convene an international conference of plenipotentiaries to conclude a convention on the basis of the text adopted by the Commission. The General Assembly has followed the recommendation of the Commission in each case. When a draft convention is to be considered by a conference of plenipotentiaries, the General Assembly requests the Secretariat to circulate the draft convention

---

[18] General Assembly resolution 31/99, para. 10 *(c)* [*Yearbook 1977,* part one, chap. I, sect. C]; see also General Assembly resolution 36/32, para. 9 [*Yearbook 1981,* part one, sect. D].

[19] *Official Records of the General Assembly, Twenty-third Session, Supplement No. 16* (A/7216), para. 18 [*Yearbook 1968-1970,* part two, chap. I, sect. A].

[20] See chapter VIII.

adopted by the Commission to Governments and interested international organizations for their comments. The Commission may also request the Secretariat to prepare a commentary on the text as adopted by the Commission; if so, the commentary is circulated with the text. The Secretariat prepares an analysis of the comments received and this analysis, together with the text itself and the commentary, if any, is placed before the conference of plenipotentiaries. In one instance, the conference of plenipotentiaries requested the Secretariat to prepare a commentary on a convention that it had concluded.[21]

6. Techniques to promote harmonization and unification of the law of international trade

23. The Commission has adopted a flexible and functional approach with respect to the techniques that it uses to further the harmonization and unification of the law of international trade.[22] The techniques that have been used by the Commission to date include the following:

(a) International conventions;

(b) Model treaty provisions, to be incorporated in future treaties or to be used in revisions of existing treaties;

(c) Uniform legal rules designed to serve as models for legislation by States (model laws);

(d) Sets of uniform rules to be incorporated by parties in their contracts or other agreements;

(e) Legal guides, identifying legal issues arising in a particular area, discussing various approaches and suggesting possible solutions, in order to establish international common understanding in particular fields, or to promote healthier and more uniform practices in such fields;

(f) Recommendations encouraging Governments and international organizations that elaborate legal texts to eliminate unnecessary legal hindrances to international trade.

24. The Commission considers a number of factors in deciding upon the most appropriate technique to use in a particular case. In some areas, such as the international sale of goods,[23] carriage of goods by sea,[24] and international commercial arbitration,[25] the Commission has sought to harmonize and unify the law by elaborating uniform legal rules. In these areas the law under various national legal systems is well developed and the jurisprudential bases and the practical consequences of the existing legal rules are well known. On the basis of its consideration and evaluation of these factors, the Commission has been

---

[21]The Convention on the Limitation Period in the International Sale of Goods (New York, 1974); see chapter IV, section A.

[22]In this connection, see also "Question of co-ordination: direction of the work of the Commission: report of the Secretary-General" (A/CN.9/203), paragraphs 99-122 [Yearbook 1981, part two, chap. V, sect. 8]; "Alternative methods for the final adoption of conventions emanating from the work of the Commission: note by the Secretariat" (A/CN.9/204) [Yearbook 1981, part two, chap. VIII].

[23]See chapter IV.

[24]See chapter VII, section A.

[25]See chapter VI, section A.

able to harmonize and unify divergent and often conflicting approaches to the issues in question by elaborating uniform legal rules governing these issues.

25.   The Commission has sometimes cast its uniform rules in the form of a multilateral convention where, for example, it has considered it desirable and possible to deal comprehensively with an area and to achieve complete uniformity of law through the elaboration of rules in a mandatory form. This technique was adopted in the international sale of goods and the carriage of goods by sea. In other cases, however, it has cast its uniform rules in different, non-mandatory, forms. For example, in the area covered by the UNCITRAL Model Law on International Commercial Arbitration,[26] the Commission considered that complete uniformity was desirable but not absolutely necessary. Moreover, it considered that the objective of harmonization of law in this area could be achieved most effectively and efficiently by enabling States to agree on a set of uniform rules that was a model and that their legislatures could, if necessary, adapt to the circumstances and requirements of their countries in implementing the rules. The desirability of elaborating rules to be used by parties to a commercial transaction at their option, and to be adapted by the parties to their particular needs, also underlies the formulation, by the Commission, of the UNCITRAL Arbitration Rules.[27]

26.   In some areas the Commission has not considered it appropriate to elaborate uniform legal rules—for example, owing to the lack of maturity of the national legal rules governing the area and the fact that States have not had sufficient occasion to evolve their positions on the issues concerned (as in the cases of electronic funds transfers[28] and the legal value of computer records[29]), owing to the difficulty of formulating a single set of rules governing a wide variety of different situations (as in the case of industrial works contracts[30]) or because approaches under national law are too disparate to permit effective unification by means of uniform rules at that particular time. In such cases the Commission has sought first to establish an international common understanding as to the legal issues emerging or existing in these areas. In the cases of industrial works contracts and electronic funds transfers, it decided to prepare legal guides discussing the issues arising in these areas and recommending possible solutions to them, in order to assist the relevant parties to deal with the issues in their respective contexts. In the case of the legal value of computer records, it adopted a recommendation encouraging Governments and international organizations elaborating legal texts relating to trade to review their existing rules in order to remove obstacles to the use of automatic data processing and facilitate the use of this technique where appropriate.

---

[26]See chapter VI, section A.3.

[27]See chapter VI, section A.1.

[28]See chapter XI, section A.

[29]See chapter XI, section B.

[30]See chapter VIII.

III. Other activities of the Commission

A. Co-ordinating the work of other organizations

27. An important part of the mandate of UNCITRAL is to co-ordinate the activities of organizations in the field of international trade law, in order to avoid duplication of efforts and to promote efficiency, consistency and coherence in the unification and harmonization of law in this field. The Secretariat regularly prepares studies to assist the Commission in monitoring activities and developments worldwide in international trade law. These studies are of two types: the first consists of general surveys of the activities of other organizations related to international trade law;[1] in the second, the Secretariat selects particular areas of international trade law and reports in depth on the activities of organizations in those areas.[2] In addition, at the annual sessions of UNCITRAL, reports are presented by various international organizations of their activities in the field of international trade law.

B. Promoting the work of other organizations

28. The Commission, when appropriate, takes concrete steps with respect to work performed by other bodies. For example, the Commission has endorsed the Convention on the Recognition and Enforcement of Foreign Arbitral Awards,[3] expressing its opinion that the Convention should be adhered to by the largest possible number of States, and has encouraged ratification of the European Convention on International Commercial Arbitration (Geneva,

---

[1]Pursuant to General Assembly resolution 34/142 [*Yearbook 1980,* part one, chap. I, sect. C]; see, for example, "Current activities of international organizations related to the harmonization and unification of international trade law: report of the Secretary-General" (A/CN.9/237 and Add.1-3 and Add.1/Corr.1 (English only)) [*Yearbook 1983,* part two, chap. V, sect. B].

[2]*Official Records of the General Assembly, Thirty-sixth Session, Supplement No. 17* (A/36/17), para. 100 [*Yearbook 1981,* part one, sect. A]; see, for example, "Co-ordination of work: international transport documents: report of the Secretary-General" (A/CN.9/225 and Corr.1 (French only)) [*Yearbook 1982,* part two, chap. VI, sect. B].

[3]United Nations, *Treaty Series,* vol. 330, p. 38, No. 4739 (1959). See *Official Records of the General Assembly, Twenty-fourth Session, Supplement No. 18* (A/7618), para. 112 [*Yearbook 1968-1970,* part two, chap. II, sect. A]; *ibid., Twenty-fifth Session, Supplement No. 17* (A/8017), para. 156 [*Yearbook 1968-1970,* part two, chap. III, sect. A]. See also *Official Records of the General Assembly, Twenty-eighth Session, Supplement No. 17* (A/9017), para. 85 [*Yearbook 1973,* part one, chap. II, sect. A]; *ibid., Thirty-fourth Session, Supplement No. 17* (A/34/17), para. 81 [*Yearbook 1979,* part one, chap. II, sect. A].

1961).[4] It has also recommended the use of Incoterms[5] and the Uniform Customs and Practice for Documentary Credits,[6] both of which have been prepared by the International Chamber of Commerce (ICC). The Commission has also assisted in the dissemination of general conditions of sale, promulgated by the United Nations Economic Commission for Europe and by the Council for Mutual Economic Assistance.[7]

29. The Commission actively co-operates and consults with other organs and organizations. It co-operated with UNCTAD in connection with UNCITRAL's work on the United Nations Convention on the Carriage of Goods by Sea, 1978 (Hamburg).[8] It consulted with various organs and organizations concerned with international commercial arbitration in connection with its own work in this area,[9] and with the ICC in the areas of bankers' commercial credits and bank guarantees.[10] In addition, it has taken up a project of the International Institute for the Unification of Private Law (UNIDROIT) on the liability of operators of transport terminals, and is receiving the co-operation of UNCTAD in this project.[11] The UNCITRAL secretariat further assists the Commission in the performance of its co-ordinating function by attending meetings and seminars and participating in activities sponsored by other organizations.

C.   Training and assistance in the field of international trade law

30.   The Commission is actively pursuing its mandate to promote training and assistance in international trade law by sponsoring symposia and seminars in this field. The Commission has itself held UNCITRAL Symposia on International Trade Law.[12] It has also organized regional seminars in this field jointly with regional organizations and with Governments.[13] These symposia and seminars are designed to promote awareness by lawyers and other interested parties, particularly from developing countries, of issues and

---

[4]*Official Records of the General Assembly, Twenty-eighth Session, Supplement No. 17* (A/9017), para. 85 [*Yearbook 1973*, part one, chap. II, sect. A].

[5]*Official Records of the General Assembly, Twenty-fourth Session, Supplement No. 18* (A/7618), para. 60 (3) [*Yearbook 1968-1970*, part two, chap. II, sect. A].

[6]*Official Records of the General Assembly, Thirtieth Session, Supplement No. 17* (A/10017), para. 41 [*Yearbook 1975*, part one, chap. II, sect. A]; *Official Records of the General Assembly, Thirty-ninth Session, Supplement No. 17* (A/39/17), para. 129; see also chapter XII.

[7]*Official Records of the General Assembly, Twenty-fourth Session, Supplement No. 18* (A/7618), para. 60 [*Yearbook 1968-1970*, part two, chap. II, sect. A].

[8]See chapter VII, section A and annex VII, section A.

[9]See chapter VI.

[10]See chapter XII.

[11]See chapter VII, section B.

[12]See *Official Records of the General Assembly, Thirtieth Session, Supplement No. 17* (A/10017), paras. 106, 107, 113 [*Yearbook 1975*, part one, chap. II, sect. A]; *Official Records of the General Assembly, Thirty-sixth Session, Supplement No. 17* (A/36/17), paras. 102-104 [*Yearbook 1981*, part one, sect. A].

[13]See *Official Records of the General Assembly, Thirty-eighth Session, Supplement No. 17* (A/38/17), paras. 125-130 [*Yearbook 1983*, part one, sect. A]; *Official Records of the General Assembly, Thirty-ninth Session, Supplement No. 17* (A/39/17), paras. 137-143 [*Yearbook 1984*, part one, sect. A].

developments in international trade law, and also to promote widespread utilization of the Commission's work in this field.

31. Each year, a limited number of persons who have recently obtained a law degree, or who have nearly completed their work towards such a degree, are given the opportunity to serve as interns in the International Trade Law Branch. Interns are assigned specific tasks in connection with projects being worked on by the Secretariat. Persons participating in this internship programme are thus able to become familiar with the work of UNCITRAL and to increase their knowledge of specific areas in the field of international trade law. The Branch also accommodates scholars and legal practitioners occasionally for limited periods of time and grants them access to the UNCITRAL Law Library in connection with work on their own projects in international trade law.

D. Disseminating information

32. The Commission takes various other steps to disseminate information about its work and about international trade law in general. Annually, the Commission publishes a *Yearbook* relating to its work during the year covered. The *Yearbook* reproduces nearly all of the documents prepared by the Secretariat over the course of the year for the Commission and its working groups. It also reproduces reports of sessions of the Commission and its working groups, as well as other information, including reports of the Sixth Committee of the General Assembly, General Assembly resolutions relating to the work of UNCITRAL, and a bibliography of writings related to this work.

33. The Commission has also published a two-volume *Register of Texts of Conventions and other Instruments concerning International Trade Law.*[14] Volume I reproduces texts emanating from organizations and sources other than UNCITRAL in the areas of international sale of goods and international payments, and lists texts in the areas of international commercial arbitration and international legislation on shipping. Volume II reproduces texts in the areas of international commercial arbitration and international legislation on shipping.

---

[14]United Nations publications, Sales Nos. E.71.V.3 (vol. I) and E.73.V.3 (vol. II).

Part Two

Topics dealt with by the Commission

IV. International sale of goods

34. International sale of goods was one of the topics on the original programme of work of UNCITRAL that was accorded priority by the Commission at its first session.[1] In view of the wide scope and complex nature of this topic, the Commission decided to focus on particular aspects of it, including time-limits and limitations (prescription) in the international sale of goods, and the two Hague Conventions of 1964, which set forth uniform legal rules governing the international sale of goods (Convention relating to a Uniform Law on the International Sale of Goods (The Hague, 1 July 1964), Convention relating to a Uniform Law on the Formation of Contracts for the International Sale of Goods (The Hague, 1 July 1964)).[2] The work of the Commission in these areas led to the Convention on the Limitation Period in the International Sale of Goods (New York, 1974) and to the United Nations Convention on Contracts for the International Sale of Goods (Vienna, 1980).

A. Limitation (prescription) period in the international sale of goods

35. During the second session of the Commission in 1969,[3] it was observed that there were numerous disparities among national legal systems with respect to rules according to which legal claims would be extinguished or barred unless presented to a tribunal within a specified period of time. Such disparities were seen to create practical difficulties with respect to claims arising from international commercial transactions. In view of the time that might be needed for negotiations and then for the institution of legal proceedings in a foreign and, often, distant country, some limitation or prescription periods seemed too short to meet the practical requirements of such transactions. Other periods seemed inappropriately long for transactions involving the international sale of goods and failed to provide the basic protection that limitation or prescription rules were intended to accord, such as protection from the uncertainty and threat to business stability posed by the delayed presentation of claims and from the loss or staleness of evidence pertaining to claims presented with undue delay. Not only did national rules differ, but in many instances they were also difficult to apply in claims arising from international sales transactions, a problem that was magnified by the fact that merchants and their lawyers were

---

[1] See chapter II, section A.1.

[2] *Official Records of the General Assembly, Twenty-third Session, Supplement No. 16* (A/7216), para. 48 (II) [*Yearbook 1968-1970,* part two, chap. I, sect. A]. The two Conventions are hereinafter referred to as the Hague Conventions and the annexed uniform laws are hereinafter referred to as the Uniform Laws.

[3] *Official Records of the General Assembly, Twenty-fourth Session, Supplement No. 18* (A/7618), paras. 40-47 [*Yearbook 1968-1970,* part two, chap. II, sect. A].

often unfamiliar with the import of legal rules and with techniques of interpretation used in foreign legal systems.

36.   Perhaps even more serious was the uncertainty as to which national law would be applicable in an international sales transaction. Apart from the problems of choice of law that customarily arose in an international transaction, prescription or limitation presented a special problem because of the differences in characterization or qualification given to these rules: some legal systems considered them to be substantive, and therefore subject to choice of law rules; some systems considered them to be part of the procedural rules of the forum; and other systems followed a combination of these two approaches.

37.   It was believed that the problems arising from the divergencies among national rules in this area were sufficiently serious to justify the preparation of uniform international legal rules on prescription or limitation of claims arising from the international sale of goods. The Commission established the Working Group on Time-limits and Limitations (Prescription) in the International Sale of Goods, and instructed it to study the topic with a view to the preparation of a preliminary draft of an international convention.[4]

38.   In 1972, the Commission approved the text of a draft Convention on Prescription (Limitation) in the International Sale of Goods, which had been prepared by the working group, and recommended that the General Assembly convene an international conference of plenipotentiaries to adopt a convention on this subject.[5] The General Assembly convened the United Nations Conference on Prescription (Limitation) in the International Sale of Goods from 20 May to 14 June 1974, at United Nations Headquarters.[6] The Convention on the Limitation Period in the International Sale of Goods (New York, 1974) was adopted by the Conference on 12 June 1974.[7] At the request of the Conference,[8] a Commentary on the Convention was subsequently prepared.[9] The General Assembly has invited all States to consider the possibility of signing, ratifying or acceding to the Convention.[10]

---

[4]*Ibid.*, para. 46 [*Yearbook 1968-1970*, part two, chap. II, sect. A].

[5]*Official Records of the General Assembly, Twenty-seventh Session, Supplement No. 17* (A/8717), para. 20 [*Yearbook 1972*, part one, chap. II, sect. A]. The text of the draft Convention as approved by the Commission is contained in paragraph 21 of the report and in A/CONF.63/4 (reproduced in *Official Records of the United Nations Conference on Prescription (Limitation) in the International Sale of Goods*, part one, sect. B) (United Nations publication, Sales No. E.74.V.8). The text of a commentary on the draft Convention prepared by the Secretariat appears in A/CN.9/73 [*Yearbook 1972*, part two, chap. I, sect. B.3] and in A/CONF.63/5 (reproduced in *Official Records of the United Nations Conference on Prescription (Limitation) in the International Sale of Goods*, part one, sect. C).

[6]General Assembly resolution 3104 (XXVIII) [*Yearbook 1974*, part one, chap. I, sect. C]; see also General Assembly resolution 2929 (XXVII) [*Yearbook 1973*, part one, chap. I, sect. C].

[7]"Final act of the United Nations Conference on Prescription (Limitation) in the International Sale of Goods" (A/CONF.63/14 and Corr.1) [*Yearbook 1974*, part three, chap. I, sect. A] (reproduced in *Official Records of the United Nations Conference on Prescription (Limitation) in the International Sale of Goods, . . .*, part one). The Convention appears in A/CONF.63/15 [*Yearbook 1974*, part three, chap. I, sect. B] (reproduced in *Official Records of the United Nations Conference on Prescription (Limitation) in the International Sale of Goods, . . .*, part one); see also annex II, A, below.

[8]Summary records of the 10th plenary meeting, paras. 74-77, *Official Records of the United Nations Conference on Prescription (Limitation) in the International Sale of Goods, . . .*, part two.

[9]A/CONF.63/17 [*Yearbook 1979*, part three, chap. I]; see also annex II, B, below.

[10]General Assembly resolution 3317 (XXIX) [*Yearbook 1975*, part three, chap. I, sect. B]; see also annex II, C, below.

39. In 1980, the Convention was amended by a protocol adopted by the United Nations Conference on Contracts for the International Sale of Goods, in order to harmonize the Convention with the United Nations Convention on Contracts for the International Sale of Goods (Vienna, 1980).[11]

B. Contracts for the international sale of goods

40. The work of the Commission in the area of contracts for the international sale of goods was the culmination of a long process of unification in this area, the origins of which go back to a decision of the International Institute for the Unification of Private Law (UNIDROIT) in 1930 to proceed with the preparation of a uniform law on the international sale of goods.[12] The work of UNIDROIT, with an interruption between 1939 and 1951 due to the Second World War, carried on into the early 1960s, and resulted in the convening of a diplomatic conference at The Hague in 1964. The conference had before it two draft texts prepared by UNIDROIT, one of a uniform law on the international sale of goods, and the other of a uniform law on formation of contracts for the international sale of goods. The Hague conference adopted the two uniform laws, annexing them to the two Hague Conventions.

41. By the time of the first session of UNCITRAL (1968), the Hague Conventions had not yet come into force, since they had each received only three of the five necessary ratifications. The Commission considered it desirable to determine the position of States with respect to the Hague Conventions and requested the Secretary-General to circulate a questionnaire to that end to States Members of the United Nations and to States members of any of its specialized agencies. At the same time, the Commission also invited States to submit to it studies on the two Hague Conventions.[13]

42. The replies and studies received[14] were considered by the Commission at its second (1969) and third (1970) sessions. At the second session, some representatives expressed the view that the Uniform Laws annexed to the Hague Conventions were suitable and practical instruments, and that an effort should not at that time be undertaken to revise them. Other representatives, however, believed that the Uniform Laws were not suitable for world-wide

[11]Protocol amending the Convention on the Limitation Period in the International Sale of Goods, "Final Act of the United Nations Conference on Contracts for the International Sale of Goods" (A/CONF.97/18), annex II [*Yearbook 1980*, part three, chap. I, sect. C] (reproduced in *Official Records of the United Nations Conference on Contracts for the International Sale of Goods*, United Nations publication, Sales No. 81.IV.3, part one). See also annex II, D, below.

[12]See "Historical introduction to the draft Convention on Contracts for the International Sale of Goods", prepared by the Secretariat (reproduced in *Official Records of the United Nations Conference on Contracts for the International Sale of Goods*, , part one, sect. B) (originally published as the introduction to document A/CONF.97/5).

[13]*Official Records of the General Assembly, Twenty-third Session, Supplement No. 16* (A/7216), para. 48 (13-15) [*Yearbook 1968-1970*, part two, chap. I, sect. A].

[14]"Replies and studies by States concerning the Hague Conventions of 1964: note by the Secretary-General" (A/CN.9/11 and Corr.1, and Add.1-4). See also the analyses of these replies and studies prepared by the Secretariat: "International sale of goods: The Hague Conventions of 1964: Analysis of the replies and studies received from Governments: report of the Secretary-General" (A/CN.9/17); "Analysis of the studies and comments by Governments on the Hague Conventions of 1964: report of the Secretary-General" (A/CN.9/31) [*Yearbook 1968-1970*, part three, chap. I, sect. A.1].

acceptance.[15] The Commission decided to create a Working Group on the International Sale of Goods, and instructed it to ascertain whether the Uniform Laws could be modified so as to render them capable of wider acceptance by countries of different legal, social and economic systems, or whether it would be necessary to elaborate a new text. The working group was also instructed to consider ways of preparing and promoting a more widely acceptable text.[16] The working group gave priority to the consideration of the Uniform Law on the International Sale of Goods (ULIS), and took up the Uniform Law on the Formation of Contracts for the International Sale of Goods (ULFC) upon completion of its work on ULIS.[17]

43.   By 1975, the working group had considered and prepared revisions of a number of articles of ULIS, and it decided to draft the revised text in the form of an integrated convention, rather than in the form of a uniform law annexed to a convention, as had been the case with ULIS.[18] The working group approved the text of a draft Convention on the International Sale of Goods in 1976.[19] On the basis of the draft text prepared by the working group, the Commission approved a draft Convention on the International Sale of Goods in 1977.[20]

44.   After completing the revision of ULIS, the working group devoted its eighth and ninth sessions to a consideration of the formation and validity of contracts for the international sale of goods. It based its deliberations on the 1964 Hague Uniform Law on the Formation of Contracts for the International Sale of Goods and a draft prepared by UNIDROIT of a law for the unification of certain rules relating to the validity of contracts of international sale of goods. In 1977 the working group approved the text of a draft Convention on the Formation of Contracts for the International Sale of Goods.[21] At the request of the working group the Secretariat prepared a commentary on the draft Convention.[22]

45.   The Commission decided to integrate the draft Convention on the Formation of Contracts and the draft Convention on the International Sale of

---

[15] *Official Records of the General Assembly, Twenty-fourth Session, Supplement No. 18* (A/7618), paras. 18-31 [*Yearbook 1968-1970*, part two, chap. II, sect. A].

[16] *Ibid.*, para. 38 [*Yearbook 1968-1970*, part two, chap. II, sect. A].

[17] See *Official Records of the General Assembly, Twenty-fifth Session, Supplement No. 17* (A/8017), para. 72 [*Yearbook 1968-1970*, part two, chap. III, sect. A].

[18] "Report of the Working Group on the International Sale of Goods on the work of its sixth session" (A/CN.9/100), para. 13 [*Yearbook 1975*, part two, chap. I, sect. 1].

[19] "Report of the Working Group on the International Sale of Goods on the work of its seventh session" (A/CN.9/116) [*Yearbook 1976*, part two, chap. I, sect. 1]; the draft Convention approved by the working group is set forth in annex I to the report and a commentary prepared by the Secretariat is set forth in annex II.

[20] *Official Records of the General Assembly, Thirty-second Session, Supplement No. 17* (A/32/17), para. 34 [*Yearbook 1977*, part one, chap. II, sect. A]. The text of the draft Convention approved by the Commission is set forth in paragraph 35 of the report.

[21] "Report of the Working Group on the International Sale of Goods on the work of its ninth session" (A/CN.9/142) [*Yearbook 1978*, part two, chap. I, sect. A]. The text of the draft Convention as approved by the working group is set forth in A/CN.9/142/Add.1.

[22] "Commentary on the draft Convention on the Formation of Contracts for the International Sale of Goods: report of the Secretary-General" (A/CN.9/144) [*Yearbook 1978*, part two, chap. I, sect. D].

Goods into a single text,[23] which became the draft Convention on Contracts for the International Sale of Goods.[24]

46. Upon the recommendation of the Commission, the General Assembly convened the United Nations Conference on Contracts for the International Sale of Goods from 10 March to 11 April 1980 at Vienna.[25] The United Nations Convention on Contracts for the International Sale of Goods (Vienna, 1980) was adopted on 10 April 1980.[26] The Conference also adopted a protocol amending the Convention on the Limitation Period in the International Sale of Goods (New York, 1974),[27] in order to harmonize the provisions of that Convention,[28] in respect of sphere of application, with those of the Convention on Contracts for the International Sale of Goods.[29]

---

[23] *Official Records of the General Assembly, Thirty-third Session, Supplement No. 17* (A/33/17), para. 18 [*Yearbook 1978,* part one, chap. II, sect. A].

[24] *Ibid.,* para. 27 [*Yearbook 1978,* part one, chap. II, sect. A]. The text of the draft Convention as approved by the Commission is set forth in paragraph 28 of the report.

[25] General Assembly resolution 33/93 [*Yearbook 1979,* part one, chap. I, sect. C] (reproduced in *Official Records of the United Nations Conference on Contracts for the International Sale of Goods, . . .).*

[26] "Final Act of the United Nations Conference on Contracts for the International Sale of Goods" (A/CONF.97/18) [*Yearbook 1980,* part three, chap. I, sect. A] (reproduced in *Official Records of the United Nations Conference on Contracts for the International Sale of Goods, . . .,* part one). The Convention is set forth in annex I to the Final Act. See also annex III, below.

[27] *Ibid.* [*Yearbook 1980,* part three, chap. I, sect. C] (reproduced in *Official Records of the United Nations Conference on Contracts for the International Sale of Goods, . . .,* annex II). See also annex II, D, below.

[28] See section A, above.

[29] *Official Records of the General Assembly, Thirty-third Session, Supplement No. 17* (A/33/17), para. 27 [*Yearbook 1978,* part one, chap. II, sect. A].

V. International negotiable instruments

47. International payments was one of the priority topics on the Commission's original programme of work.[1] Within that topic the Commission decided to devote attention to the law relating to international negotiable instruments.

48. At the outset of its deliberations on this topic, the Commission observed that there were two principal systems of negotiable instruments law: that represented by the Geneva Conventions of 1930 and 1931;[2] and that represented by the English Bills of Exchange Act and the United States Negotiable Instruments Law (superseded by article 3 of the Uniform Commercial Code). The Commission recognized that disparities existed in the way these two systems dealt with various issues, and that even within these systems complete unification of law had not been achieved.[3] There was a general consensus within the Commission that the work towards unification of law in this area should concentrate on finding a solution that would reduce the problems arising from the coexistence of these systems.[4]

49. The Commission considered various methods for achieving unification of the law relating to international negotiable instruments.[5] It concluded that the only viable approach at that time was to focus on the formulation of uniform legal rules that would be applicable to a special negotiable instrument for use in international transactions. Unification of law would be confined to payment transactions that were international in character and, consequently, the proposed uniform rules would not supersede national laws and practices insofar as those laws and practices related to domestic transactions. Moreover, the uniform rules would apply only to international transactions where the drawer of a negotiable instrument had opted for the application of the uniform

---

[1]See chapter II, section A.1.

[2]Convention providing a Uniform Law for Bills of Exchange and Promissory Notes (Geneva, 1930); Convention providing a Uniform Law for Cheques (Geneva, 1931). Both are reproduced in *Register of Texts of Conventions and other Instruments concerning International Trade Law*, vol. 1 (United Nations publication, Sales No. E.71.V.3), chapter II, section A.1.

[3]See *Official Records of the General Assembly, Twenty-fourth Session, Supplement No. 18* (A/7618), para. 66 [*Yearbook 1968-1970*, part two, chap. II, sect. A]; *Official Records of the General Assembly, Twenty-sixth Session, Supplement No. 17* (A/8417), para. 28 [*Yearbook 1971*, part one, chap. II, sect. A].

[4]*Official Records of the General Assembly, Twenty-fourth Session, Supplement No. 18* (A/7618), para. 66 [*Yearbook 1968-1970*, part two, chap. II, sect. A].

[5]See *Official Records of the General Assembly, Twenty-fourth Session, Supplement No. 18* (A/7618), paras. 69-81 and 85-87 [*Yearbook 1968-1970*, part two, chap. II, sect. A]; *Official Records of the General Assembly, Twenty-fifth Session, Supplement No. 17* (A/8017), para. 111 [*Yearbook 1968-1970*, part two, chap. III, sect. A].

rules by the use of an international instrument bearing an appropriate designation.[6]

50. At the request of the Commission,[7] the Secretariat prepared an initial draft, and a commentary thereon,[8] of uniform rules governing international bills of exchange. Thereafter, in view of the results of inquiries among banking and trade circles concerning the use and importance of promissory notes in international trade, the Commission agreed that the scope of the draft uniform rules should be extended to cover promissory notes.[9] It set up a Working Group on International Negotiable Instruments, and entrusted it with the task of preparing final draft uniform legal rules on international bills of exchange and promissory notes.[10]

51. The working group proceeded to prepare uniform legal rules relating to international bills of exchange and international promissory notes, based on draft uniform legal rules prepared by the Secretariat, and in consultation with the UNCITRAL Study Group on International Payments.[11] In the course of that work, the working group decided to recommend that the uniform rules be set forth in the form of a convention rather than in the form of a model law.[12]

52. With respect to international cheques, the Commission authorized the working group to embark on the drafting of uniform legal rules relating to international cheques if the group was of the view that the formulation of such rules was desirable and that the application of the uniform rules relating to international bills of exchange and promissory notes could be extended to include international cheques.[13] The working group had been advised by the Study Group on International Payments that cheques were widely used for settling international commercial transactions, and that there was substantial support for the establishment of uniform legal rules applicable to international cheques. It therefore decided to undertake the preparation of such uniform rules.[14]

53. In 1981, the working group adopted a draft Convention on International Bills of Exchange and International Promissory Notes and a draft

---

[6] *Official Records of the General Assembly, Twenty-fifth Session, Supplement No. 17* (A/8017), para. 112 [*Yearbook 1968-1970,* part two, chap. III, sect. A]; *Official Records of the General Assembly, Twenty-sixth Session, Supplement No. 17* (A/8417), para. 27 [*Yearbook 1971,* part one, chap. II, sect. A].

[7] *Official Records of the General Assembly, Twenty-sixth Session, Supplement No. 17* (A/8417), para. 35 [*Yearbook 1971,* part one, chap. II, sect. A].

[8] "International payments: negotiable instruments: draft uniform law on international bills of exchange and commentary: report of the Secretary-General" (A/CN.9/67 and Corr.1 (English only)) [*Yearbook 1972,* part two, chap. II, sect. 1].

[9] *Official Records of the General Assembly, Twenty-seventh Session, Supplement No. 17* (A/8717), para. 55 [*Yearbook 1972,* part one, chap. II, sect. A].

[10] *Ibid.,* para. 61 [*Yearbook 1972,* part one, chap. II, sect. A].

[11] See chapter II, paragraph 18.

[12] "Report of the Working Group on International Negotiable Instruments on the work of its fifth session" (A/CN.9/141), para. 13 [*Yearbook 1978,* part two, chap. II, sect. A].

[13] *Official Records of the General Assembly, Thirty-fourth Session, Supplement No. 17* (A/34/17), para. 44 [*Yearbook 1979,* part one, chap. II, sect. A].

[14] "Report of the Working Group on International Negotiable Instruments on the work of its eighth session" (A/CN.9/178), paras. 102 and 103 [*Yearbook 1980,* part two, chap. III, sect. A].

Convention on International Cheques.[15] The Secretariat subsequently prepared a commentary for each draft Convention.[16]

54. The Commission engaged in a substantive discussion on the draft Convention on International Bills of Exchange and International Promissory Notes at its seventeenth session (1984), and instructed the working group to revise the draft Convention in the light of that discussion, taking into account comments on the draft Convention that had been submitted by Governments and international organizations.[17] The Commission decided to postpone work on the draft Convention on International Cheques, and to take a decision as to further work on that draft Convention after completion of the work on the draft Convention on International Bills of Exchange and International Promissory Notes.[18]

---

[15]"Report of the Working Group on International Negotiable Instruments on the work of its eleventh session" (A/CN.9/210) [*Yearbook 1982*, part two, chap. II, sect. A.1]. The text of the draft Convention on International Bills of Exchange and International Promissory Notes is contained in document A/CN.9/211 [*Yearbook 1982*, part two, chap. II, sect. A.3]; the text of the draft Convention on International Cheques is contained in document A/CN.9/212 and Corr.1 (Spanish only) [*Yearbook 1982*, part two, chap. II, sect. A.5].

[16]The Commentary on the draft Convention on International Bills of Exchange and International Promissory Notes is contained in document A/CN.9/213 [*Yearbook 1982*, part two, chap. II, sect. A.4]; the commentary on the draft Convention on International Cheques is contained in document A/CN.9/214 [*Yearbook 1982*, part two, chap. II, sect. A.6].

[17]*Official Records of the General Assembly, Thirty-ninth Session, Supplement No. 17* (A/39/17), paras. 14-88 [*Yearbook 1984*, part one, sect. A].

[18]*Ibid.*, para. 88 [*Yearbook 1984*, part one, sect. A].

VI. International commercial arbitration and conciliation

A. Arbitration

55. The harmonization and unification of the law relating to international commercial arbitration was another topic accorded priority status by the Commission at its first session.[1] Having noted that several organs and organizations had been working on various aspects of this topic,[2] the Commission appointed a special rapporteur to consider the most important problems concerning the application and interpretation of existing conventions in this area, and other related problems.[3]

56. In a report[4] submitted to the Commission the special rapporteur presented a general account, including results, of activities undertaken by various organs and organizations in the area of international commercial arbitration. A number of problems were also discussed with respect to the application and interpretation of existing multilateral international conventions in this area. One of the recommendations made by the special rapporteur was that the Commission should consider drawing up a model set of arbitration rules to cover proceedings arising from international commercial relationships, and a model law designed to unify and simplify national legislation concerning such proceedings.[5]

1. *UNCITRAL arbitration rules*

57. Based on the report of the special rapporteur, the Commission requested the Secretary-General to prepare a draft set of arbitration rules for optional use in *ad hoc* arbitration relating to international trade.[6] A preliminary draft set of arbitration rules, with commentaries, prepared by the Secretariat in consultation

---

[1]See chapter II, para. 11.

[2]*Official Records of the General Assembly, Twenty-third Session, Supplement No. 16* (A/7216), para. 48 (31) [*Yearbook 1968-1970*, part two, chap. I, sect. A].

[3]*Ibid., Twenty-fourth Session, Supplement No. 18* (A/7618), para. 112 [*Yearbook 1968-1970*, part two, chap. II, sect. A].

[4]"Problems concerning the application and interpretation of existing multilateral conventions on international commercial arbitration and related matters", report by Mr. Ion Nestor (Romania), Special Rapporteur (A/CN.9/64) [*Yearbook 1972*, part two, chap. III].

[5]*Ibid.,* paras. 180 and 181 [*Yearbook 1972*, part two, chap. III].

[6]*Official Records of the General Assembly, Twenty-eighth Session, Supplement No. 17* (A/9017), para. 85 [*Yearbook 1973*, part one, chap. II, sect. A].

with experts in this field,[7] was presented to the Commission[8] and revised by the Secretariat in light of the Commission's deliberations.[9] A commentary on the revised draft rules was also prepared.[10] The Commission finalized and adopted the UNCITRAL Arbitration Rules at its ninth session in 1976.[11]

58. The United Nations General Assembly has recommended the use of the UNCITRAL Arbitration Rules in the settlement of disputes arising in the context of international commercial relations,[12] as has the Asian-African Legal Consultative Committee (AALCC).[13] Since gaining these endorsements, the Rules have become widely accepted and used in manifold contexts.

2. Guidelines for administering arbitrations under the UNCITRAL Arbitration Rules

59. Although the UNCITRAL Arbitration Rules, in their final form,[14] are designed for non-administered arbitration (i.e. when the parties agree to arbitration but do not select an arbitral institution to administer the arbitration), they are also suitable for use in administered arbitration (i.e. when the parties agreeing to arbitration select such an institution). In a study prepared for the Commission in 1979, the Secretariat reported that several arbitral institutions had either declared their willingness to administer

---

[7]"Preliminary draft set of arbitration rules for optional use in *ad hoc* arbitration relating to international trade (UNCITRAL Arbitration Rules): report of the Secretary-General" (A/CN.9/97) [*Yearbook 1975*, part two, chap. III, sect. 1]. The experts consisted of Professor Pieter Sanders of the Netherlands, who served as a consultant to the Secretariat on the subject, as well as a Consultative Group of four experts appointed by the International Committee on Commercial Arbitration of the International Arbitration Congress, a body composed of representatives of centres of international commercial arbitration and of experts in this field; see section 1 of A/CN.9/97.

[8]*Official Records of the General Assembly, Thirtieth Session, Supplement No. 17* (A/10017), paras. 79-83 and annex I [*Yearbook 1975*, part one, chap. II, sect. A].

[9]"Revised draft set of arbitration rules for optional use in *ad hoc* arbitration relating to international trade (UNCITRAL Arbitration Rules): report of the Secretary-General" (A/CN.9/112) [*Yearbook 1976*, part two, chap. III, sect. 1].

[10]"Revised draft set of arbitration rules for optional use in *ad hoc* arbitration relating to international trade (UNCITRAL Arbitration Rules) (addendum): commentary on the draft UNCITRAL Arbitration Rules: report of the Secretary-General" (A/CN.9/112/Add.1) [*Yearbook 1976*, part two, chap. III, sect. 2].

[11]*Official Records of the General Assembly, Thirty-first Session, Supplement No. 17* (A/31/17), paras. 51-56 and annex II [*Yearbook 1976*, part one, chap. II, sect. A]. The text of the UNCITRAL Arbitration Rules is set forth in para. 57. For convenience of use, the Rules have also been published in booklet form: *UNCITRAL Arbitration Rules* (United Nations publication, Sales No. E.77.V.6). See also annex IV, A, below.

[12]General Assembly resolution 31/98 [*Yearbook 1977*, part one, chap. I, sect. C]. See annex IV, B, below.

[13]Decision by the Asian-African Legal Consultative Committee on international commercial arbitration, reproduced in "International commercial arbitration: note by the Secretary-General" (A/CN.9/127), annex [*Yearbook 1977*, part two, chap. III].

[14]In their preliminary form (see A/CN.9/97, footnote 7, above), they consisted of draft rules for administered and for non-administered arbitration. However, the prevailing view among representatives at the Commission's eighth session was to exclude, for the time being, administered arbitration from the scope of the Rules, but to permit parties to designate in advance a person or institution to carry out the functions of an appointing authority as specified in the Rules. *Official Records of the General Assembly, Thirtieth Session, Supplement No. 17* (A/10017), annex I, para. 8 [*Yearbook 1975*, part one, chap. II, sect. A].

arbitrations under the rules or had adopted the rules as their own; however, the institutions had adopted different approaches with respect to the use of the rules.[15]

60. The Commission deemed it desirable that the UNCITRAL Arbitration Rules be applied without change, even when arbitral institutions administered arbitration under the rules, and that disparities in the use of the rules be avoided. Modifications, where required, to adjust the rules to administered arbitration, could be achieved if the parties agreed to have their arbitration conducted under the administrative rules of the arbitral institution.[16] Accordingly, the Commission requested the Secretariat to prepare guidelines for administering arbitration under the UNCITRAL Arbitration Rules in order to assist arbitral institutions and other bodies, such as chambers of commerce, in adopting procedures for acting as appointing authorities or providing administrative services in cases conducted under the UNCITRAL Arbitration Rules.[17] On the basis of drafts prepared by the Secretariat,[18] the Commission finalized and adopted in 1982 a set of non-binding Recommendations to Assist Arbitral Institutions and other Interested Bodies with regard to Arbitrations under the UNCITRAL Arbitration Rules.[19]

3. UNCITRAL Model Law on International Commercial Arbitration

61. When AALCC gave its endorsement to the UNCITRAL Arbitration Rules,[20] it made certain additional recommendations aimed at: ensuring the autonomy of parties to agree on arbitration rules irrespective of any contrary provision of the law applicable to the arbitration; safeguarding fairness in arbitral proceedings; and excluding reliance on sovereign immunity in international commercial arbitration.[21] It was suggested by AALCC that these issues could be clarified in a protocol to the Convention on the Recognition and Enforcement of Foreign Arbitral Awards (New York, 1958) (the "New York Convention").

62. In this connection, the Secretariat prepared two studies for the Commission. One was a report on the application and interpretation of the New York Convention. It identified ambiguities, divergencies and problems

---

[15]"Issues relevant in the context of the UNCITRAL Arbitration Rules: note by the Secretariat" (A/CN.9/170) [*Yearbook 1979*, part two, chap. III, sect. E].

[16]*Official Records of the General Assembly, Thirty-fourth Session, Supplement No. 17* (A/34/17), para. 66 [*Yearbook 1979*, part one, chap. II, sect. A].

[17]*Ibid.*, para. 71 [*Yearbook 1979*, part one, chap. II, sect. A]; *Official Records of the General Assembly, Thirty-sixth Session, Supplement No. 17* (A/36/17), para. 59 [*Yearbook 1981*, part one, sect. A].

[18]"Issues relating to the use of the UNCITRAL Arbitration Rules and the designation of an appointing authority: note by the Secretary-General" (A/CN.9/189), para. 15 [*Yearbook 1980*, part two, chap. IV, sect. D]; "Recommendations concerning administrative services provided in arbitrations under the UNCITRAL Arbitration Rules: note by the Secretary-General" (A/CN.9/222), annex [*Yearbook 1982*, part two, chap. III, sect. C].

[19]*Official Records of the General Assembly, Thirty-seventh Session, Supplement No. 17* (A/37/17), paras. 74-85 [*Yearbook 1982*, part one, sect. A]. The text of the recommendations is set forth in annex I to the report. See also annex IV, C, below.

[20]See paragraph 58.

[21]A/CN.9/127, annex (see footnote 13 above).

encountered in the application of the convention and ascertained its practical value for the promotion of international commercial arbitration. The report concluded that, despite some minor deficiencies, the convention had satisfactorily met the general purpose for which it was adopted and that it was therefore inadvisable to amend it.[22]

63.　The second report discussed the need for greater uniformity in national laws on arbitral procedure and the desirability of establishing standards for modern and fair arbitral procedures. The report suggested that the Commission commence work on a model law on arbitral procedure, which could help both to overcome most of the problems that had been identified in the first report with respect to the New York Convention and to meet the concerns expressed in the recommendations of the AALCC.[23]

64.　The Commission agreed that such a model law could assist States in reforming and modernizing their laws on arbitral procedure so as to take into account the particular features and meet the needs of international commercial arbitration. It would help reduce the divergencies encountered in the interpretation of the New York Convention. In addition, it would meet in large measure the concerns expressed by the AALCC in that, if the model law were accepted by States, it would minimize the possible conflicts between national laws and arbitration rules.[24] The Commission therefore requested the Secretariat to prepare a preliminary draft of a model law on international commercial arbitration,[25] and assigned the preparation of the draft model law[26] to its Working Group on International Contract Practices.

65.　The working group completed the work by adopting a draft Model Law on International Commercial Arbitration.[27] The Commission adopted the UNCITRAL Model Law on International Commercial Arbitration in 1985.[28] The General Assembly has recommended that all States give due consideration to the Model Law, in view of the desirability of uniformity of the law of arbitral procedures and the specific needs of international commercial arbitration practice.[29]

---

[22]"Study on the application and interpretation of the Convention on the Recognition and Enforcement of Foreign Arbitral Awards (New York, 1958): report of the Secretary-General" (A/CN.9/168) [*Yearbook 1979*, part two, chap. III, sect. C].

[23]"Further work in respect of international commercial arbitration: note by the Secretariat" (A/CN.9/169) [*Yearbook 1979*, part two, chap. III, sect. D].

[24]*Official Records of the General Assembly, Thirty-fourth Session, Supplement No. 17* (A/34/17), para. 78 [*Yearbook 1979*, part one, chap. II, sect. A].

[25]*Ibid.*, para. 81 [*Yearbook 1979*, part one, chap. II, sect. A]; see also *Official Records of the General Assembly, Thirty-sixth Session, Supplement No. 17* (A/36/17), para. 70 [*Yearbook 1981*, part one, sect. A].

[26]*Ibid., Thirty-sixth Session, Supplement No. 17* (A/36/17), para. 70 [*Yearbook 1981*, part one, sect. A].

[27]"Report of the Working Group on International Contract Practices on the work of its seventh session" (A/CN.9/246) [*Yearbook 1984*, part two, chap. II, sect. B.1]. The text of the draft Model Law is contained in the annex to the report.

[28]*Official Records of the General Assembly, Fortieth Session, Supplement No. 17* (A/40/17), para. 332 [*Yearbook 1985*, part one, sect. A]. The text of the UNCITRAL Model Law on International Commercial Arbitration is contained in annex I to the report. See also annex V, A, below.

[29]General Assembly resolution 40/72. See annex V, B, below.

B. Conciliation: UNCITRAL Conciliation Rules

66. One of the priority topics on the programme of work adopted by the Commission at its eleventh session (1978) was conciliation of international trade disputes.[30] A report prepared for the Commission by the Secretariat[31] dealt with the nature of conciliation, and discussed the purpose, potential advantages and particular features of conciliation in comparison with other methods of dispute settlement.

67. On the basis of draft texts and commentaries prepared by the Secretariat,[32] the Commission finalized and adopted the UNCITRAL Conciliation Rules in 1980.[33] The General Assembly has recommended the use of the rules in cases where a dispute arises in the context of international commercial relations and the parties seek an amicable settlement of that dispute by recourse to conciliation.[34]

---

[30] *Official Records of the General Assembly, Thirty-third Session, Supplement No. 17* (A/33/17), paras. 67 *(c)* (iv), 68 and 69 [*Yearbook 1978,* part one, chap. II, sect. A].

[31] "Conciliation of international trade disputes: report of the Secretary-General" (A/CN.9/167) [*Yearbook 1979,* part two, chap. III, sect. B].

[32] "Draft UNCITRAL Conciliation Rules: preliminary draft prepared by the Secretary-General" (A/CN.9/166) [*Yearbook 1979,* part two, chap. III, sect. A]; a commentary is contained in "Conciliation of international trade disputes: report of the Secretary-General" (A/CN.9/167) [*Yearbook 1979,* part two, chap. III, sect. B]. "Revised draft UNCITRAL Conciliation Rules: draft prepared by the Secretary-General" (A/CN.9/179) [*Yearbook 1980,* part two, chap. IV, sect. A]; a commentary is contained in "Commentary on the revised draft UNCITRAL Conciliation Rules: report of the Secretary-General" (A/CN.9/180) [*Yearbook 1980,* part two, chap. IV, sect. B].

[33] *Official Records of the General Assembly, Thirty-fifth Session, Supplement No. 17* (A/35/17), paras. 105 and 106 [*Yearbook 1980,* part one, chap. II, sect. A]. The text of the UNCITRAL Conciliation Rules as adopted by the Commission is set forth in *ibid.,* paragraph 106. For convenience of use, the Rules have been published in booklet form: UNCITRAL Conciliation Rules (United Nations publication, Sales No. E.81.V.6). See also annex VI, A, below.

[34] General Assembly resolution 35/52 [*Yearbook 1980,* part one, chap. II, sect. D]. See also annex VI, B, below.

VII. International transport of goods

A. Carriage of goods by sea

68. In 1968, UNCTAD, noting that UNCITRAL had not at its first session included international shipping legislation in its initial programme of work, recommended the creation within the UNCTAD Committee on Shipping of a Working Group on International Shipping Legislation. It further recommended that the working group should review commercial and economic aspects of international legislation on shipping in order to identify areas where modifications were needed and to make recommendations as to new legislation. It was contemplated that, on the basis of the recommendations of the working group, the Committee on Shipping might ask UNCITRAL to undertake the drafting of such new legislation.[1]

69. During the twenty-third session of the General Assembly (1968), views were expressed in the Sixth Committee in favour of some form of involvement by UNCITRAL in the area of international legislation on shipping.[2] On the basis of a recommendation by the Sixth Committee, the General Assembly recommended that UNCITRAL should consider the inclusion of international shipping legislation among the priority topics in its work programme.[3]

70. In considering this matter at its annual session in 1969, the Commission referred to the desirability of collaboration with the organs and organizations already working in this field, and expressed a wish for close co-operation between UNCITRAL and UNCTAD. Accordingly, it decided to include international legislation on shipping among the priority items in its programme of work and set up a Working Group on International Legislation on Shipping, instructing it to consider the topics and methods of work that should be pursued.[4]

71. Subsequently, the UNCTAD Committee on Shipping set up its own Working Group on Shipping Legislation as had been recommended by UNCTAD. It instructed its working group to make recommendations and

---

[1]UNCTAD resolution 14 (II) and related matters are discussed in "Consideration of inclusion of international shipping legislation among the priority topics in the work programme: note by the Secretary-General" (A/CN.9/23).

[2]A/7408, para. 17 (see document A/CN.9/23, footnote 1, above, para. 11).

[3]General Assembly resolution 2421 (XXIII), para. 6 *(b)* [*Yearbook 1968-1970,* part two, chap. I, sect. B.3]; see also General Assembly resolution 2502 (XXIV), paras. 2 and 10 *(a)* [*Yearbook 1968-1970,* part two, chap. II, sect. B.3].

[4]*Official Records of the General Assembly, Twenty-third Session, Supplement No. 18* (A/7618), para. 133 [*Yearbook 1968-1970,* part two, chap. II, sect. A].

prepare the necessary documentation to serve as a basis for further work by UNCITRAL on the drafting of new legislation or other appropriate action.[5]

72. The UNCTAD working group decided that its first priority topic would be to deal with the law and practice relating to bills of lading.[6] In 1971, it reviewed existing rules and practices concerning bills of lading and their effect on cargo interests. It considered that some of the rules and practices created uncertainties in the application of laws and the interpretation of terms. The removal of those uncertainties would in various instances reduce costs in international trade, which were onerous for cargo-owners, especially in developing countries. It therefore considered that those rules and practices, including rules contained in the International Convention for the Unification of Certain Rules relating to Bills of Lading (the Brussels Convention 1924) and in the protocol to amend that convention (the Brussels Protocol 1968), should be examined and, where appropriate, revised and amplified, and that it might be appropriate for a new international convention to be prepared. In addition to removing the existing uncertainties and ambiguities, the main objective of this work would be to establish a balanced allocation of risks between the cargo owner and the carrier. The working group established broad policy guidelines for the reform and recommended that this work, including the preparation of the necessary draft texts, should be undertaken by UNCITRAL.[7] The UNCITRAL working group endorsed the recommendations of the UNCTAD working group,[8] and in 1971 the Commission instructed the UNCITRAL working group to proceed accordingly.[9]

73. The UNCITRAL working group completed its preparation of a draft Convention on the Carriage of Goods by Sea in 1975.[10] The Secretariat prepared draft provisions concerning implementation, reservations and other final clauses for the draft Convention.[11] In 1976, the Commission finalized and approved the text of a draft Convention on the Carriage of Goods by Sea, and recommended that the General Assembly convene an international conference of plenipotentiaries to conclude a convention on the subject.[12]

---

[5]UNCTAD Resolution 7 (III), "Official Records of the Trade and Development Board, ninth session, Report of the Committee on Shipping on its third session" (TD/B/240), annex I.

[6]TD/B/289, paras. 27 and 31; see also "A survey of the work in the field of international legislation on shipping undertaken by various international organizations and co-ordination of future work in this field: report of the Secretary-General" (A/CN.9/41) [*Yearbook 1968-1970*, part three, chap. II, sect. A].

[7]TD/B/C.4/86, annex I; see "Working Group on International Legislation on Shipping: report on the work of the first session" (A/CN.9/55), para. 8 and annex II [*Yearbook 1971*, part two, chap. III].

[8]*Ibid.*, para. 13 [*Yearbook 1971*, part two, chap. III].

[9]*Official Records of the General Assembly, Twenty-sixth Session, Supplement No. 17* (A/8417), para. 19 [*Yearbook 1971*, part one, chap. II, sect. A].

[10]"Report of the Working Group on International Legislation on Shipping on the work of its eighth session" (A/CN.9/105) [*Yearbook 1975*, part two, chap. IV, sect. 3]. The text of the draft Convention as approved by the working group is set forth in the annex.

[11]"Draft Convention on the Carriage of Goods by Sea: draft provisions concerning implementation, reservations and other final clauses" (A/CN.9/115) [*Yearbook 1976*, part two, chap. IV, sect. 5].

[12]*Official Records of the General Assembly, Thirty-first Session, Supplement No. 17* (A/31/17), para. 44 [*Yearbook 1976*, part one, chap. II, sect. A]. The text of the draft Convention as approved by the Commission is set forth in paragraph 45.

74.   Based upon the recommendation of the Commission, the General Assembly convened the United Nations Conference on the Carriage of Goods by Sea.[13] The Conference, which was held on the invitation of the Federal Republic of Germany at Hamburg from 6 to 31 March 1978, adopted on 30 March 1978 the United Nations Convention on the Carriage of Goods by Sea, 1978 (Hamburg) (also known as the Hamburg Rules), together with a Common Understanding relating to the Convention.[14]

B.   Liability of operators of transport terminals

75.   In recent years, the law governing the international transport of goods by various modes of transport has become increasingly harmonized and unified through international transport conventions. The legal regime governing international transport will become even more unified when the United Nations Convention on the Carriage of Goods by Sea, 1978 (Hamburg)[15] and the United Nations Convention on International Multimodal Transport of Goods (1980)[16] come into force. Notwithstanding this trend, however, the liability of operators of transport terminals for loss of and damage to goods before, during and after international transport has remained regulated exclusively by widely disparate national laws. Moreover, some national legal systems permit terminal operators to modify the legal rules applicable in those systems and to restrict their liability through contractual conditions.

76.   In the 1970s, work was begun within UNIDROIT towards the preparation of uniform legal rules governing the liability of operators of transport terminals. The objective of this work was to fill the gaps left in the harmonized legal regime created by international transport conventions. Uniform rules in this area are considered desirable in order to give due protection to parties with interests in cargo in the custody of transport terminal operators, and to facilitate recourse against terminal operators by carriers, multi-modal transport operators, freight forwarders and similar entities when held liable for loss of or damage to goods in the custody of terminal operators.

77.   In 1983, the UNIDROIT Governing Council adopted a preliminary draft Convention on Operators of Transport Terminals.[17] The central features of the liability regime set forth in the preliminary draft Convention paralleled those of the Hamburg Rules and the Multimodal Convention.

78.   In response to initiatives taken by UNIDROIT, the Commission in 1983 added the topic of liability of operators of transport terminals to its programme

---

[13]General Assembly resolution 31/100 [*Yearbook 1977,* part one, chap. I, sect. C].

[14]"Final Act of the United Nations Conference on the Carriage of Goods by Sea" (A/CONF.89/13) [*Yearbook 1978,* part three, chap. I]. The Convention is set forth in annex I to the Final Act, and the Common Understanding is set forth in annex II. See also annex VII, below.

[15]See paragraph 74.

[16]TD/MT/CONF/160. This Convention, hereinafter referred to as the Multimodal Convention, resulted from work carried out by UNCTAD.

[17]The preliminary draft Convention as adopted by the UNIDROIT Governing Council is set forth in "Liability of operators of transport terminals: report of the Secretary-General" (A/CN.9/252), annex II [*Yearbook 1984,* part two, chap. IV, sect. A].

of work, and requested the Secretariat to prepare a study of important issues arising from the UNIDROIT preliminary draft Convention.[18] After considering this study,[19] the Commission assigned the task of formulating uniform legal rules in this area to its Working Group on International Contract Practices.[20]

C. International transport documents[21]

79. In 1982, the Secretariat prepared for the Commission a study discussing the legal regime in respect of transport documentation under the principal multilateral transport conventions and some of the current developments in this field. The report concluded that there might be a greater need in the future than there had been in the past for harmonization of the rules governing such transport documentation.[22]

80. The Secretariat is closely monitoring developments in this field, and the Commission has requested to be kept informed of any future course of action that it might take.[23]

---

[18]*Official Records of the General Assembly, Thirty-eighth Session, Supplement No. 17* (A/38/17), para. 115 [*Yearbook 1983,* part one, sect. A].

[19]"Liability of operators of transport terminals: report of the Secretary-General" (A/CN.9/252) [*Yearbook 1984,* part two, chap. IV, sect. A].

[20]*Official Records of the General Assembly, Thirty-ninth Session, Supplement No. 17* (A/39/17), para. 113 [*Yearbook 1984,* part one, sect. A].

[21]See also chapter XI.

[22]"Co-ordination of work: international transport documents: report of the Secretary-General" (A/CN.9/225 and Corr.1) [*Yearbook 1982,* part two, chap. VI, sect. B].

[23]*Official Records of the General Assembly, Thirty-seventh Session, Supplement No. 17* (A/37/17), para. 104 [*Yearbook 1982,* part one, sect. A].

VIII. Legal implications of the new international economic order: industrial contracts

81.   In 1974 and 1975, the United Nations General Assembly, at its sixth and seventh special sessions, adopted a series of resolutions dealing with economic development and the establishment of a new international economic order. As one of the organs of the United Nations, the Commission was called upon by the General Assembly to take account of the relevant provisions of these resolutions. The Commission responded by including in the programme of work, which it adopted at its eleventh session (1978), the topic of legal implications of the new international economic order,[1] and considered how, having regard to its special expertise and within the context of its mandate, it could most effectively advance the objectives set forth in the General Assembly resolutions. The Commission established a Working Group on the New International Economic Order and charged it with the task of recommending specific topics that could appropriately form a part of the programme of work of the Commission. To assist the working group, the Commission requested the Secretariat to prepare a report setting forth subject-matters that were relevant in this context and that would be suitable for consideration, accompanied by background studies and recommendations as appropriate. It also invited Governments to submit their views and proposals as to subject-matters that might be pursued by the Commission.[2]

82.   The working group reported to the Commission that its discussion had revealed that the harmonization, unification and review of contractual provisions commonly occurring in international contracts in the field of industrial development, including, *inter alia,* contracts for the supply and construction of large industrial works, would be of special importance to developing countries and to the work of the Commission in the context of the

---

[1] *Official Records of the General Assembly, Thirty-third Session, Supplement No. 17* (A/33/17), paras. 67 *(c)* (vi), 68, 69 [*Yearbook 1978,* part one, chap. II, sect. A]. In reaching this decision the Commission took into consideration a recommendation made by the Asian-African Legal Consultative Committee (AALCC) that the Commission include this topic in its programme of work: "Recommendations of the Asian-African Legal Consultative Committee: note by the Secretary-General" (A/CN.9/155), annex [*Yearbook 1978,* part two, chap. IV, sect. B]; see *Official Records of the General Assembly, Thirty-third Session, Supplement No. 17* (A/33/17), para. 55 [*Yearbook 1978,* part one, chap. II, sect. A].

[2] *Official Records of the General Assembly, Thirty-third Session, Supplement No. 17* (A/33/17), para. 71 [*Yearbook 1978,* part one, chap. II, sect. A]; *Official Records of the General Assembly, Thirty-fourth Session, Supplement No. 17* (A/34/17), para. 100 [*Yearbook 1979,* part one, chap. II, sect. A].

new international economic order.[3] The Commission agreed to accord priority to work related to contracts in the field of industrial development. It assigned this work to the working group and enlarged its composition to include all 36 States members of the Commission.[4] The Commission instructed the working group to prepare a Legal Guide on drawing up International Contracts for the Construction of Industrial Works. This legal guide will identify the legal issues involved in such contracts and suggest possible solutions to assist parties, in particular from developing countries, in negotiating contracts that are balanced and equitable.[5]

83.   Work on the drafting of the legal guide has progressed in two stages. In the first stage, the Secretariat prepared for the working group a study of clauses commonly found in international contracts for the construction of industrial works.[6] Views regarding the various issues presented in the studies were expressed at sessions of the working group and possible solutions discussed.[7] The purpose of this discussion was to provide guidance to the Secretariat when it commenced the drafting of the legal guide.[8]

84.   Once this stage of the work had been completed, the working group instructed the Secretariat to begin work on the second stage, namely, the preparation of draft chapters of the legal guide.[9] In the preparation of these draft chapters, the Secretariat consulted with an *ad hoc* group of experts, which reviewed and commented upon initial drafts at meetings of the group convened by the Secretariat. These drafts were revised in light of comments made by the group and then submitted to the working group. The draft chapters were revised again by the Secretariat in light of the views expressed and decisions taken at sessions of the working group. After all of the draft chapters of the legal guide have been examined by the working group and revised by the Secretariat, the entire draft legal guide will be submitted to, and finalized by, the Commission.

---

[3]"Report of the Working Group on the New International Economic Order on the work of its session" (A/CN.9/176), paras. 31 (4) and 32 [*Yearbook 1980*, part two, chap. V, sect. A]. See also the recommendation of AALCC, reproduced in "Legal implications of the new international economic order: note by the Secretariat" (A/CN.9/194) [*Yearbook 1980*, part two, chap. V, sect. D].

[4]*Official Records of the General Assembly, Thirty-fifth Session, Supplement No. 17* (A/35/17), para. 143 [*Yearbook 1980*, part one, chap. II, sect. A].

[5]*Official Records of the General Assembly, Thirty sixth Session, Supplement No. 17* (A/36/17), para. 84 [*Yearbook 1981*, part one, sect. A].

[6]"Clauses related to contracts for the supply and construction of large industrial works: study of the Secretary-General" (A/CN.9/WG.V/WP.4 and Add.1-8) [*Yearbook 1981*, part two, chap. IV, sect. B]; (A/CN.9/WG.V/WP.7 and Add.1-6) [*Yearbook 1982*, part two, chap. IV, sect. B].

[7]"Report of the Working Group on the New International Economic Order on the work of its second session" (A/CN.9/198) [*Yearbook 1981*, part two, chap. IV, sect. A]; "Report of the Working Group on the New International Economic Order on the work of its third session" (A/CN.9/217) [*Yearbook 1982*, part two, chap. IV, sect. A].

[8]"Report of the Working Group on the New International Economic Order on the work of its second session" (A/CN.9/198), para. 20 [*Yearbook 1981*, part two, chap. IV, sect. A].

[9]"Report of the Working Group on the New International Economic Order on the work of its third session" (A/CN.9/217), para. 130 [*Yearbook 1982*, part two, chap. IV, sect. A].

IX. Liquidated damages and penalty clauses

85. Commercial contracts often contain clauses providing for the payment by a party of a specified sum of money as damages or as a penalty in the event of the failure of the party to perform its contractual obligations. However, the common law and civil law systems have very different approaches to the validity and application of these clauses.

86. With these considerations before it,[1] the Commission included the topic of liquidated damages and penalty clauses in the programme of work that it adopted at its eleventh session (1978) and requested the Secretariat to prepare a study of the subject.[2] The study prepared by the Secretariat discussed the treatment of liquidated damages and penalty clauses under different legal systems and the use of such clauses in international trade contracts and general conditions, and examined the possibilities of unifying the law relating to such clauses.[3]

87. After considering this study, the Commission, in 1979, decided to undertake work towards the formulation of uniform legal rules regulating liquidated damages and penalty clauses. It entrusted this work to its Working Group on International Contract Practices, and it requested the working group to consider the feasibility of formulating the uniform rules so as to be applicable to a wide range of international trade contracts.[4]

88. The working group prepared and adopted a set of draft Uniform Rules on Liquidated Damages and Penalty Clauses.[5] The draft rules were presented in 1981 to the Commission, which then discussed the form that the rules should take (e.g. convention, model law or general conditions of contract).[6]

---

[1]See "Liquidated damages and penalty clauses: note by the Secretariat" (A/CN.9/149/Corr.1 and 2) [*Yearbook 1978*, part two, chap. IV, sect. A].

[2]*Official Records of the General Assembly, Thirty-third Session, Supplement No. 17* (A/33/17), paras. 67 *(c)* (i) *(b)*, 68, 69 [*Yearbook 1978*, part one, chap. II, sect. A].

[3]"Liquidated damages and penalty clauses: report of the Secretary-General" (A/CN.9/161) [*Yearbook 1979*, part two, chap. I, sect. C].

[4]*Official Records of the General Assembly, Thirty-fourth Session, Supplement No. 17* (A/34/17), para. 31 [*Yearbook 1979*, part one, chap. II, sect. A].

[5]"Report of the Working Group on International Contract Practices on the work of its second session" (A/CN.9/197) [*Yearbook 1981*, part two, chap. I, sect. A]. The text of the draft Rules on Liquidated Damages and Penalty Clauses as adopted by the Working Group is set forth in the annex to the report.

[6]*Official Records of the General Assembly, Thirty-fourth Session, Supplement No. 17* (A/34/17), paras. 37-44 [*Yearbook 1981*, part one, sect. A].

89.   At the request of the Commission,[7] the Secretariat drafted supplementary provisions to the draft rules, which might be required if the rules were to take the form of either a convention or a model law, and also prepared a commentary on the draft rules.[8]

90.   With this preparatory work before it, the Commission, in 1983, adopted a text of uniform rules on this subject, with the title "Uniform Rules on Contract Clauses for an Agreed Sum due upon Failure of Performance".[9] However, the Commission did not decide upon the form that the Uniform Rules should take, considering that, in view of the importance of this issue, such a decision might be taken by the Sixth Committee of the General Assembly.[10]

91.   Upon the recommendation of the Sixth Committee, the General Assembly recommended that States should give serious consideration to the Uniform Rules and, where appropriate, implement them in the form of either a model law or a convention. This action was taken by the General Assembly without prejudice to its making a further recommendation or taking further action with respect to the uniform rules if circumstances so warranted.[11]

---

[7]*Ibid.*, para. 44 [*Yearbook 1981*, part one, sect. A].

[8]See "Text of draft uniform rules on liquidated damages and penalty clauses, together with a commentary thereon: report of the Secretary-General" (A/CN.9/218) [*Yearbook 1982*, part two, chap. I, sect. A]; "Revised text of draft uniform rules on liquidated damages and penalty clauses: report of the Secretary-General" (A/CN.9/235) [*Yearbook 1983*, part two, chap. I].

[9]*Official Records of the General Assembly, Thirty-eighth Session, Supplement No. 17* (A/38/17), paras. 75 and 76 [*Yearbook 1983*, part one, sect. A]. The text of the Uniform Rules as adopted by the Commission is set forth in annex I to the report. See also annex VIII, A, below.

[10]*Ibid.*, para. 78 [*Yearbook 1983*, part one, sect. A].

[11]General Assembly resolution 38/135 [*Yearbook 1983*, part one, sect. D]. See annex VIII, B, below.

X. Universal unit of account for international conventions

92.   A number of international transport, maritime and other conventions impose liability for damage or injury occurring during carriage or resulting from the activities covered by the convention. Many of these conventions establish maximum limits on the amount of compensation that the party held liable must pay. In treaties concluded prior to 1975, it was common for these liability limits to be expressed in units of account consisting of defined quantities of gold, such as the Germinal franc or the Poincaré franc. In order to apply such liability limitation provisions in particular cases, the limits as expressed in units of account must be converted into the appropriate national currency. The abolition of an official price for gold by the International Monetary Fund in 1978, the existence of a widely fluctuating market price for gold and the advent of floating currencies have produced uncertainty and lack of uniformity in liability limits calculated on the basis of these units of account.

93.   In recent years, alternatives to these units of account have been sought. One such alternative, which has been used in recently adopted or revised conventions, is the Special Drawing Right (SDR) of the International Monetary Fund.[1] The use of the SDR as a unit of account has been regarded as a significant improvement over the use of gold or of a national currency. However, it has not been without problems. First, the national laws of some non-member States of the International Monetary Fund have not permitted the use of the SDR. Secondly, the purchasing power of liability limits expressed in fixed quantities of SDRs erodes over time due to inflation.

94.   These problems were considered, but not resolved, in debates within UNCITRAL during its drafting of the United Nations Convention on the Carriage of Goods by Sea, 1978 (Hamburg), and in the diplomatic conference that adopted that Convention.[2] Shortly thereafter, pursuant to a proposal by the Government of France,[3] UNCITRAL decided to consider the establishment of a unit of account that could be used in conventions universally and that would maintain its value over time.[4]

---

[1]See, for example, United Nations Convention on the Carriage of Goods by Sea, 1978 (Hamburg) (see chapter VII, footnote 14), art. 26.

[2]See chapter VII.

[3]"Proposal by France: note by the Secretariat" (A/CN.9/156) [*Yearbook 1978,* part two, chaps. I, IV, sect. C].

[4]*Official Records of the General Assembly, Thirty-third Session, Supplement No. 17* (A/33/17), paras. 67 *(c)* (iii), 68 and 69 [*Yearbook 1978,* part one, chap. II, sect. A].

95. The subject was examined by the UNCITRAL Study Group on International Payments[5] in 1978, 1979 and 1980. The views of the study group were considered by the Commission at its fourteenth session (1981), at which time the Commission referred the subject to its Working Group on International Negotiable Instruments.[6]

96. After considering the matter at a session held in 1982, the working group decided to recommend to the Commission that a draft article be prepared for use in international conventions, which would designate the SDR as the unit of account for expressing monetary amounts in limitation of liability provisions.[7] It also drafted two alternative sample provisions designed to preserve the value of liability limits expressed in units of account. Under one sample text the limits of liability would be revised through the use of a price index; the other sample text set forth an expedited procedure for revising the limits.[8]

97. The recommendation and sample provisions were before the Commission at its fifteenth session. The Commission adopted a provision designating the SDR as the unit of account in limitation of liability provisions, and two alternative sample provisions for revising the limits of liability.[9] The General Assembly recommended that, in the preparation of future international conventions containing limitation of liability provisions or in the revision of existing conventions, the unit of account provision and one of the two alternative provisions for adjustment of the limits of liability should be used.[10]

[5]See chapter II, paragraph 18.

[6]*Official Records of the General Assembly, Thirty-sixth Session, Supplement No. 17* (A/36/17), paras. 23-32 [*Yearbook 1981,* part one, sect. A].

[7]"Report of the Working Group on International Negotiable Instruments on the work of its twelfth session" (A/CN.9/215), para. 97 [*Yearbook 1982,* part two, chap. II, sect. B.1].

[8]*Ibid.,* paras. 53, 54 and 90 [*Yearbook 1982,* part two, chap. II, sect. B.1].

[9]*Official Records of the General Assembly, Thirty-seventh Session, Supplement No. 17* (A/37/17), para. 63 [*Yearbook 1982,* part one, sect. A]. See annex IX, A and B, below.

[10]General Assembly resolution 37/107 [*Yearbook 1982,* part one, sect. D]. See annex IX, C, below.

XI. Legal issues arising from automatic data processing

A. Electronic funds transfers

98. Developments in electronics and in computer technology have greatly increased the efficiency and speed with which it is possible to compute, store and transmit data. One way in which international trade is benefiting from such developments is that transfers of funds between parties to a transaction can now be effected rapidly by electronics, rather than by the physical movement and handling of paper. Certain legal issues have arisen, however, with the advent of this technological advance and the accompanying changes in international payment and banking practices.[1]

99. These issues have been under consideration within UNCITRAL since the mid-1970s. They first came to the attention of the Commission during its work on the preparation of draft conventions dealing with international negotiable instruments,[2] in particular in relation to the impact of electronic funds transfers on the use of cheques for making international payments.[3] In advising the UNCITRAL secretariat in connection with the preparation of these draft conventions, the UNCITRAL Study Group on International Payments[4] considered the influence of electronic techniques on the future course of development of the international funds transfer system.

100. These circumstances prompted the Secretariat to prepare for the Commission a preliminary report on electronic funds transfers,[5] in connection with the adoption by the Commission in 1978 of its current programme of work. Partly on the basis of that report, the Commission included the topic of electronic funds transfers in its work programme.[6]

---

[1]See also chapter VII, section C.

[2]Draft Convention on International Bills of Exchange and International Promissory Notes; draft Convention on International Cheques; see chapter V.

[3]*Official Records of the General Assembly, Twenty-seventh Session, Supplement No. 17* (A/8717), para. 57 [*Yearbook 1972,* part one, chap. II, sect. A]; "Report of the Working Group on International Negotiable Instruments on the work of its third session" (A/CN.9/99), para. 136 [*Yearbook 1975,* part two, chap. II, sect. 1].

[4]See chapter II, paragraph 18.

[5]"Some legal aspects of international electronic funds transfer: note by the Secretariat" (A/CN.9/149/Add.3) [*Yearbook 1978,* part two, chap. IV, sect. A]. This note includes a summary of deliberations of the UNCITRAL Study Group on International Payments on issues connected with electronic funds transfers.

[6]*Official Records of the General Assembly, Thirty-third Session, Supplement No. 17* (A/33/17), paras. 67 *(c)* (ii) *(b),* 68 and 69 [*Yearbook 1978,* part one, chap. II, sect. A].

101. In connection with its preparatory work on this topic, the Secretariat prepared a report describing some of the legal problems arising in this field and containing the recommendations of the study group on the future work that the Commission might undertake.[7] The report noted that electronic funds transfer systems had developed in a partial legal vacuum. In many countries it was assumed that the law relating to paper-based transfers also applied, at least in part, to electronic funds transfers. However, it was seldom clear to what extent this was the case. Moreover, the law that had developed to govern paper-based funds transfers might not be appropriate in all respects for electronic funds transfers. These problems were magnified in the case of international funds transfers, where no adequate legal framework existed within which such problems could be settled.[8]

102. On the basis of this report and the recommendations contained in it, the Commission decided in 1982 to prepare a legal guide on electronic funds transfers.[9] The guide is intended to identify the legal issues arising from such transfers, discuss the various approaches for dealing with them and suggest alternative solutions. It will be oriented towards providing guidance for legislators or lawyers preparing rules governing particular funds transfer systems.

103. The preparation of the legal guide has been undertaken by the Secretariat in co-operation with the Study Group on International Payments. The Secretariat prepared initial drafts of chapters, which were submitted to the study group, at meetings convened by the Secretariat for its review and comments. Thereafter the draft chapters were re-drafted by the Secretariat, and submitted to the Commission.[10] The Commission decided at its eighteenth session in 1985 to circulate the draft legal guide to Governments and interested international organizations for their comments. The draft legal guide will be revised by the Secretariat in light of the comments received and then submitted to the Commission at its nineteenth session in 1986 for consideration and possible adoption.[11]

B. Legal value of computer records

104. In the report on electronic funds transfers prepared by the Secretariat for the fifteenth session of the Commission (1982),[12] it was noted that problems associated with the legal value of computer records concerned not only transfers of funds but also all other aspects of international trade. It was concluded in the report that generalized solutions to these problems would be

---

[7]"Electronic funds transfer: report of the Secretary-General" (A/CN.9/221 and Corr.1 (French only)) [*Yearbook 1982*, part two, chap. II, sect. C].

[8]*Ibid.*, paras. 82 and 83 [*Yearbook 1982*, part two, chap. II, sect. C].

[9]*Official Records of the General Assembly, Thirty-seventh Session, Supplement No. 17* (A/37/17), para. 73 [*Yearbook 1982*, part one, sect. A].

[10]The draft chapters of the legal guide are contained in A/CN.9/250/Add.1-4 [*Yearbook 1984*, part two, chap. I, sect. B] and A/CN.9/266/Add.1 and 2.

[11]*Official Records of the General Assembly, Fortieth Session, Supplement No. 17* (A/40/17), para. 342 [*Yearbook 1985*, part one, sect. A].

[12]See paragraph 101.

desirable.[13] A similar conclusion was reached in a report describing the legal problems arising in the teletransmission of trade data, which was prepared by the Working Party on Facilitation of International Trade Procedures, a body jointly sponsored by the ECE and UNCTAD.[14] Accordingly, the Commission requested the Secretariat to prepare a study of the problems associated with the legal value of computer records.[15] In preparing this study, the Secretariat sent a questionnaire to Governments eliciting information on the use of computer-readable data as evidence in court proceedings in their countries. At the same time, and in co-operation with the Secretariat, the Customs Co-operation Council prepared a questionnaire on issues relating to the submission to customs authorities of goods declarations in computer-readable form.

105. The conclusion was reached in the study[16] that the existence of traditional differences among systems of adjudication, to which the rules of evidence were closely tied, did not allow for a single approach to the use of computer records as evidence, and that the experience in regard to the rules of evidence as they applied to the paper-based system of trade documentation had shown that substantial differences in the rules themselves had so far caused no noticeable harm to the development of international trade. As a result, there was no need to unify the rules of evidence regarding the use of computer records in international trade. The study found, however, that legal requirements that documents be signed or that documents be in paper-based form constituted a more serious obstacle to the use of computers and computer-to-computer telecommunications in international trade. Furthermore, the study concluded that legal rules based upon paper-based means of documenting international trade might create an obstacle to the use of automatic data processing in that they led to insecurity or impeded the efficient use of automatic data processing where its use was otherwise justified.

106. On the basis of this study, the Commission recommended to Governments and to international organizations elaborating legal texts relating to trade that they review the rules within their competence relating to automatic data processing with an end towards eliminating unnecessary obstacles to the use of automatic data processing in international trade.[17]

C. Other legal aspects of automatic data processing

107. Other issues arising in connection with the teletransmission of trade data were discussed in the report of the ECE/UNCTAD Working Party,[18] and

---

[13]"Electronic funds transfer: report of the Secretary-General" (A/CN.9/221 and Corr.1 (French only)), para. 81 [*Yearbook 1982*, part two, chap. II, sect. C].

[14]"Legal aspects of automatic trade data interchange" (TRADE/WP.4/R.185/Rev.1), contained in "Co-ordination of work: legal aspects of automatic data processing: note by the Secretariat" (A/CN.9/238), annex II [*Yearbook 1983*, part two, chap. V, sect. D].

[15]*Official Records of the General Assembly, Thirty-seventh Session, Supplement No. 17* (A/37/17), para. 73 [*Yearbook 1982*, part one, sect. A].

[16]"Legal value of computer records: report of the Secretary-General" (A/CN.9/265). An analytical summary of the replies to the questionnaire is contained in the annex to the report.

[17]*Official Records of the General Assembly, Fortieth Session, Supplement No. 17* (A/40/17), para. 360 [*Yearbook 1985*, part one, sect. A]. See annex X, below.

[18]See paragraph 104.

also in a report prepared by the Secretariat for the seventeenth session of the Commission (1984).[19] On the basis of these reports, the Commission placed the topic of legal aspects of automatic data processing on its programme of work as a priority item.[20] Further reports on this topic will be prepared by the Secretariat for the Commission.

[19]"Co-ordination of work: legal aspects of automatic data processing: report of the Secretary-General" (A/CN.9/254) [*Yearbook 1984,* part two, chap. V, sect. D].

[20]*Official Records of the General Assembly, Thirty-ninth Session, Supplement No. 17* (A/39/17), para. 136 [*Yearbook 1984,* part one, sect. A].

XII. Additional topics dealt with by the Commission

108.   The Commission has dealt with several topics in addition to those discussed in the preceding chapters. The work has principally involved studying issues associated with those topics and monitoring the relevant activities of other organizations. With respect to certain topics, such as bankers' commercial credits and bank guarantees, the Commission has also contributed procedurally and substantively to work being carried out by other organizations.[1]

Clauses protecting parties against the effects of currency fluctuations

109.   A report prepared for the Commission by the Secretariat in 1979 dealt with clauses designed to protect creditors against changes in the value of a currency in relation to other currencies, and clauses by which creditors seek to maintain the purchasing value of monetary obligations under contracts.[2] The Commission recognized that this subject was of interest because of the floating of the major currencies used in international trade.[3] It was also pointed out that the fluctuations in the value of those currencies created problems for developing countries as well as for countries whose currencies were in use. The Commission has requested the Secretariat to keep the question of currency fluctuation clauses under study and to submit a report on this subject to a future session.[4]

110.   Problems caused by currency fluctuations have also been dealt with by the Commission in the contexts of its work on the Legal Guide on drawing up International Contracts for the Construction of Industrial Works[5] and on a universal unit of account for international conventions.[6]

Bankers' commercial credits and bank guarantees

111.   From its earliest sessions, the Commission has taken an active interest in the work of the International Chamber of Commerce (ICC) in the areas of bankers' commercial credits and bank guarantees. This work includes the

---

[1]See paragraphs 111-114.

[2]"Clauses protecting parties against the effects of currency fluctuations: report of the Secretary-General" (A/CN.9/164) [*Yearbook 1979,* part two, chap. I, sect. D].

[3]*Official Records of the General Assembly, Thirty-fourth Session, Supplement No. 17* (A/34/17), para. 37 [*Yearbook 1979,* part one, chap. II, sect. A].

[4]*Ibid., Thirty-sixth Session, Supplement No. 17* (A/36/17), para. 49 [*Yearbook 1981,* part one, sect. A].

[5]See chapter VIII.

[6]See chapter X.

Uniform Customs and Practice for Documentary Credits, drawn up by the ICC in 1933 and revised by it in 1962, 1974 and 1983, and an examination of the law and practice relating to various types of bank guarantees used in international trade, such as performance guarantees, bid or tender guarantees, and guarantees of the repayment of advance payments made by purchasers. The **Uniform Rules for Contract Guarantees were drawn up by the ICC following its work on bank guarantees.**[7]

112. At the suggestion of the Commission and in conjunction with the UNCITRAL secretariat, the ICC also dealt with the subject of stand-by letters of credit.[8] One result of this work was the inclusion, in the 1983 revision of the Uniform Customs and Practice for Documentary Credits, of a specific reference to the applicability of the Uniform Customs and Practice to stand-by letters of credit.

113. Pursuant to its co-ordinating role in the area of international trade law, the Commission has closely monitored the progress of the work of the ICC in these areas. It has also co-operated with the ICC by serving as a channel through which States and interested banking and trade institutions not represented in the ICC could express their views on those subjects to the ICC.[9] On a substantive level, it has discussed at its annual sessions issues arising in connection with the work of the ICC,[10] and its secretariat has participated in

---

[7]The 1983 revision of *Documentary Credits: Uniform Customs and Practice for Documentary Credits* is contained in ICC publication no. 400 (Paris, ICC Publishing S.A., 1983) and reprinted in A/CN.9/251, annex II [*Yearbook 1984*, part two, chap. V, sect. B]. The text of *Uniform Rules for Contract Guarantees* is printed in ICC publication no. 325 (Paris, ICC Publishing S.A.).

[8]In formulating its current programme of work in 1978, the Commission decided to include the subject of stand-by letters of credit, to be studied in conjunction with the ICC. *Official Records of the General Assembly, Thirty-third Session, Supplement No. 17* (A/33/17), paras. 67 *(c)* (ii) *(a)*), 68 and 69 [*Yearbook 1978*, part one, chap. II, sect. A]. See also "Stand-by letters of credit: report of the Secretary-General" (A/CN.9/163), paras. 13-15) [*Yearbook 1979*, part two, chap. II, sect. B]; *Official Records of the General Assembly, Thirty-fourth Session, Supplement No. 17* (A/34/17), para. 48 [*Yearbook 1979*, part one, chap. II, sect. A]; "Current activities of international organizations related to the harmonization and unification of international trade law: report of the Secretary-General" (A/CN.9/202/Add.1), para. 132 [*Yearbook 1981*, part two, chap. V, sect. A]; "Documentary credits: note by the Secretariat" (A/CN.9/229), paras. 9-12 and footnote 10 [*Yearbook 1982*, part two, chap. VI, sect. C].

[9]For work on documentary credits, see, for example, *Official Records of the General Assembly, Twenty-fourth Session, Supplement No. 18* (A/7618), para. 95 [*Yearbook 1968-1970*, part two, chap. II, sect. A]; *ibid., Twenty-fifth Session, Supplement No. 17* (A/8017), para. 126 [*Yearbook 1968-1970*, part two, chap. III, sect. A]; *ibid., Twenty-seventh Session, Supplement No. 17* (A/8717), para. 78 [*Yearbook 1972*, part one, chap. II, sect. A]; *ibid., Twenty-eighth Session, Supplement No. 17* (A/9017), para. 38 [*Yearbook 1973*, part one, chap. II, sect. A]; A/CN.9/229, para. 11 [*Yearbook 1982*, part two, chap. VI, sect. C]. For work on bank guarantees, see, for example, *Official Records of the General Assembly, Twenty-fifth Session, Supplement No. 17* (A/8017), para. 138 [*Yearbook 1968-1970*, part two, chap. III, sect. A]; *ibid., Twenty-seventh Session, Supplement No. 17* (A/8717), para. 78 [*Yearbook 1972*, part one, chap. II, sect. A].

[10]For work on documentary credits, see, for example, *Official Records of the General Assembly, Twenty-fourth Session, Supplement No. 18* (A/7618), paras. 92 and 93 [*Yearbook 1968-1970*, part two, chap. II, sect. A]; *ibid., Twenty-fifth Session, Supplement No. 17* (A/8017), paras. 121-124 [*Yearbook 1968-1970*, part two, chap. IV, sect. A]; *ibid., Twenty-eighth Session, Supplement No. 17* (A/9017), para. 41 [*Yearbook 1973*, part one, chap. II, sect. A]. For work on bank guarantees, see, for example, *Official Records of the General Assembly, Twenty-fifth Session, Supplement No. 17* (A/8017), paras. 130-132 [*Yearbook 1968-1970*, part two, chap. III, sect. A]; *ibid., Twenty-seventh Session, Supplement No. 17* (A/8717), paras. 69-72 [*Yearbook 1972*, part one, chap. II, sect. A]; *ibid., Twenty-ninth Session, Supplement No. 17* (A/9617), para. 37 [*Yearbook 1974*, part one, chap. II, sect. B].

meetings of ICC bodies in which that work was carried out.[11] The Commission has requested its secretariat to prepare a further study on letters of credit and their operation in order to identify legal problems arising from their use, especially in connection with contracts other than those for the sale of goods.[12]

114.   Recognizing the important contribution made by the ICC's Uniform Customs and Practice for Documentary Credits to the unification of rules and practices relating to letters of credit, the Commission has endorsed and promoted the use of the 1962, 1974 and 1983 revisions of the Uniform Customs and Practice in transactions involving the establishment of a documentary credit.[13]

General conditions of sale

115.   During its early sessions the Commission discussed the important role played by general conditions of sale in the international sale of goods. At the request of the Commission,[14] the Secretariat prepared a series of studies on the feasibility of advancing the harmonization and unification of law in this area by formulating a set of general conditions to be applicable to the international sale of a broad range of goods and commodities.[15] The Commission's consideration of this subject was performed concurrently with its work leading to the signing at Vienna in 1980 of the United Nations Convention on Contracts for the International Sale of Goods (the "Vienna Sales Convention").[16] As work on these two aspects of the international sale of goods progressed, it became clear to the Commission that general conditions of sale, on the one hand, and comprehensive legal rules governing sales (such as those contained in the evolving Vienna Sales Convention), on the other hand, would cover many of the same issues, and that in these respects the provisions of one text might duplicate the provisions of the other. Accordingly, the Commission decided to concentrate its efforts in this area on the elaboration of the Vienna Sales Convention.[17]

---

[11]See, for example, *Official Records of the General Assembly, Twenty-seventh Session, Supplement No. 17* (A/8717), para. 78 [*Yearbook 1972,* part one, chap. II, sect. A]; *ibid., Twenty-ninth Session, Supplement No. 17* (A/9617), para. 37 [*Yearbook 1974,* part one, chap. II, sect. B]; A/CN.9/229, para. 11 [*Yearbook 1982,* part two, chap. VI, sect. C].

[12]*Official Records of the General Assembly, Thirty-seventh Session, Supplement No. 17* (A/37/17), para. 112 [*Yearbook 1982,* part one, sect. A].

[13]See *Official Records of the General Assembly, Twenty-fourth Session, Supplement No. 18* (A/7618), para. 95 [*Yearbook 1968-1970,* part two, chap. II, sect. A]; *ibid., Thirtieth Session, Supplement No. 17* (A/10017), para. 41 [*Yearbook 1975,* part one, chap. II, sect. A]; *ibid., Thirty-ninth Session, Supplement No. 17* (A/39/17), para. 129.

[14]*Official Records of the General Assembly, Twenty-fourth Session, Supplement No. 18* (A/7618), para. 60 (1) *(g)* [*Yearbook 1968-1970,* part two, chap. II, sect. A]; *ibid., Twenty-fifth Session, Supplement No. 17* (A/8017), para. 102 *(b)* [*Yearbook 1968-1970,* part two, chap. III, sect. A].

[15]"Implementation of the Commission's decisions relating to general conditions of sale and standard contracts: report of the Secretary-General" (A/CN.9/54) [*Yearbook 1971,* part two, chap. I, sect. B]; "General conditions of sale and standard contracts: report by the Secretary-General" (A/CN.9/69); "The feasibility of developing general conditions of sale embracing a wide scope of commodities: report of the Secretary-General" (A/CN.9/78) [*Yearbook 1973,* part two, chap. I, sect. B]; "General conditions of sale and standard contracts: report of the Secretary-General" (A/CN.9/98) [*Yearbook 1975,* part two, chap. I, sect. 6]; "General conditions of sale and standard contracts: report of the Secretary-General" (A/CN.9/136).

[16]See chapter IV, section B.

[17]See *Official Records of the General Assembly, Thirty-second Session, Supplement No. 17* (A/32/17), para. 36 [*Yearbook 1977,* part one, chap. II, sect. A].

116.   The Commission has dealt with specific types of clauses that may appear in general conditions in connection with its work on liquidated damages and penalty clauses and on the Legal Guide on drawing up International Contracts for the Construction of Industrial Works.[18]

Barter and barter-like transactions

117.   Recognizing that barter-like transactions are a significant factor in international trade,[19] the Commission has examined some of the factual and legal aspects relating to barter and barter-like transactions, and is monitoring the work of United Nations organs and other organizations in this field.[20]

Multinational enterprises

118.   In response to a request by the General Assembly in 1972,[21] the Commission considered the subject of multinational enterprises.[22] The Secretariat obtained information from Governments and interested international organizations on legal problems presented by different kinds of multinational enterprises. It also prepared a study for the Commission dealing with existing national legislation concerning multinational enterprises, analysing legal problems presented by such enterprises, and describing activities in this area engaged in by other United Nations organs.[23] The information and study presented by the Secretariat and the deliberations within UNCITRAL revealed no specific legal issues that could be acted on by the Commission.[24] In the meantime, the Economic and Social Council had created the United Nations Commission on Transnational Corporations, with the Centre for Transnational Corporations as its secretariat. UNCITRAL requested its secretariat to monitor developments in this field within the Commission on Transnational Corporations and other United Nations bodies and to inform UNCITRAL of any developments that might be of interest to it.[25]

---

[18]See chapters IX and VIII, respectively; see, also, *Official Records of the General Assembly, Thirty-third Session, Supplement No. 17* (A/33/17), para. 67 *(c)* (i) *(b)* [*Yearbook 1978*, part one, chap. II, sect. A].

[19]*Official Records of the General Assembly, Thirty-fourth Session, Supplement No. 17* (A/34/17), para. 21 [*Yearbook 1979*, part one, chap. II, sect. A].

[20]Reports of activities of other bodies in this field are contained in various documents within the series on co-ordination of work of other organizations: see chapter III, section A.

[21]General Assembly resolution 2928 (XXVII), para. 5 [*Yearbook 1973*, part one, chap. I, sect. C].

[22]*Official Records of the General Assembly, Twenty-eighth Session, Supplement No. 17* (A/9017), paras. 108 116 [*Yearbook 1973*, part one, chap. II, sect. A].

[23]"Multinational enterprises: report of the Secretary-General" (A/CN.9/104) [*Yearbook 1975*, part two, chaps. I and VI].

[24]See *Official Records of the General Assembly, Thirtieth Session, Supplement No. 17* (A/10017), para. 89 [*Yearbook 1975*, part one, chap. II, sect. A].

[25]*Official Records of the General Assembly, Thirtieth Session, Supplement No. 17* (A/10017), paras. 91-93 [*Yearbook 1975*, part one, chap. II, sect. A]; *ibid., Thirty-first Session, Supplement No. 17* (A/31/17), para. 73 [*Yearbook 1976*, part one, chap. II, sect. A]. See also "Multinational enterprises: note by the Secretary-General" (A/CN.9/148) [*Yearbook 1978*, part two, chap. III], which contains an exchange of letters between the Chairman of UNCITRAL and the Chairman of the Commission on Transnational Corporations.

Security interests in goods

119.   The Commission has examined the area of security interests in goods, focusing on the differing treatment of security interests under national legal systems and the desirability and feasibility of harmonizing the law in respect of security interests used in international trade transactions. Studies of various aspects of these questions were prepared in order to assist the Commission in this work, including a comprehensive comparative study of the law relating to security interests in a number of countries prepared by Professor Ulrich Drobnig of the Max Planck Institute of Foreign and Private International Law in Hamburg.[26]

120.   These studies, and the discussions within the Commission, underscored the complexity of the subject, its relationship with other areas of law (such as bankruptcy) and the fundamental differences in approach to the subject among legal systems. The Commission did not consider it desirable at that stage to undertake a world-wide unification of the law of security interests in goods, and decided not to engage in further work on the topic.[27]

Liability for damage caused by products intended for or involved in international trade

121.   In response to a request by the General Assembly,[28] the Commission examined the area of products liability in the context of goods intended for or involved in international trade, and the desirability and feasibility of formulating uniform legal rules in that area. The Secretariat prepared a series of studies relating to those matters, and circulated a questionnaire to Governments eliciting information on various aspects of the law relating to products liability in national legal systems.[29] After considering the preparatory work supplied by the Secretariat, the Commission decided not to pursue work towards the formulation of uniform rules.[30] It noted, however, that the studies performed by the Secretariat, and the information that it obtained from Governments could be useful to any country that wished to draft national legislation dealing with the question of products liability.[31]

---

[26]This study, supplemented in limited respects by the Secretariat, is set forth in "Study on security interests: report of the Secretary-General" (A/CN.9/131), annex [*Yearbook 1977*, part two, chap. II, sect. A].

[27]*Official Records of the General Assembly, Thirty-fifth Session, Supplement No. 17* (A/35/17), para. 28 [*Yearbook 1980*, part one, chap. II, sect. A].

[28]General Assembly resolution 3108 (XXVIII), para. 7 [*Yearbook 1974*, part one, chap. I, sect. C].

[29]The questionnaire, and analysis of replies received by the Secretariat, are contained in "Analysis of the replies of Governments to the questionnaire on liability for damage caused by products: report of the Secretary-General" (A/CN.9/139) [*Yearbook 1977*, part two, chap. IV, sect. B].

[30]*Official Records of the General Assembly, Thirty-second Session, Supplement No. 17* (A/32/17), para. 44, and annex II, paras. 38-46 [*Yearbook 1977*, part one, chap. II, sect. A].

[31]*Ibid., Thirty-second Session, Supplement No. 17* (A/32/17), para. 43 [*Yearbook 1977*, part one, chap. II, sect. A].

Most-favoured-nation clauses

122. The International Law Commission (ILC) completed work in 1978 on a set of draft articles designed to assist in the interpretation and application of most-favoured-nation clauses to which States might agree in their bilateral and multilateral relations. The General Assembly requested UNCITRAL to submit any comments and observations that it deemed appropriate on the ILC draft articles.[32] The Commission considered the matter on the basis of a study prepared by the Secretariat.[33] While no formal comments were formulated by the Commission for submission to the General Assembly,[34] the Assembly took note of the points raised during the discussion within the Commission as reflected in the report of the Commission to the Assembly.[35]

---

[32]General Assembly resolution 36/111, reproduced in "Most-favoured-nation clauses: note by the Secretariat" (A/CN.9/224), annex [*Yearbook 1982,* part two, chap. V].

[33]"Most-favoured-nation clauses: note by the Secretariat" (A/CN.9/224) [*Yearbook 1982,* part two, chap. V].

[34]*Official Records of the General Assembly, Thirty-seventh Session, Supplement No. 17* (A/37/17), paras. 133-138 [*Yearbook 1982,* part one, sect. A].

[35]General Assembly resolution 37/106, para. 1 [*Yearbook 1982,* part one, sect. D].

Annexes

Legal texts and other material relating to or emanating from the work of the Commission

ANNEX I. ORIGIN AND MANDATE OF THE COMMISSION

General Assembly resolution 2205 (XXI) of 17 December 1966

2205 (XXI). ESTABLISHMENT OF THE UNITED NATIONS COMMIS-
SION ON INTERNATIONAL TRADE LAW

The General Assembly,

Recalling its resolution 2102 (XX) of 20 December 1965, by which it requested the Secretary-General to submit to the General Assembly at its twenty-first session a comprehensive report on the progressive development of the law of international trade,

Having considered with appreciation the report of the Secretary-General on that subject,[1]

Considering that international trade co-operation among States is an important factor in the promotion of friendly relations and, consequently, in the maintenance of peace and security,

Recalling its belief that the interests of all peoples, and particularly those of developing countries, demand the betterment of conditions favouring the extensive development of international trade,

Reaffirming its conviction that divergencies arising from the laws of different States in matters relating to international trade constitute one of the obstacles to the development of world trade,

Having noted with appreciation the efforts made by intergovernmental and non-governmental organizations towards the progressive harmonization and unification of the law of international trade by promoting the adoption of international conventions, uniform laws, standard contract provisions, general conditions of sale, standard trade terms and other measures,

Noting at the same time that progress in this area has not been commensurate with the importance and urgency of the problem, owing to a number of factors, in particular insufficient co-ordination and co-operation between the organizations concerned, their limited membership or authority and the small degree of participation in this field on the part of many developing countries,

Considering it desirable that the process of harmonization and unification of the law of international trade should be substantially co-ordinated, systematized and accelerated and that a broader participation should be secured in furthering progress in this area,

Convinced that it would therefore be desirable for the United Nations to play a more active role towards reducing or removing legal obstacles to the flow of international trade,

Noting that such action would be properly within the scope and competence of the Organization under the terms of Article 1, paragraph 3, and Article 13, and of Chapters IX and X of the Charter of the United Nations,

---

[1] *Official Records of the General Assembly, Twenty-first Session, Annexes,* agenda item 88, documents A/6396 and Add.1 and 2.

Having in mind the responsibilities of the United Nations Conference on Trade and Development in the field of international trade,

Recalling that the Conference, in accordance with its General Principle Six,[2] has a particular interest in promoting the establishment of rules furthering international trade as one of the most important factors in economic development,

Recognizing that there is no existing United Nations organ which is both familiar with this technical legal subject and able to devote sufficient time to work in this field,

I

Decides to establish a United Nations Commission on International Trade Law (hereinafter referred to as the Commission), which shall have for its object the promotion of the progressive harmonization and unification of the law of international trade, in accordance with the provisions set forth in section II below;

II

Organization and functions of the United Nations Commission on International Trade Law

1. The Commission shall consist of twenty-nine States, elected by the General Assembly for a term of six years, except as provided in paragraph 2 of the present resolution. In electing the members of the Commission, the Assembly shall observe the following distribution of seats:

   (a)   Seven from African States;

   (b)   Five from Asian States;

   (c)   Four from Eastern European States;

   (d)   Five from Latin American States;

   (e)   Eight from Western European and other States.

The General Assembly shall also have due regard to the adequate representation of the principal economic and legal systems of the world, and of developed and developing countries.

2. Of the members elected at the first election, to be held at the twenty-second session of the General Assembly, the terms of fourteen members shall expire at the end of three years. The President of the General Assembly shall select these members within each of the five groups of States referred to in paragraph 1 above, by drawing lots.

3. The members elected at the first election shall take office on 1 January 1968. Subsequently, the members shall take office on 1 January of the year following each election.

4. The representatives of members on the Commission shall be appointed by Member States in so far as possible from among persons of eminence in the field of the law of international trade.

5. Retiring members shall be eligible for re-election.

6. The Commission shall normally hold one regular session a year. It shall, if there are no technical difficulties, meet alternately at United Nations Headquarters and at the United Nations Office at Geneva.

7. The Secretary-General shall make available to the Commission the appropriate staff and facilities required by the Commission to fulfil its task.

---

[2]See *Proceedings of the United Nations Conference on Trade and Development*, vol. I, *Final Act and Report* (United Nations publication, Sales No.: 64.II.B.11), annex A.I.1, p. 18.

8. The Commission shall further the progressive harmonization and unification of the law of international trade by:

(a) Co-ordinating the work of organizations active in this field and encouraging co-operation among them;

(b) Promoting wider participation in existing international conventions and wider acceptance of existing model and uniform laws;

(c) Preparing or promoting the adoption of new international conventions, model laws and uniform laws and promoting the codification and wider acceptance of international trade terms, provisions, customs and practices, in collaboration, where appropriate, with the organizations operating in this field;

(d) Promoting ways and means of ensuring a uniform interpretation and application of international conventions and uniform laws in the field of the law of international trade;

(e) Collecting and disseminating information on national legislation and modern legal developments, including case law, in the field of the law of international trade;

(f) Establishing and maintaining a close collaboration with the United Nations Conference on Trade and Development;

(g) Maintaining liaison with other United Nations organs and specialized agencies concerned with international trade;

(h) Taking any other action it may deem useful to fulfil its functions.

9. The Commission shall bear in mind the interests of all peoples, and particularly those of developing countries, in the extensive development of international trade.

10. The Commission shall submit an annual report, including its recommendations, to the General Assembly, and the report shall be submitted simultaneously to the United Nations Conference on Trade and Development for comments. Any such comments or recommendations which the Conference or the Trade and Development Board may wish to make, including suggestions on topics for inclusion in the work of the Commission, shall be transmitted to the General Assembly in accordance with the relevant provisions of Assembly resolution 1995 (XIX) of 30 December 1964. Any other recommendations relevant to the work of the Commission which the Conference or the Board may wish to make shall be similarly transmitted to the General Assembly.

11. The Commission may consult with or request the services of any international or national organization, scientific institution and individual expert, on any subject entrusted to it, if it considers such consultation or services might assist it in the performance of its functions.

12. The Commission may establish appropriate working relationships with inter-governmental organizations and international non-governmental organizations concerned with the progressive harmonization and unification of the law of international trade.

III

1. *Requests* the Secretary-General, pending the election of the Commission, to carry out the preparatory work necessary for the organization of the work of the Commission and, in particular:

(a) To invite Member States to submit in writing before 1 July 1967, taking into account in particular the report of the Secretary-General,[3] comments on a programme of work to be undertaken by the Commission in discharging its functions under paragraph 8 of section II above;

---

[3] *Official Records of the General Assembly, Twenty-first Session, Annexes,* agenda item 88, documents A/6396 and Add.1 and 2.

(b) To request similar comments from the organs and organizations referred to in paragraph 8 *(f)* and *(g)* and in paragraph 12 of section II above;

2. *Decides* to include an item entitled "Election of the members of the United Nations Commission on International Trade Law" in the provisional agenda of its twenty-second session.

1497th plenary meeting,
17 December 1966

ANNEX II. INTERNATIONAL SALE OF GOODS: LIMITATION PERIOD

A. Convention on the Limitation Period in the International Sale of Goods (New York, 1974)

Preamble

The States Parties to the present Convention,

Considering that international trade is an important factor in the promotion of friendly relations amongst States,

Believing that the adoption of uniform rules governing the limitation period in the international sale of goods would facilitate the development of world trade,

Have agreed as follows:

Part I. Substantive provisions

SPHERE OF APPLICATION

Article 1

1. This Convention shall determine when claims of a buyer and a seller against each other arising from a contract of international sale of goods or relating to its breach, termination or invalidity can no longer be exercised by reason of the expiration of a period of time. Such period of time is hereinafter referred to as "the limitation period".

2. This Convention shall not affect a particular time-limit within which one party is required, as a condition for the acquisition or exercise of his claim, to give notice to the other party or perform any act other than the institution of legal proceedings.

3. In this Convention:

(a) "Buyer", "seller" and "party" mean persons who buy or sell, or agree to buy or sell, goods, and the successors to and assigns of their rights or obligations under the contract of sale;

(b) "Creditor" means a party who asserts a claim, whether or not such a claim is for a sum of money;

(c) "Debtor" means a party against whom a creditor asserts a claim;

(d) "Breach of contract" means the failure of a party to perform the contract or any performance not in conformity with the contract;

(e) "Legal proceedings" includes judicial, arbitral and administrative proceedings;

(f) "Person" includes corporation, company, partnership, association, or entity, whether private or public, which can sue or be sued;

(g) "Writing" includes telegram and telex;

(h) "Year" means a year according to the Gregorian calendar.

Article 2

For the purposes of this Convention:

(a) A contract of sale of goods shall be considered international if, at the time of the conclusion of the contract, the buyer and the seller have their places of business in different States;

(b) The fact that the parties have their places of business in different States shall be disregarded whenever this fact does not appear either from the contract or from any dealings between, or from information disclosed by, the parties at any time before or at the conclusion of the contract;

(c) Where a party to a contract of sale of goods has places of business in more than one State, the place of business shall be that which has the closest relationship to the contract and its performance, having regard to the circumstances known to or contemplated by the parties at the time of the conclusion of the contract;

(d) Where a party does not have a place of business, reference shall be made to his habitual residence;

(e) Neither the nationality of the parties nor the civil or commercial character of the parties or of the contract shall be taken into consideration.

Article 3

1. This Convention shall apply only if, at the time of the conclusion of the contract, the places of business of the parties to a contract of international sale of goods are in Contracting States.

2. Unless this Convention provides otherwise, it shall apply irrespective of the law which would otherwise be applicable by virtue of the rules of private international law.

3. This Convention shall not apply when the parties have expressly excluded its application.

Article 4

This Convention shall not apply to sales:

(a) Of goods bought for personal, family or household use;

(b) By auction;

(c) On execution or otherwise by authority of law;

(d) Of stocks, shares, investment securities, negotiable instruments or money;

(e) Of ships, vessels or aircraft;

(f) Of electricity.

Article 5

This Convention shall not apply to claims based upon:

(a) Death of, or personal injury to, any person;

(b) Nuclear damage caused by the goods sold;

(c) A lien, mortgage or other security interest in property;

(d) A judgement or award made in legal proceedings;

(e) A document on which direct enforcement or execution can be obtained in accordance with the law of the place where such enforcement or execution is sought;

(f) A bill of exchange, cheque or promissory note.

Article 6

1. This Convention shall not apply to contracts in which the preponderant part of the obligations of the seller consists in the supply of labour or other services.

2. Contracts for the supply of goods to be manufactured or produced shall be considered to be sales, unless the party who orders the goods undertakes to supply a substantial part of the materials necessary for such manufacture or production.

Article 7

In the interpretation and application of the provisions of this Convention, regard shall be had to its international character and to the need to promote uniformity.

THE DURATION AND COMMENCEMENT OF THE LIMITATION PERIOD

Article 8

The limitation period shall be four years.

Article 9

1. Subject to the provisions of articles 10, 11 and 12 the limitation period shall commence on the date on which the claim accrues.

2. The commencement of the limitation period shall not be postponed by:

(a) A requirement that the party be given a notice as described in paragraph 2 of article 1, or

(b) A provision in an arbitration agreement that no right shall arise until an arbitration award has been made.

Article 10

1. A claim arising from a breach of contract shall accrue on the date on which such breach occurs.

2. A claim arising from a defect or other lack of conformity shall accrue on the date on which the goods are actually handed over to, or their tender is refused by, the buyer.

3. A claim based on fraud committed before or at the time of the conclusion of the contract or during its performance shall accrue on the date on which the fraud was or reasonably could have been discovered.

Article 11

If the seller has given an express undertaking relating to the goods which is stated to have effect for a certain period of time, whether expressed in terms of a specific period of time or otherwise, the limitation period in respect of any claim arising from the undertaking shall commence on the date on which the buyer notifies the seller of the fact on which the claim is based, but not later than on the date of the expiration of the period of the undertaking.

Article 12

1. If, in circumstances provided for by the law applicable to the contract, one party is entitled to declare the contract terminated before the time for performance is due, and exercises this right, the limitation period in respect of a claim based on any such circumstances shall commence on the date on which the declaration is made to the other party. If the contract is not declared to be terminated before performance becomes due, the limitation period shall commence on the date on which performance is due.

2. The limitation period in respect of a claim arising out of a breach by one party of a contract for the delivery of or payment for goods by instalments shall, in relation to each separate instalment, commence on the date on which the particular breach occurs. If, under the law applicable to the contract, one party is entitled to declare the contract

terminated by reason of such breach, and exercises this right, the limitation period in respect of all relevant instalments shall commence on the date on which the declaration is made to the other party.

CESSATION AND EXTENSION OF THE LIMITATION PERIOD

Article 13

The limitation period shall cease to run when the creditor performs any act which, under the law of the court where the proceedings are instituted, is recognized as commencing judicial proceedings against the debtor or as asserting his claim in such proceedings already instituted against the debtor, for the purpose of obtaining satisfaction or recognition of his claim.

Article 14

1. Where the parties have agreed to submit to arbitration, the limitation period shall cease to run when either party commences arbitral proceedings in the manner provided for in the arbitration agreement or by the law applicable to such proceedings.

2. In the absence of any such provision, arbitral proceedings shall be deemed to commence on the date on which a request that the claim in dispute be referred to arbitration is delivered at the habitual residence or place of business of the other party or, if he has no such residence or place of business, then at his last known residence or place of business.

Article 15

In any legal proceedings other than those mentioned in articles 13 and 14, including legal proceedings commenced upon the occurrence of:

(a) The death or incapacity of the debtor,

(b) The bankruptcy or any state of insolvency affecting the whole of the property of the debtor, or

(c) The dissolution or liquidation of a corporation, company, partnership, association or entity when it is the debtor,

the limitation period shall cease to run when the creditor asserts his claim in such proceedings for the purpose of obtaining satisfaction or recognition of the claim, subject to the law governing the proceedings.

Article 16

For the purposes of articles 13, 14 and 15, any act performed by way of counterclaim shall be deemed to have been performed on the same date as the act performed in relation to the claim against which the counterclaim is raised, provided that both the claim and the counterclaim relate to the same contract or to several contracts concluded in the course of the same transaction.

Article 17

1. Where a claim has been asserted in legal proceedings within the limitation period in accordance with articles 13, 14, 15 or 16, but such legal proceedings have ended without a decision binding on the merits of the claim, the limitation period shall be deemed to have continued to run.

2. If, at the time such legal proceedings ended, the limitation period has expired or has less than one year to run, the creditor shall be entitled to a period of one year from the date on which the legal proceedings ended.

Article 18

1.   Where legal proceedings have been commenced against one debtor, the limitation period prescribed in this Convention shall cease to run against any other party jointly and severally liable with the debtor, provided that the creditor informs such party in writing within that period that the proceedings have been commenced.

2.   Where legal proceedings have been commenced by a subpurchaser against the buyer, the limitation period prescribed in this Convention shall cease to run in relation to the buyer's claim over against the seller, if the buyer informs the seller in writing within that period that the proceedings have been commenced.

3.   Where the legal proceedings referred to in paragraphs 1 and 2 of this article have ended, the limitation period in respect of the claims of the creditor or the buyer against the party jointly and severally liable or against the seller shall be deemed not to have ceased running by virtue of paragraphs 1 and 2 of this article, but the creditor or the buyer shall be entitled to an additional year from the date on which the legal proceedings ended, if at that time the limitation period had expired or had less than one year to run.

Article 19

Where the creditor performs, in the State in which the debtor has his place of business and before the expiration of the limitation period, any act, other than the acts described in articles 13, 14, 15 and 16, which under the law of that State has the effect of recommencing a limitation period, a new limitation period of four years shall commence on the date prescribed by that law.

Article 20

1.   Where the debtor, before the expiration of the limitation period, acknowledges in writing his obligation to the creditor, a new limitation period of four years shall commence to run from the date of such acknowledgement.

2.   Payment of interest or partial performance of an obligation by the debtor shall have the same effect as an acknowledgement under paragraph (1) of this article if it can reasonably be inferred from such payment or performance that the debtor acknowledges that obligation.

Article 21

Where, as a result of a circumstance which is beyond the control of the creditor and which he could neither avoid nor overcome, the creditor has been prevented from causing the limitation period to cease to run, the limitation period shall be extended so as not to expire before the expiration of one year from the date on which the relevant circumstance ceased to exist.

MODIFICATION OF THE LIMITATION PERIOD BY THE PARTIES

Article 22

1.   The limitation period cannot be modified or affected by any declaration or agreement between the parties, except in the cases provided for in paragraph (2) of this article.

2.   The debtor may at any time during the running of the limitation period extend the period by a declaration in writing to the creditor. This declaration may be renewed.

3. The provisions of this article shall not affect the validity of a clause in the contract of sale which stipulates that arbitral proceedings shall be commenced within a shorter period of limitation than that prescribed by this Convention, provided that such clause is valid under the law applicable to the contract of sale.

GENERAL LIMIT OF THE LIMITATION PERIOD

Article 23

Notwithstanding the provisions of this Convention, a limitation period shall in any event expire not later than 10 years from the date on which it commenced to run under articles 9, 10, 11 and 12 of this Convention.

CONSEQUENCES OF THE EXPIRATION OF THE LIMITATION PERIOD

Article 24

Expiration of the limitation period shall be taken into consideration in any legal proceedings only if invoked by a party to such proceedings.

Article 25

1. Subject to the provisions of paragraph (2) of this article and of article 24, no claim shall be recognized or enforced in any legal proceedings commenced after the expiration of the limitation period.

2. Notwithstanding the expiration of the limitation period, one party may rely on his claim as a defence or for the purpose of set-off against a claim asserted by the other party, provided that in the latter case this may only be done:

   (a) If both claims relate to the same contract or to several contracts concluded in the course of the same transaction; or

   (b) If the claims could have been set-off at any time before the expiration of the limitation period.

Article 26

Where the debtor performs his obligation after the expiration of the limitation period, he shall not on that ground be entitled in any way to claim restitution even if he did not know at the time when he performed his obligation that the limitation period had expired.

Article 27

The expiration of the limitation period with respect to a principal debt shall have the same effect with respect to an obligation to pay interest on that debt.

CALCULATION OF THE PERIOD

Article 28

1. The limitation period shall be calculated in such a way that it shall expire at the end of the day which corresponds to the date on which the period commenced to run. If there is no such corresponding date, the period shall expire at the end of the last day of the last month of the limitation period.

2. The limitation period shall be calculated by reference to the date of the place where the legal proceedings are instituted.

Article 29

Where the last day of the limitation period falls on an official holiday or other *dies non juridicus* precluding the appropriate legal action in the jurisdiction where the creditor institutes legal proceedings or asserts a claim as envisaged in articles 13, 14 or 15 the limitation period shall be extended so as not to expire until the end of the first day following that official holiday or *dies non juridicus* on which such proceedings could be instituted or on which such a claim could be asserted in that jurisdiction.

INTERNATIONAL EFFECT

Article 30

The acts and circumstances referred to in articles 13 through 19 which have taken place in one Contracting State shall have effect for the purposes of this Convention in another Contracting State, provided that the creditor has taken all reasonable steps to ensure that the debtor is informed of the relevant act or circumstances as soon as possible.

Part II.   Implementation

Article 31

1.   If a Contracting State has two or more territorial units in which, according to its constitution, different systems of law are applicable in relation to the matters dealt with in this Convention, it may, at the time of signature, ratification or accession, declare that this Convention shall extend to all its territorial units or only to one or more of them, and may amend its declaration by submitting another declaration at any time.

2.   These declarations shall be notified to the Secretary-General of the United Nations and shall state expressly the territorial units to which the Convention applies.

3.   If a Contracting State described in paragraph (1) of this article makes no declaration at the time of signature, ratification or accession, the Convention shall have effect within all territorial units of that State.

Article 32

Where in this Convention reference is made to the law of a State in which different systems of law apply, such reference shall be construed to mean the law of the particular legal system concerned.

Article 33

Each Contracting State shall apply the provisions of this Convention to contracts concluded on or after the date of the entry into force of this Convention.

Part III.   Declarations and reservations

Article 34

Two or more Contracting States may at any time declare that contracts of sale between a seller having a place of business in one of these States and a buyer having a place of business in another of these States shall not be governed by this Convention, because they apply to the matters governed by this Convention the same or closely related legal rules.

Article 35

A Contracting State may declare, at the time of the deposit of its instrument of ratification or accession, that it will not apply the provisions of this Convention to actions for annulment of the contract.

Article 36

Any State may declare, at the time of the deposit of its instrument of ratification or accession, that it shall not be compelled to apply the provisions of article 24 of this Convention.

Article 37

This Convention shall not prevail over conventions already entered into or which may be entered into, and which contain provisions concerning the matters covered by this Convention, provided that the seller and buyer have their places of business in States parties to such a convention.

Article 38

1. A Contracting State which is a party to an existing convention relating to the international sale of goods may declare, at the time of the deposit of its instrument of ratification or accession, that it will apply this Convention exclusively to contracts of international sale of goods as defined in such existing convention.

2. Such declaration shall cease to be effective on the first day of the month following the expiration of 12 months after a new convention on the international sale of goods, concluded under the auspices of the United Nations, shall have entered into force.

Article 39

No reservation other than those made in accordance with articles 34, 35, 36 and 38 shall be permitted.

Article 40

1. Declarations made under this Convention shall be addressed to the Secretary-General of the United Nations and shall take effect simultaneously with the entry of this Convention into force in respect of the State concerned, except declarations made thereafter. The latter declarations shall take effect on the first day of the month following the expiration of six months after the date of their receipt by the Secretary-General of the United Nations.

2. Any State which has made a declaration under this Convention may withdraw it at any time by a notification addressed to the Secretary-General of the United Nations. Such withdrawal shall take effect on the first day of the month following the expiration of six months after the date of the receipt of the notification by the Secretary-General of the United Nations. In the case of a declaration made under article 34 of this Convention, such withdrawal shall also render inoperative, as from the date on which the withdrawal takes effect, any reciprocal declaration made by another State under that article.

Part IV. Final clauses

Article 41

This Convention shall be open until 31 December 1975 for signature by all States at the Headquarters of the United Nations.

Article 42

This Convention is subject to ratification. The instruments of ratification shall be deposited with the Secretary-General of the United Nations.

This Convention shall remain open for accession by any State. The instuments of accession shall be deposited with the Secretary-General of the United Nations.

Article 44

1. This Convention shall enter into force on the first day of the month following the expiration of six months after the date of the deposit of the tenth instrument of ratification or accession.

2. For each State ratifying or acceding to this Convention after the deposit of the tenth instrument of ratification or accession, this Convention shall enter into force on the first day of the month following the expiration of six months after the date of the deposit of its instrument of ratification or accession.

Article 45

1. Any Contracting State may denounce this Convention by notifying the Secretary-General of the United Nations to that effect.

2. The denunciation shall take effect on the first day of the month following the expiration of 12 months after receipt of the notification by the Secretary-General of the United Nations.

Article 46

The original of this Convention, of which the Chinese, English, French, Russian and Spanish texts are equally authentic, shall be deposited with the Secretary-General of the United Nations.

B. Commentary on the Convention on the Limitation Period in the International Sale of Goods, done at New York, 14 June 1974

This commentary has been prepared pursuant to a request by the United Nations Conference on Prescription (Limitation) in the International Sale of Goods (New York, 20 May-14 June 1974) at which the Convention on the Limitation Period in the International Sale of Goods was adopted. It has been written under the responsibility of the United Nations Office of Legal Affairs by Professor Kazuaki Sono of Hokkaido University, Japan, who served as Secretary of the Drafting Committee of the Conference.

CONTENTS

Preamble

The States Parties to the present Convention,

Considering that international trade is an important factor in the promotion of friendly relations amongst States,

Believing that the adoption of uniform rules governing the limitation period in the international sale of goods would facilitate the development of world trade,

Have agreed as follows:

Introduction: Objective of the Convention

1. This Convention is concerned with the period of time within which the parties to a contract of international sale of goods may commence legal proceedings for the exercise of claims arising from or relating to such contracts.

2. Differences in national laws governing the limitation of claims or the prescription of rights create serious practical difficulties. The prescription or limitation periods under national laws vary widely. Some periods seem too short (e.g. six months, one year) to meet the practical requirements of international sales transactions, in view of the time that may be needed for negotiations and then for the institution of legal proceedings in a foreign and, often, distant country. Other limitation periods (in some cases up to 30 years) are inappropriately long for transactions involving the international sale of goods and fail to provide the basic protection that limitation rules were intended to accord, such as protection from the uncertainty and threat to business stability posed by the delayed presentation of claims and from the loss or stalenesss of evidence pertaining to claims presented with undue delay.

3. National rules not only differ, but in many instances they are also difficult to apply to international sales transactions.[1] One difficulty arises from the fact that some national laws apply a single rule of prescription or limitation to a wide variety of transactions and relationships. As a result, the rules are expressed in general and

---

[1]For some illustrations of difficulties, see R. Kuratowski, Limitation of Actions Founded on Contract and Prescription of Contractual Obligations in Private International Law, Estratto Paglivatti del Terzo Congresso di Diritto Comparato, vol. III—Paris IV, pp. 447-460; E. Harris, Time-Limits for Claims and Actions, in Unification of the Law Governing International Sale of Goods (J. Honnold, ed. 1966), pp. 201-223. Also see H. Trammer, Time-Limits for Claims and Actions in International Trade, *ibid.,* pp. 225-233.

sometimes vague terms that are difficult to apply to the specific problems of an international sale. This difficulty is magnified for international transactions, since merchants and their lawyers will often be unfamiliar with the import of these general terms and with the techniques of interpretation used in a foreign legal system.

4. Perhaps even more serious is the uncertainty as to which national law will be applicable to an international sales transaction. Apart from the problems of choice of law that customarily arise in an international transaction, problems of prescription or limitation present a special difficulty of characterization or qualification: some legal systems consider these rules as "substantive" and therefore must decide which national law is applicable; other systems consider them as part of the "procedural" rules of the forum; still other legal systems follow a combination of the above approaches.[2]

5. In light of the difficulties mentioned in paragraphs 2-4 above, i.e. the differences in the time periods for bringing claims under various national laws, the problems in determining which national law is to apply and what effect it is to have, and the need to provide specific rules in this area adapted to the practical needs of international commerce, it was felt that the problems were sufficiently serious to justify the preparation of uniform rules on prescription or limitation of claims arising from the international sale of goods. In addition, substantive unification of the national laws on the prescription or limitation of claims would not only remove doubt and uncertainty in legal relations arising from the international sale of goods but would also serve the interests of justice and equity: under present conditions it is possible that an unexpected or severe application of a national rule on prescription or limitation of claims will prevent redress of a just claim, or that a lax application of such a rule will fail to provide adequate protection against claims that are stale or unfounded.

6. In view of the widely varying concepts and approaches prevailing under national laws with respect to the limitation of claims and the prescription of rights, it has been considered advisable to provide in a convention uniform rules that are as concrete and complete as possible. A brief and general uniform law (such as a law merely specifying the length of the prescription or limitation period) would do little in actual practice to achieve unification, since the divergent rules of national law would then be brought into play in "interpreting" such a brief and general provision. Since this Convention is confined to one type of transaction—the purchase and sale of goods—it is possible to state uniform rules for this type of transaction with a degree of concreteness and specificity that is not feasible in statutes that deal with many different types of transactions and claims. The loss of uniformity in the application of this Convention through the use of divergent rules and concepts of national law may not be wholly avoided, but this Convention seeks to minimize the danger by dealing with the problems that are inherent in this field as specifically as feasible within the scope of a convention of manageable length.[3]

Part I. Substantive provisions

Sphere of application

Article 1
[Introductory provisions: subject-matter and definitions]*

1. This Convention shall determine when claims of a buyer and a seller against each other arising from a contract of international sale of goods or relating to its breach, termination or invalidity can no longer be exercised by reason of the

---

*Captions are not contained in the Convention; they are added to this commentary only for ease of reference and should not be considered as forming part of the Convention.

[2]See para. 5 of commentary on art. 3.

[3]See also art. 7, on rules for interpretation and application of the provisions of this Convention.

expiration of a period of time. Such period of time is hereinafter referred to as "the limitation period".

2. This Convention shall not affect a particular time-limit within which one party is required, as a condition for the acquisition or exercise of his claim, to give notice to the other party or perform any act other than the institution of legal proceedings.

3. In this Convention:

(a) "Buyer", "seller" and "party" means persons who buy or sell, or agree to buy or sell, goods, and the successors to and assigns of their rights or obligations under the contract of sale;

(b) "Creditor" means a party who asserts a claim, whether or not such a claim is for a sum of money;

(c) "Debtor" means a party against whom a creditor asserts a claim;

(d) "Breach of contract" means the failure of a party to perform the contract of any performance not in conformity with the contract;

(e) "Legal proceedings" includes judicial, arbitral and administrative proceedings;

(f) "Persons" includes corporation, company, partnership, association or entity, whether private or public, which can sue or be sued;

(g) "Writing" includes telegram and telex;

(h) "Year" means a year according to the Gregorian calendar.

Commentary

I. *The subject-matter covered by the Convention, paragraph (1)*

1. Under paragraph (1) of article 1, this Convention governs *the period* within which the parties to a contract of international sale of goods must exercise against each other any claim arising from or relating to such contract or be time-barred from asserting it. The characterization of this period and the legal effect of its expiration on the rights or claims of the parties differ widely under the various national legal systems. In view of the international character of this Convention and in order to promote uniformity in its interpretation and application, the use of traditional terms, such as "prescription of rights", "limitation of claims" or "limitation of legal proceedings", having differing connotations in the various legal systems, was avoided in the Convention. Consequently, paragraph (1) employs the neutral expression "when claims . . . can no longer be exercised by reason of the expiration of a period of time" to denote the subject-matter covered by the Convention. Thus the Convention is applicable irrespective of the particular theoretical approach or terminology employed by the applicable national law, as long as the period of time in question performs the function described in the first sentence of article 1 (1). The second sentence of paragraph (1) of this article provides that in the Convention such a time-period shall be called "the limitation period".

2. Specific aspects of the Convention's sphere of application will be discussed in relation to: *(a)* the parties governed by the Convention, and *(b)* the types of claims that are subject to the limitation period.

(a) *The parties*

3. Paragraph (1) of article 1 shows that this Convention is directed to claims arising from the relationship of *buyer and seller*. The terms "buyer", "seller" and "party", as defined in article 1 (3) *(a)*, include the "successors to and assigns of their rights or obligations under the contract of sale". Thus the Convention also governs the limitation period for the assertion of rights and obligations which are acquired through succession by operation of law (as on death or bankruptcy) or through voluntary assignment or delegation by a party to an international sales contract. Other important "successors" include insurers who become subrogated to the rights of a party under a sales contract

and the surviving company which results from a merger of companies or from a corporate reorganization.

4. It should be noted that, under article 1 (3) *(a)*, to be a "buyer" or "seller" a person must "buy or sell, or agree to buy or sell, goods". Thus a party who has only the right (or "option") *to conclude* a sales contract is not a "buyer" or "seller" unless and until the sales contract is in fact concluded. Thus, rights under the option agreement (as contrasted with rights under a contract that may result from the exercise of the option) are not governed by the Convention.

(b) *Transactions subject to the Convention; types of claims*

5. Under article 1 (1), this Convention applies to *"claims . . . arising from* a contract of international sale of goods or *relating to* its breach, termination or invalidity". Article 2 determines whether a contract of sale of goods is "international"; article 3 details the circumstances under which a Contracting State must apply the rules of this Convention; and articles 4 through 6 exclude from the scope of the Convention certain defined types of sales, goods, claims and contracts.

6. Paragraph (1) of article 1 provides that this Convention governs claims "arising from a contract of international sale of goods" as well as claims "relating to its breach, termination or invalidity". The requirement that claims "arise from" a sales contract serves to exclude claims that arise independently of the contract, such as claims based on tort or *delict*. The language "relating to" the breach, termination or invalidity in article 1 (1) is broad enough to cover not only claims arising from but also claims "relating to" the breach, termination or invalidity of an international sales contract. For example, the buyer may have made an advance payment to the seller under a sales contract which the seller fails to perform alleging impossibility, government regulation or some similar supervening event. The seller might also claim that the contract was invalid for some other reasons. Whether these events constitute an excuse for the seller's failure to perform may often be in dispute. Hence, the buyer may need to bring an action against the seller presenting, in the alternative, claims both for breach of contract and for restitution of the advance payment. Because of the frequent connexion, in practice, between these two types of claims, both are governed by this Convention.[4]

7. The references in article 1 (1) to the "contract" and to the relationship between "a buyer and a seller against each other" serve to exclude from the coverage of the Convention claims against a seller by a person who has purchased the goods from someone other than the seller. For example, where a manufacturer sells goods to a distributor who resells the goods to a subpurchaser, a claim by the subpurchaser against the manufacturer would not be governed by the Convention. See also paragraph 3, above. Nor does this Convention apply to claims of the buyer or seller against a person who is neither a "buyer" nor "seller", but who had guaranteed the performance by the buyer or seller of an obligation under the contract of sale.[5]

---

[4]The language "relating to" is also relevant where the applicable law of the contract requires that the invalidity of a contract must first be established by way of an *action for annulment.* In such a case, a mere assertion that a contract is terminated or invalid does not create a basis for the assertion of claims against the other party until the termination or invalidity itself has been established by the courts. Under the broad language of article 1 (1), the period for bringing such an action for annulment falls within the scope of this Convention. (As to the possibility of excluding actions for annulment from the application of this Convention by way of a reservation, see art. 35 and its accompanying commentary.) Of course, where the termination or invalidity need not first be established by an action for annulment, this Convention does not affect provisions in the applicable national law that may require the assertion of termination or invalidity against the other party by means other than the institution of legal proceedings within a fixed time-limit. See art. 1 (2) and para. 9 below.

[5]For similar reasons, claims based upon a documentary letter of credit will not come within the scope of this Convention. The documentary letter of credit is an undertaking by banks independent of the underlying sales contract and does not constitute the legal relationship of "a buyer and a seller against each other".

II. *This Convention is not applicable to "time-limits" (déchéance), paragraph (2)*

8. Paragraph (2) of article 1 makes it clear that this Convention only governs *the limitation period* within which parties to a contract of international sale of goods must commence legal proceedings (as defined in article 1 (3) *(e)*) for the exercise of any claim arising from the contract or relating to its breach, termination or invalidity. Thus, the Convention has no effect on any rules under the applicable law concerning "time-limits" *(déchéance)*, that make giving notice to the other party a prerequisite for the acquisition or exercise of a particular type of claim. Typical examples include the requirements that within a specified period of time the other party be given notice of the alleged defects in the goods delivered or of the refusal to accept such goods on grounds of non-conformity or defects. These notice requirements are designed to permit the parties to take prompt action in adjustment of their current performance under a sales transaction—e.g. making tests to ascertain the quality of goods on delivery, or retaking and salvaging rejected goods. In such cases, failure by a party to give notice as required may deprive that party of the right to assert claims based on the alleged defects or non-conformity of the goods.[6] A further example of such "time-limits" *(déchéance)*, which are not governed by this Convention, is a requirement under the applicable law that notice of termination or rescission of a contract be given to the other party within a specified period of time.[7]

9. Paragraph (2) of article 1 also preserves the validity of "time-limits" under national laws within which one party is required, as a condition for the acquisition or exercise of his claim, to perform any act "other than the institution of legal proceedings". Thus, this paragraph preserves "time-limits" which, while variously expressed, are not comparable to the general limitation period governed by this Convention in that they are addressed to something "other than the institution of legal proceedings".[8] When the parties have stipulated in their sales contract a "time-limit" which is not directed at "the institution of legal proceedings", the question of the validity of this stipulation shall be determined by the applicable law.

III. *Definitions, paragraph (3)*

10. "Person" is defined in article 1 (3) *(f)* to include "corporation, company, partnership, association or entity, whether public or private, which can sue or be sued". This definition is intended to show that this Convention is applicable without regard to the form of the organization that enters into a contract of international sale of goods. "Public" entities often engage in commercial activities and it is important to make it clear that such entities are subject to this Convention in the same way as "private" entities. Furthermore, the term public entity covers not only governmental agencies but also States, to the extent that they can sue or be sued. (The question of the immunity of a Contracting State before its own or foreign courts is not affected by this Convention.) An organization need not be corporate to be a "person". A partnership, an association or an "entity" "which can sue or be sued" in its own name under the applicable national law, is a "person" for the purpose of this Convention.

11. Most of the other definitions of terms in paragraph (3) of article 1 can best be considered in connexion with the provisions in the Convention that employ the term in question. For example, the definition of "legal proceedings" in paragraph (3) *(c)* can best be considered in connexion with article 15; the definition of "breach of contract" in paragraph (3) *(d)* can best be considered in connexion with articles 10 (1) and 12 (2); and the definition of "year" in paragraph (3) *(h)* in connexion with articles 8 and 28.

---

[6]For example, art. 39 (1) of the Uniform Law on the International Sale of Goods (ULIS), annexed to the Hague Convention of 1964, provides that "the buyer shall lose the right to rely on a lack of conformity of the goods if he has not given the seller notice thereof *promptly* after he has discovered the lack of conformity or ought to have discovered it".

[7]A number of articles of ULIS provide that a party may avoid the contract only if he has made a declaration to the other party of his intention to avoid the contract, under varying circumstances, "within a reasonable time" (arts. 26, 30, 62 (1)), or "promptly" (arts. 32, 43, 62 (2), 66 (2), 67, 75).

[8]See also art. 9 (2) *(a)* and accompanying commentary, para. 3.

12.   Certain other terms used in this Convention (such as "claims" and "rights") are not defined, since their meaning can best be seen in the light of the context in which they are used and of the objectives of this Convention.[9] It is important to note that the construction of these terms by reference to the varying conceptions found in national laws would be inconsistent with the international character of the Convention and with its objective to promote uniformity in interpretation and application.[10]

Article 2
[Definition of a contract of international sale]

For the purposes of this Convention:

(a)   A contract of sale of goods shall be considered international if, at the time of the conclusion of the contract, the buyer and the seller have their places of business in different States;

(b)   The fact that the parties have their places of business in different States shall be disregarded whenever this fact does not appear either from the contract or from any dealings between, or from information disclosed by, the parties at any time before or at the conclusion of the contract;

(c)   Where a party to a contract of sale of goods has places of business in more than one State, the place of business shall be that which has the closest relationship to the contract and its performance, having regard to the circumstances known to or contemplated by the parties at the time of the conclusion of the contract;

(d)   Where a party does not have a place of business, reference shall be made to his habitual residence;

(e)   Neither the nationality of the parties nor the civil or commercial character of the parties or of the contract shall be taken into consideration.

Commentary

1.   This article deals with the degree of internationality that makes a contract of sale of goods an "international" one for the purposes of this Convention.

I.   *The basic criteria subparagraphs* (a) *and* (b)

2.   Subparagraph *(a)* provides that for a contract of sale of goods to be considered international, the contract must satisfy the following three requirements: (i) *at the time of the conclusion of the contract,* (ii) the parties must have their *places of business* (and not simply centres of only formal significance, such as places of incorporation), (iii) *in different States* (whether these are Contracting or non-Contracting States). In short, the parties' places of business at the time of the conclusion of the contract may *not* be in the same State. The simplicity and clarity of these basic criteria will contribute to certainty in establishing whether a sale of goods is "international" for the purposes of this Convention.

3.   The simplicity and clarity of the criteria contained in subparagraph *(a)* are further enhanced by subparagraph *(b)* of this article. Under subparagraph *(b)*, the contract will not be considered "international", and hence the Convention will not govern, where one of the parties to the contract neither knew or had reason to know "at any time before or at the conclusion of the contract" that the place of business of the other party was in a different State. One example of such a situation is where one of the parties was acting as agent for a foreign undisclosed principal. Subparagraph *(b)* is designed to protect a

---

[9]Representatives at the Diplomatic Conference which adopted this Convention were generally agreed that the term "goods" means tangible movables. The term, however, was not defined formally, partly because the use of the words "*objets mobiliers corporels*" in the French text of the Convention already implied this and partly because the exclusions from the scope of the Convention provided in arts. 4 through 6 also made this point clear.

[10]See art. 7 and accompanying commentary.

party who enters into a contract of sale with another party, justifiably assuming that the places of both parties are in the same State, from finding out later to his surprise that he had entered into an international sales contract that is subject to this Convention.[11]

II. *Place of business, subparagraph* (c)

4.   This subparagraph deals with the situation where one of the parties to a sales contract has more than one place of business. Characterizing the sales contract as "international" for purposes of article 2 *(a)* in cases where a party has a number of places of business, causes no problem where all the places of business of one party (X) are situated in States other than the one where the other party (Y) has his place of business; whichever place is designated as the relevant place of business of X, the places of business of X and Y will be in *different* States. The problem arises only when one of X's places of business is situated in the *same* State as the place of business of Y. In such a case it becomes crucial to determine which of the different places of business of X is the relevant place of business within the meaning of subparagraph *(a)* of this article.

5.   Subparagraph *(c)* lays down the criterion for determining the relevant place of business for the purposes of this Convention where a party has more than one place of business: it is the place of business "which has the closest relationship to the contract and its performance". The phrase "the contract and its performance" refers to the transaction as a whole, including factors relating to the offer and the acceptance as well as the performance of the contract. In determining the place of business which has the "closest relationship", subparagraph *(c)* states that regard shall be given to "the circumstances known to or contemplated by the parties at the time of the conclusion of the contract". Circumstances that may not be known to one of the parties at the time of entering into the contract would include supervision over the making of the contract by a head office located in another State or the foreign origin or final destination of the goods. When these circumstances are not known to or contemplated by both parties, they are not to be taken into consideration.

III. *Habitual residence, subparagraph* (d)

6.   This subparagraph deals with the case where one of the parties does not have a place of business. Most international contracts are entered into by businessmen who have recognized places of business. Occasionally, however, a person who does not have an established "place of business" may enter into a contract of international sale of goods where the goods are intended for commercial purposes, and not simply for "personal, family or household use" within the meaning of article 4 of this Convention. The present provision provides that, in this situation, the reference shall be to the habitual residence of such a party.

IV. *Nationality of the parties; civil or commercial character of the parties or the contract, subparagraph* (e)

7.   This paragraph provides that neither the nationality of the parties nor the civil or commercial character of the parties or the contract shall be taken into consideration for the purposes of this Convention. Classification of a contract of sale of goods as "international" under article 2 *(a)* depends primarily on a determination that "the seller and buyer have their places of business in different States". In defining "place of business" in article 2 *(c)* and in referring to "habitual residence" in article 2 *(d)* there are no references to the nationality, place of incorporation or place of the head office of any party. Subparagraph *(e)* emphasizes this fact by providing specifically that the nationality of the parties shall not be taken into consideration.

---

[11]As to the possibility of making a reservation with respect to the definition of an international sale, see art. 38 and accompanying commentary.

8. In some legal systems the national law relating to contracts of sale of goods has different provisions for cases where the parties or the contract are classified as "commercial" than for cases where the parties or the contract are classified as "civil". In other legal systems the distinction between "civil" and "commercial" parties or contracts is not known. In order to avoid possible differences in interpretation by national courts applying this Convention, subparagraph *(e)* of article 2 provides that, for the purposes of this Convention, the *"commercial or civil character of the parties or of the contract"* under the applicable national law shall be disregarded.[12]

Article 3

[Application of the Convention; exclusion of the rules of private international law]

1. This Convention shall apply only if, at the time of the conclusion of the contract the places of business of the parties to a contract of international sale of goods are in Contracting States.

2. Unless this Convention provides otherwise, it shall apply irrespective of the law which would otherwise be applicable by virtue of the rules of private international law.

3. This Convention shall not apply when the parties have expressly excluded its application.

Commentary

1. Paragraphs (1) and (2) of this article deal with the question: when must a Contracting State apply the rules of this Convention? Paragraph (3) deals with the freedom of the parties to exclude the application of the Convention.

I. Application of the Convention, paragraph (1)

2. Article 3 (1) provides that this Convention *must* be applied if, "at the time of the conclusion of the contract, the places of business of the parties to a contract of international sale of goods are in *Contracting* States". Thus, a Contracting State is *not bound* under this Convention to apply the rules of the Convention when one party has his relevant place of business in a non-Contracting State even if the sales contract in question falls within the definition of "a contract of international sale of goods" under article 2 *(a)*. (See also art. 33.)

3. It must be emphasized in this connexion that the nationality of a party is not relevant for the purposes of the application of this Convention (art. 2 *(e)*). Thus, whether the place of incorporation or the head office of the parties is in a Contracting or a non-Contracting State is not relevant for determining the applicability of this Convention. The only relevant question is whether for each party the place of business having "the closest relationship to the contract and its performance" is located in a *Contracting State* (art. 2 *(c)*).[13]

II. Exclusion of the rules of private international law, paragraph (2)

4. Paragraph (2) of this article provides that, subject to any contrary provisions in this Convention, the Convention must be applied without regard to "the law which would otherwise be applicable by virtue of the rules of private international law". This language is designed to emphasize the fact that the applicability of this Convention depends on the basic test established in article 3 (1) rather than on the general rules of private international law.

---

[12]See also para. 3 of commentary to art. 3.

[13]As to the possibility of further limiting the application of the Convention by way of reservation, see art. 34 and accompanying commentary. See also art. 37.

5. If the applicability of this Convention were linked to the rules of private international law, special difficulties would have been presented because of the unusually divergent approaches in different legal systems to the characterization of the subject-matter of this Convention. For example, while most civil law systems characterize problems of prescription as substantive questions and apply the proper law of the contract *(lex causae contractus)* (and in some cases, the "proper law of prescription"), most common law jurisdictions characterize limitation problems as questions of procedure and, on this ground, apply the rules of the *forum (lex fori)*. In some jurisdictions, a combination of the two characterizations may be possible. It has already been pointed out that this Convention governs regardless of the different theoretical approaches to the problem under national law as long as the period in question has the function described under article 1 (1) and (2).[14] The combined effect of paragraphs (1) and (2) of article 3 is certainty and uniformity in the application of this Convention.

6. The opening phrase of the paragraph, "unless this Convention provides otherwise", is occasioned by specific provisions of the Convention which make room for national law to modify certain rules under the Convention. One such instance is paragraph (3) of article 22 which provides, *inter alia,* that the validity of a clause defined therein shall not be affected by the provisions in the other paragraphs of article 22, "provided that such clause is valid under the law applicable to the contract of sale". Another example is the last phrase of article 15, which provides that the rule under that article is "subject to the law governing the proceedings".

III. *Exclusion of the applicability of the Convention by agreement of the parties, paragraph (3)*

7. Paragraph (3) allows the parties to agree to exclude the application of the Convention, provided that this is done "expressly". Thus, for example, where the parties have chosen as "the law applicable *to the contract*" the law of a non-Contracting State, which treats the question of limitation as substantive, an implication might arise that the parties have excluded the application of this Convention because of their implied choice of the prescription rules contained in the chosen national law. Such an interpretation is more likely to arise if the legal proceedings are brought in a form of one of those Contracting States which also characterizes the limitation question as substantive. However, in such a case this Convention still applies because the exclusion of the application of this Convention was not "express". Furthermore, permitting an implied exclusion of the application of this Convention would defeat the purpose of article 3 (2).[15]

8. There is no requirement as to the time and form in which the agreement of the parties for the exclusion of this Convention must be expressed. Where, under article 3 (3), the parties have expressly excluded the application of this Convention, their claims will be regulated according to the law deemed to be applicable under the rules of private international law of the forum (cf. art. 3 (2)).

Article 4
[*Exclusion of certain sales and types of goods*]

This Convention shall not apply to sales:

(a) Of goods bought for personal, family or household use;

(b) By auction;

(c) On execution or otherwise by authority of law;

(d) Of stocks, shares, investment securities, negotiable instruments or money;

(e) Of ships, vessels or aircraft;

(f) Of electricity.

---

[14]See para. 1 of commentary on art. 1.

[15]See paras. 4 and 5, *supra.*

Commentary

I. *Exclusion of consumer sales, subparagraph* (a)

1. Subparagraph *(a)* of this article excludes consumer sales from the scope of this Convention. A particular sale is outside the scope of this Convention if the goods are bought "for personal, family or household use". The usage of the word "personal" in conjunction with the words "family or household" indicates that the intended use must be non-commercial. Thus, for example, none of the following situations is excluded from the Convention: a camera bought by a professional photographer for use in his business, soap or other toiletries bought by a corporation for the personal use of its employees, and a single automobile bought by a car dealer for resale.

2. The rationale for excluding consumer sales from the Convention is that in a number of countries such transactions are subject to various types of national laws that are designed to protect consumers. In order to avoid any risk of impairing the effectiveness of such national laws, it was considered advisable that questions of prescription or limitation relating to consumer sales should be excluded from this Convention. In addition, most consumer sales are domestic transactions and it was felt that the Convention should not apply to the relatively few cases where consumer sales were international transactions (e.g. because the buyer was a tourist with his habitual residence in another country).[16]

II. *Exclusion of sales by auction, subparagraph* (b)

3. Subparagraph *(b)* of this article excludes from the scope of this Convention sales by auction. Because sales by auction are often subject to special rules under various national laws, it was considered desirable that they should in all respects remain subject to these special rules. In addition, the length of the limitation period should not be affected by the location of the place of business of the successful bidder at an auction since at the opening of the auction the seller could not know which buyer would make a particular purchase.

III. *Exclusion of sales on execution or otherwise by authority of law, subparagraph* (c)

4. Subparagraph *(c)* of this article excludes sales on judicial or administrative execution or otherwise by authority of law, because such sales are usually governed by special rules in the State under whose authority the execution sale is made. Furthermore, such sales do not constitute a significant part of international trade and may, therefore, safely be regarded as purely domestic operations.

IV. *Exclusion of sales of stocks, shares, investment securities, negotiable instruments or money, subparagraph* (d)

5. This subparagraph excludes sales of stocks, shares, investment securities, negotiable instruments and money.[17] Such transactions present problems that are different from the usual international sale of *goods* and, in addition, in many countries, are subject to special mandatory rules.

V. *Exclusion of sales of ships, vessels and aircraft, subparagraph* (e)

6. This subparagraph excludes from the scope of the Convention all sales of ships, vessels and aircraft, items which are often subject to different special rules under the various national legal systems. In some legal systems there may be a question whether such items are "goods". Under most national laws at least certain types of ships, vessels and aircraft are subject to special registration requirements. The rules under various

---

[16]See art. 2 *(b)*.

[17]As to whether commercial paper of the type enumerated might be "goods", see foot-note 5 to commentary on art. 1.

national laws, specifying the ships, vessels and aircraft that must be registered, differ widely. Since the relevant place of registration, and therefore the law which would govern the registration, might not be known at the time of the sale, the sale of all ships, vesels and aircraft was excluded in order to make uniform the application of this Convention.

VI. *Exclusion of sales of electricity, subparagraph* (f)

7. This subparagraph excludes sales of electricity from the scope of the Convention on the ground that international sales of electricity present unique problems that are different from those presented by the usual international sale of goods.

Article 5
[*Exclusion of certain claims*]

This Convention shall not apply to claims based upon;

(a) Death of, or personal injury to, any person;

(b) Nuclear damage caused by the goods sold;

(c) A lien, mortgage or other security interest in property;

(d) A judgement or award made in legal proceedings;

(e) A document on which direct enforcement or execution can be obtained in accordance with the law of the place where such enforcement or execution is sought;

(f) A bill of exchange, cheque or promissory note.

Commentary

1. Subparagraph *(a)* excludes from the Convention claims based on the death of or personal injury to any person. If such a claim is based on tort (or *delict*), the claim would be excluded from this Convention by virtue of the provisions of article 1 (1).[18] However, under some circumstances, claims for liability for the death or personal injury of the buyer or of some other person might be based on the failure of the goods to comply with the contract; furthermore, a claim by the buyer against the seller for pecuniary loss or damage might arise because of personal injuries suffered by persons *other than himself* (including by a subpurchaser). While such claims based on personal injuries, under some legal systems, may be regarded as contractual, in other legal systems the characterization is in doubt and in still others all such claims may be regarded as delictual. Therefore, in order to avoid possible doubt and diversity in interpretation, this subparagraph excludes *all* claims based on "death of, or personal injury to, any person"; it would also be often inappropriate to subject such claims to the same limitation period as the one applicable to the usual type of commercial claims based on contract.

2. Subparagraph *(b)* excludes claims based on "nuclear damage caused by the goods sold". The effects of such damage may not appear until a long period after exposure to radio-active materials. In addition, special periods for the extinction of actions based on nuclear damage are contained in the Vienna Convention on Civil Liability for Nuclear Damage of 21 May 1963.[19]

3. Subparagraph *(c)* excludes claims based on "a lien, mortgage or other security interest in property". It should be noted that this subparagraph excludes rights based not only on "lien" and "mortgage" but also rights based on "other security interest in property". This latter phrase is sufficiently broad to exclude rights asserted by a seller for the recovery of property sold under a "conditional sale" or similar arrangement designed to permit the seizure of property on default of payment. Liens, mortgages and

---

[18]See para. 6 of commentary on art. 1.

[19]See art. VI (basic periods of 10 or 20 years, subject to certain adjustments); art. I (1) *(k)* (definition of "nuclear damage").

other security interests involve rights *in rem* which traditionally have been governed by the *lex situs* and are enmeshed with a wide variety of rights affecting other creditors; expanding the scope of the Convention to include such claims would have impeded the adoption of the Convention.

4.   Of course, the expiration of the limitation period applicable to a claim based on a sales contract may have serious consequences with respect to the enforcement of a lien, mortgage or other interest securing that claim. However, for the reasons given in connexion with article 25 (1) (para. 2 of commentary on art. 25), this Convention does not attempt to prescribe uniform rules with respect to such consequences, and leaves these questions to the applicable national law. It may be expected that the tribunals of Contracting States in solving these problems will give full effect to the basic policies of this Convention with respect to the institution of legal proceedings for the enforcement of stale claims.

5.   Under subparagraph *(d)*, claims based on "a judgement or award made in legal proceedings" are excluded even though the judgement or award may have resulted from a claim arising from an international sale. This exclusion is consistent with the purpose of this Convention to regulate the period within which the parties to a contract of international sale of goods must *bring legal proceedings* for the exercise of any claims arising under that contract.[20] Moreover, in actions to enforce a judgement or award, it may be difficult to ascertain whether the underlying claim arose from an international sale of goods and satisfied the other requirements for the applicability of this Convention. In addition, the enforcement of a judgement or award involves the procedural rules of the forum (including rules concerning "merger" of the claim in the judgement) and thus would be difficult to subject to a uniform rule limited to claims derived from the international sale of goods.

6.   Subparagraph *(e)* excludes claims based on "a document on which direct enforcement or execution can be obtained in accordance with the law of the place where such enforcement or execution is sought". Such documents are given different names and rules in various national jurisdictions (e.g. *titre exécutoire*), but they have an independent legal effect that differentiates them from claims that must first be established by way of legal proceedings in which the breach of the contract of sale must be proved. In addition, these documents present some of the problems mentioned with respect to subparagraph *(d)* (para. 5, above). (Subparagraph *(e)* is also analogous to the exclusion under subparagraph *(f)* of claims based on documents having a legal identity distinct from the sales contract.)

7.   Subparagraph *(f)* excludes claims based on "a bill of exchange, cheque or promissory note". Such an instrument may be given (or accepted) in connexion with the obligation to pay for goods sold in an international transaction subject to this Convention. Such instruments are in many cases governed by international conventions or national laws that state special periods of limitation. In addition, such instruments are often circulated among third persons who have no connexion with or knowledge of the underlying sales transactions; moreover, the obligation under the instrument may be distinct (or "abstracted") from the sales transaction that occasioned the issuance of the instrument. In view of these facts, claims under the instruments described in subparagraph *(f)* are excluded from this Convention.[21]

Article 6

[Mixed contracts]

1.   This Convention shall not apply to contracts in which the preponderant part of the obligations of the seller consists in the supply of labour or other services.

---

[20]See para. 1 of commentary on art 1.

[21]Contrast the treatment of assignees of rights under the sales contract (art. 1 (3) *(a)*).

2. Contracts for the supply of goods to be manufactured or produced shall be considered to be sales, unless the party who orders the goods undertakes to supply a substantial part of the materials necessary for such manufacture or production.

Commentary

1. This article deals with two different situations relating to mixed contracts.

I. *Sale of goods and supply of labour or other services by the seller, paragraph (1)*

2. This paragraph deals with contracts under which the seller undertakes to sell goods as well as to supply labour or other services. An example of such a contract is where the seller agrees to sell machinery and undertakes to set it up in a plant in working condition or to supervise its installation. In such cases, paragraph (1) provides that where the "preponderant part" of the obligation of the seller consists in the supply of labour or other services, the contract is not subject to the provisions of this Convention.

3. It is important to note that this paragraph does not attempt to determine whether obligations created by one instrument or transaction comprise essentially one or two contracts. Thus, the question whether the seller's obligations relating to the sale of goods and those relating to the supply of labour or other services can be considered as two separate contracts (under what is sometimes called the doctrine of "severability" of contracts) will be resolved in accordance with the applicable national law.

II. *Supply of materials by the buyer, paragraph (2)*

4. The opening phrase of paragraph (2) of this article provides that the sale of goods to be manufactured by the seller to the buyer's order is as much subject to the provisions of this Convention as the sale of ready-made goods.

5. However, the concluding phrase in this paragraph, "unless the party who orders the goods undertakes to supply a substantial part of the materials necessary for such manufacture or production", is designed to exclude from the scope of this Convention those contracts under which *the buyer undertakes to supply the seller* (the manufacturer) with a *substantial* part of the necessary materials from which the goods are to be manufactured or produced. Since such contracts are more akin to contracts for the supply of services or labour than to contracts for sale of goods, they are excluded from the scope of this Convention, in line with the basic rule of paragraph (1).

Article 7

[Interpretation to promote uniformity]

In the interpretation and application of the provisions of this Convention, regard shall be had to its international character and to the need to promote uniformity.

Commentary

National rules on limitation (prescription) are subject to sharp divergencies in approach and concept. Thus, it is especially important to avoid differing constructions of the provisions of this Convention by national courts, each dependent upon the varying concepts of the particular national law that it was applying. To this end, article 7 emphasizes the importance, in interpreting and applying the provisions of the Convention, of having due regard for the international character of the Convention and the need to promote uniformity. Illustrations of the application of this article may be found elsewhere in the commentary, e.g. in article 1 at paragraphs 10-12; article 14, foot-note 38; and article 22, foot-note 53.

Article 8
[Length of the period]

The limitation period shall be four years.

Commentary

1. Establishing the length of the limitation period required the reconciliation of various conflicting considerations. On the one hand, the limitation period must be adequate for the investigation of claims, negotiation for possible settlements making the arrangements necessary for bringing legal proceedings. In assessing the time required, consideration was given to the special problems resulting from the distance that often separates the parties to an international sale and the complications resulting from differences in language and legal systems. On the other hand, the limitation period should not be so long as to fail to provide protection against the dangers of uncertainty and injustice that would result from the extended passage of time without the resolution of disputed claims. (These dangers include the loss of evidence and the possible threat to business stability or solvency resulting from extended delays.)

2. In the course of drafting this Convention, it was generally considered that a limitation period within the range of three to five years would be appropriate.[22] The limitation period of four years established in this article is a product of compromise. In reaching this decision, account was taken of other provisions in this Convention affecting the running of the limitation period. These provisions include articles 9 to 12 (rules relating to the commencement of the running of the period), article 19 (a new period commences to run afresh when the creditor performs an act which has the effect of recommencing the original limitation period in a given jurisdiction), article 20 (a new period commences to run when the debt is acknowledged by the debtor), articles 17, 18 and 21 (rules extending the limitation period), and article 22 (modification of the period by the parties).

Article 9
[Basic rule on commencement of the period]

1. Subject to the provisions of articles 10, 11 and 12, the limitation period shall commence on the date on which the claim accrues.

2. The commencement of the limitation period shall not be postponed by:

(a) A requirement that the party be given a notice as described in paragraph 2 of article 1, or

(b) A provision in an arbitration agreement that no right shall arise until an arbitration award has been made.

Commentary

1. Articles 9 to 12 govern the point in time at which the limitation period starts to run with regard to all claims covered by this Convention. Article 9 (1) provides the basic rule as to the commencement of the period: the limitation period commences to run "on the date on which the claim accrues". Article 10 provides special rules for the purpose of the application of the basic rule provided in article 9 (1) with regard to claims arising from breach, non-conformity of goods, and fraud. Article 11 deals with the situation

---

[22]To help resolve the question of the length of the limitation period and other relevant issues, a questionnaire was addressed to Governments and interested international organizations, and the replies, reporting national rules and suggestions from each region, were analysed in a report of the Secretary-General (A/CN.9/70/Add.2, sect. 14; *Yearbook 1972*, part two, I, B, 1).

where the seller gives an express undertaking relating to the goods. Article 12 covers the cases where the contract was terminated before the time when the performance would have become due.

2. While many claims will be governed by the rules under article 10, claims may also arise without breach or fraud. One example is a claim for the restitution of advance payments where the performance under the contract is excused under the applicable national law because of impossibility of performance, *force majeure,* and the like.[23] Such claims will be governed by the basic rule provided in article 9 (1). Whether such a claim exists and, if it does, when it accrues, is not governed by this Convention and must be decided under the applicable national law.

3. Article 9 (2) *(a)* was designed to eliminate any difference in the starting point of the running of the limitation period under the Convention where under the applicable national law one party is required, as a prerequisite for the acquisition or exercise of his claim, to give notice to the other party, or where the parties agreed, validly under the applicable national law, that notice be given to the other party of any claim within a specified period of time. Where such notice is required, either by statute or by contract, the time when a claim is considered to "accrue" may be determined in a number of ways. Thus, under some national laws, such claims "accrue" when the necessary notice is given; under other national laws claims may "accrue" before the notice, provided the notice is then in fact given within a prescribed period. Under article 9 (2) *(a)* the commencement of the limitation period "shall not be postponed" by the requirement of such notices.[24]

4. Article 9 (2) *(b)* deals with the effect of a provision in an arbitration agreement stating that "no right shall *arise* until an arbitration award has been made". Under article 9 (2) *(b)* such a contractual provision will be disregarded for the purpose of determining the starting point for the running of the limitation period under the Convention. The reason behind this provision is similar to that behind the rule in article 9 (2) *(a)*. (See para. 3, above.)

Article 10

[Special rules: breach; defect or non-conformity of the goods; fraud]

1. A claim arising from a breach of contract shall accrue on the date on which such breach occurs.

2. A claim arising from a defect or other lack of conformity shall accrue on the date on which the goods are actually handed over to, or their tender is refused by, the buyer.

3. A claim based on fraud committed before or at the time of the conclusion of the contract or during its performance shall accrue on the date on which the fraud was or reasonably could have been discovered.

Commentary

1. The basic rule as to the commencement of the limitation period is provided in article 9 (1): "The limitation period shall commence on the date on which the claim *accrues*". Article 10 is designed to eliminate difficulties in determining when a claim "accrues" by providing specific rules as to the time when a claim arising from a breach of contract, from a defect or other lack of conformity, or based on fraud, should be deemed to have "accrued".

---

[23]As to other examples of such claims, see para. 6 of commentary on art. 1.

[24]This rule, of course, has no effect on the rules of the applicable national law requiring notice. See art. 1 (2) and accompanying commentary, paras. 8 and 9.

I. *Breach of contract, paragraph (1)*

2. With respect to a claim arising from breach of contract, article 10 (1) provides that the claim "shall accrue on the date on which such breach occurs".[25] "Breach of contract" is defined in article 1 (3) *(d)* to mean "the failure of a party to perform the contract or any performance not in conformity with the contract". The application of this rule may be illustrated by the following examples:

Example 10A: The sales contract required the seller to place goods at the buyer's disposal on 1 June. The seller failed to supply or tender any goods under the contract on 1 June or on any subsequent date. The limitation period for bringing any legal proceedings by the buyer in respect of the breach of the contract commences to run on the date on which the breach of contract occurred, i.e., in this example, on 1 June, the date for performance required under the contract.

Example 10B: The sales contract required the seller to place goods at the buyer's disposal on 1 June. The seller failed to supply or tender any goods under the contract on 1 June. However, a few weeks thereafter the buyer agreed to the extension of the time for delivery until 1 December. On 1 December, the seller again failed to perform. If the above extension of the time for delivery was valid, the limitation period commences to run on 1 December, the date of "breach" of the contract.

Example 10C: The sales contract provided that the buyer may pay the price at the time of delivery of the goods and obtain a 2 per cent discount. The contract also provided that the buyer must, at the latest, pay within 60 days of the delivery. The buyer did not pay on delivery of the goods. The limitation period does not commence to run until the end of the 60-day period because there was no "breach" of contract by the buyer until the time for his performance expired.

Example 10D: The sales contract provided that the goods should be shipped in a specified year on a date to be named by the buyer. The buyer might have requested shipment in January, but he only requested shipment on 30 December of that year. The seller did not perform. The limitation period with respect to this failure to perform did not commence until 30 December since, under the terms of the contract, there was no "breach" of the contract until the date specified by the buyer for shipment had arrived.

II. *Claims by buyers relying on non-conformity of the goods, paragraph (2)*

3. With regard to a claim by the buyer of a breach of contract "arising from a defect or other lack of conformity" of the delivered goods, article 10 (2) provides a special rule: the claim "shall accrue on the date on which the goods are actually handed over to, or their tender is refused by, the buyer". The phrase "a claim arising from a defect or other lack of conformity" of the goods is sufficiently broad to include any respect in which the goods may fail to comply with the requirements of the contract.

4. The phrase "the goods are actually handed over to . . . the buyer" refers to the existence of circumstances which constitute placing the goods under the buyer's "actual" control regardless of whether or not this occurs on the due date or at the place contemplated by the contract.[26] Unless the goods have reached the stage where "actual" inspection of the goods by the buyer is possible, the goods cannot be regarded to have been "actually handed over to . . . the buyer".

Example 10E: Seller in Santiago agreed to ship goods to a buyer in Bombay: the terms of shipment were "F.O.B. Santiago". Pursuant to the contract, the seller loaded the goods on board a ship in Santiago on 1 June. The goods reached Bombay on

---

[25]Art. 10 (2) contains a special rule applicable to those breaches of contract that take the form of a defect or lack of conformity of the goods.

[26]The term "delivery" was intentionally avoided because of the differences in the definition of this legal concept in various legal systems, particularly where there was purported "delivery" of non-conforming goods.

1 August, and on the same date the carrier notified the buyer that he could take possession of the goods. On 15 August the buyer took possession of the goods. Under these facts, the goods are "actually handed over" to the buyer on 15 August.

5. The result in example 10E is not affected by the fact that under the terms of the contract the risk of loss during the ocean voyage rested on the buyer. Nor is this result affected by the fact that, under some legal systems, it might be concluded that "title" or "ownership" in the goods passed to the buyer when the goods were loaded on the ship in Santiago. Alternative forms of price quotation (F.O.B. seller's city; F.O.B. buyer's city; F.A.S.; C.I.F. and the like) have significance in relation to possible changes in freight rates and the manner of arranging for insurance, but they have no significance in relationship to the time when the goods were "actually" handed over to the buyer.[27]

6. In a case where the buyer refuses to accept the goods although the seller placed them at his disposal, there is no date on which the goods are *actually handed over* to the buyer. For this reason, article 10 (2) contains an alternative rule which provides that where the buyer refuses to accept the tendered goods, the claim shall accrue on the date on which the *tender* of the goods *was refused* by the buyer. The commencement of the limitation period will not be affected, once the buyer refused to accept the tendered goods, by the buyer thereafter taking possession of the goods under the contract.[28]

III. *Claims based on fraud, paragraph (3)*

7. Fraud committed while the contract was being negotiated or at the time of the conclusion of the contract or during its performance may give rise to various claims. Where a claim based on fraud arises in tort (or *delict*), it is, of course, outside the scope of this Convention.[29] However, the defrauded party may be entitled to avoid or rescind the contract under the applicable national law. If the contract is avoided, the defrauded party may want to ask for the restitution of advance payments, if any. This claim for restitution of any advance payments falls within the scope of this Convention.[30] For such a claim, article 10 (3) provides that it should be deemed to have accrued "on the date on which the fraud was or reasonably could have been discovered".

Article 11
[Express undertaking]

If the seller has given an express undertaking relating to the goods which is stated to have effect for a certain period of time, whether expressed in terms of a specific period of time or otherwise, the limitation period in respect of any claim arising from the undertaking shall commence on the date on which the buyer notifies the seller of the fact on which the claim is based, but not later than on the date of the expiration of the period of the undertaking.

---

[27]Of course, if the buyer takes effective physical control over the goods in the seller's city and thereafter ships the goods, then the goods would have been actually handed over to the buyer in the seller's city. It may also be noted that goods may be handed over to agents or assigns of the buyer who are authorized to receive them. Cf. art. 1 (3) *(a)*. For the purpose of illustration, assume that the buyer in example 10E, above, resells the goods to C during the transit of the goods and transfers the bill of lading to C. The goods are handed over to the "buyer" when C actually takes possession of the goods.

[28]The over-all fairness of the rules contained in arts. 9 and 10 needs to be considered in the light of the following factors: *(a)* exclusion from the Convention (art. 5 *(a)*) of claims based on "death of, or personal injury to, any person"; *(b)* confining the scope of this Convention to claims that arise in relation to a *contract*—thereby excluding claims based on tort or *delict* (see discussion in para. 6 of commentary on art. (1)); *(c)* exclusion of consumer sales from the Convention (art. 4 *(a)*); *(d)* the special provisions for claims based on an express undertaking given by the seller which is stated to have effect for a period of time (art. 11).

[29]See para. 6 of commentary on art. 1.

[30]See para. 6 of commentary on art. 1.

Commentary

1.   Article 11 provides a special rule for cases where the seller has given the buyer an express undertaking (such as a warranty or guarantee) relating to the goods, which is stated to have effect for a certain period of time. This period may be expressed in terms of a specific period of time or otherwise, such as in terms of an amount of performance. Under this article if the notice is given before the expiration of the period of the undertaking, the commencement of the limitation period for claims arising from the undertaking is from "the date on which the buyer notifies the seller of the fact on which the claim is based". Where the notice has not been given before the expiration of the period of the undertaking, article 11 provides that the limitation period shall commence "on the date of the expiration of the period of the undertaking".[31]

2.   Article 11 does not specify when the seller's "express undertaking" must be given. The seller, after delivering the goods, might adjust certain components and in this connexion might give an express warranty at that time. Such an express undertaking, although given after the delivery of the goods, would be governed by this article.

Article 12
[Termination before performance is due; instalment contracts]

1.   If, in circumstances provided for by the law applicable to the contract, one party is entitled to declare the contract terminated before the time for performance is due, and exercises this right, the limitation period in respect of a claim based on any such circumstances shall commence on the date on which the declaration is made to the other party. If the contract is not declared to be terminated before performance becomes due, the limitation period shall commence on the date on which performance is due.

2.   The limitation period in respect of a claim arising out of a breach by one party of a contract for the delivery of or payment for goods by instalments shall, in relation to each separate instalment, commence on the date on which the particular breach occurs. If, under the law applicable to the contract, one party is entitled to declare the contract terminated by reason of such breach, and exercises this right, the limitation period in respect of all relevant instalments shall commence on the date on which the declaration is made to the other party.

Commentary

1.   Both paragraphs (1) and (2) of article 12 deal with problems that arise when a party is entitled to terminate the contract before performance is due. Paragraph (1) establishes the basic general rule; paragraph (2) deals with the special problems that arise when a contract calls for the delivery of goods, or the payment for goods, in instalments.

I.   *Basic rule, paragraph (1)*

2.   The basic rule of paragraph (1) may be illustrated by the following:

Example 12A: Under a contract of sale made on 1 June the seller is to deliver the goods on 1 December. On 1 July the seller (without a valid excuse) notifies the buyer that he will not deliver the goods required by the contract. On 15 July the buyer declares to the seller that in view of the seller's repudiation the contract is terminated.

3.   Under some legal systems, notification, in advance of refusal to perform an obligation that will be due in the future is regarded as an anticipatory breach upon which both an election to terminate and a legal action for breach may be based.

---

[31]This article does not affect the time-limit within which such notice must be given for the exercise of a claim under the undertaking. See art. 1 (2) and para. 8 of accompanying commentary.

Circumstances such as bankruptcy or other events manifesting an inability to perform may also become grounds upon which one party *may* terminate the contract before the performance is due under the contract. In such circumstances, where a party who is entitled to declare the contract terminated "exercises this right", the limitation period runs from "the date on which the declaration is made to the other party". On the facts in the above example, this date is 15 July.

4. It will be noted that paragraph (1) is only applicable in cases where a party elects to exercise his right to declare the contract terminated. If in the above case, such an election (i.e., by the notification of termination made on 15 July) had not taken place, "the limitation period shall commence on the date on which performance is due", 1 December in the above example.[32] This result is in conformity with the general rule of article 10 (1) concerning the point of time at which a claim for breach of contract "accrues".[33]

5. In the interest of definiteness and uniformity, under this paragraph the period commences on the earlier date (15 July) only when a party affirmatively "declares" the contract terminated. Thus, termination resulting from a rule of the applicable national law to the effect that in certain circumstances the contract shall be automatically considered as terminated is not termination resulting from a "declaration" by a party within the meaning of paragraph (1). It should also be noted that article 12 does not govern the situation, existing under some legal systems, whereby circumstances such as repudiation or bankruptcy prior to the time performance is due entitle one party to declare that the performance is *due immediately*.[34]

II. *Instalment contracts, paragraph (2)*

6. For claims arising out of breaches of instalment contracts for the delivery of or payment for goods, article 12 (2) follows the same approach as article 10 (1). The limitation period "shall, in relation to each separate instalment, commence on the date on which the particular *breach occurs*".[35] This rule will minimize the theoretical difficulties as to whether a particular instalment contract should be regarded as a set of several contracts or as a single contract. The application of article 12 (2) may be illustrated by the following example:

Example 12B: A contract of sale made on 1 June required the seller to sell the buyer 4,000 kg of sugar, with deliveries of 1,000 kg on 1 July, 1 August, 1 September and 1 October. Each of the four instalments was delivered late. The buyer, while he complained to the seller of these late deliveries, did not elect to terminate the contract although he was entitled to do so under the national law applicable to the contract. Under these facts, the limitation period would be applied separately to each claim arising from the late delivery in July, August, September, and October.

---

[32]This Convention does not specify the time when a notification of termination must be given. However, the second sentence of paragraph (1) of article 12 restricts the application of this rule to those instances where the declaration to terminate the contract is made "before performance becomes due".

[33]While the second sentence of article 12 (1) is intended to attain the same result as under article 10 (1), the expression "the date on which *performance is due*" was employed in article 12 (1) rather than the words "breach occurs" to avoid possible confusion, particularly in a jurisdiction where "anticipatory *breach*" is a recognized legal concept.

[34]Under these circumstances, where a party validly declares that performance is due immediately and the other party then does not perform, the acceleration of the "due date" will lead to a "breach" at an earlier date, and hence to the earlier commencement of the running of the limitation period.

[35]The reference to "breach" in the first sentence of art. 12 (2) does not preclude the application of art. 10 (2) for determining the date on which the breach occurred, in cases where the breach consisted of non-conformity of the goods; art. 10 (2) is a special rule while art. 10 (1) deals with breach in general. See also art. 1 (3) *(d)*.

7. However, if one party does exercise his right to declare the instalment contract terminated by reason of such breach, article 12 (2) provides that "the limitation period in respect of all relevant instalments" commences when such declaration was made. This rule may be illustrated as follows:

Example 12C: The contract is the same as in Example 12B above. The first instalment, delivered on 1 July, proved on examination to be so seriously defective that the buyer rightfully took two steps: he rejected the defective instalment and he notified the seller on 5 July that the contract was terminated as to future instalments. Once termination is thus effected, the single limitation period for claims arising from all relevant instalments (i.e., here the July, August, September, and October instalments) commences on the date of the declaration that the contract is terminated, i.e., 5 July.

8. For the purpose of paragraph (2), the determining factor is the buyer's election to "declare the contract terminated" as to future instalments. The term "all relevant instalments" embraces all instalments, whether preceding or subsequent to the event giving rise to the declaration of the termination of the instalment contract, which are covered by or affected by the termination of the contract. This approach reflects the fact that the right to terminate the contract may arise from the cumulative effect of breaches in the performance of a number of instalments.

CESSATION AND EXTENSION OF THE LIMITATION PERIOD

Article 13

[Judicial proceedings]

The limitation period shall cease to run when the creditor performs any act which, under the law of the court where the proceedings are instituted, is recognized as commencing judicial proceedings against the debtor or as asserting his claim in such proceedings already instituted against the debtor, for the purpose of obtaining satisfaction or recognition of his claim.

Commentary

1. As was noted earlier (introduction, para. 1), this Convention is essentially concerned with the time within which the parties to a contract for the international sale of goods may bring legal proceedings to exercise claims arising from such contract. Article 8 states the length of the limitation period. Articles 24 to 27 state the consequences of the expiration of the period; these include the rule (art. 25 (1)) that no claim for which the limitation period has expired "shall be recognized or enforced in any legal proceedings". To complete this structure, article 13 provides that the "limitation period shall cease to run" when the creditor commences judicial proceedings against the debtor for the purpose of obtaining satisfaction or recognition of his claim (provision for "legal" proceedings other than "judicial" proceedings—e.g., arbitral and adminis- trative proceedings—is made in arts. 14 and 15). The net effect of these rules is substantially the same as providing that a proceeding for the enforcement of claims may only be brought before the limitation period has expired. However, the approach of this Convention, in stating that the limitation period shall "cease ro run" when the proceeding is instituted, provides a basis for dealing with problems that arise when such proceeding fails to result in a decision on the merits or is otherwise abortive (see art. 17).

2. Article 13 is designed to identify the stage which the judicial proceedings must reach in order to halt the running of the limitation period. Under the various legal systems judicial proceedings may be started in different ways. Under some national laws a claim may be filed or pleaded in court only after the plaintiff has taken certain preliminary steps (e.g., service of a "summons" or "complaint"). In some national jurisdictions these preliminary steps may be taken by the parties or their attorneys without resort to a court; nevertheless, these steps are regarded as commencing the

judicial proceedings. In some other national jurisdictions judicial proceedings are considered to commence only at some later stage in the proceedings. For this reason, article 13 refers to the creditor's performance of "any act which, *under the law of the court where the proceedings are instituted,* is recognized as commencing judicial proceedings", rather than to any particular procedural steps that must be taken by the creditor. The limitation period ceases to run if the creditor performs any act recognized by the law of the forum as commencing judicial proceedings against the debtor for the purpose of satisfying the creditor's claim.[36]

3. This article also covers the case where the creditor *adds* a claim to a judicial proceeding he had instituted earlier against the debtor. In such a case, the procedural step that stops the running of the limitation period depends on when, under the law of the forum, the creditor is regarded to have performed the act of "asserting his claim" in the pending proceeding.[37]

Article 14
[*Arbitration*]

1. Where the parties have agreed to submit to arbitration, the limitation period shall cease to run when either party commences arbitral proceedings in the manner provided for in the arbitration agreement or by the law applicable to such proceedings.

2. In the absence of any such provision, arbitral proceedings shall be deemed to commence on the date on which a request that the claim in dispute be referred to arbitration is delivered at the habitual residence or place of business of the other party or, if he has no such residence or place of business, then at his last known residence or place of business.

Commentary

1. Article 14 applies to arbitration based on an actual agreement of the parties to submit certain disputes to arbitration.[38] Article 13 relies on the law of the judicial forum to determine the point in the judicial proceedings at which the limitation period shall cease to run. The same approach cannot be used in relation to arbitral proceedings since under many national laws the manner of commencing arbitral proceedings is left to the agreement of the parties. Thus, article 14 (1) provides that any question as to what acts constitute the commencement of arbitral proceedings is to be answered by "the arbitration agreement or by the law applicable to such proceedings".

2. If the arbitration agreement or the applicable law does not regulate the manner of commencing arbitral proceedings, under paragraph (2) the decisive point is the date on which "a request that the claim in dispute be referred to arbitration is delivered at the habitual residence or place of business of the other party"; if he has no such residence or place of business, the request may be delivered at his last-known residence or place of business. Under paragraph (2), the request for arbitration must be "delivered" at the designated place. Thus, the risk of a failure or error in transmission falls on the sender of the request to arbitrate, but the sender need not establish that it actually came into

---

[36]Initiation by the creditor against the debtor of a criminal proceeding for fraud or active participation by the creditor in state-initiated criminal proceedings against the debtor, under some legal systems, would stop the running of the limitation period under this Convention if, under the local law, the creditor's act constitutes institution of a proceeding "for the purpose of obtaining satisfaction or recognition of his claim".

[37]The permissibility of amendment of claims in a pending proceeding and its effect are questions left to the law of the forum.

[38]Art. 14 applies only where the parties *"have agreed* to submit to arbitration". Obligatory "arbitration" not based on an agreement of the parties would be characterized as "judicial proceedings" for the purpose of the Convention. See arts. 1 (3) *(e),* and 13.

the hands of the other party in view of the practical difficulties involved in proving receipt by a designated person following delivery of the request at the place specified in the article.

Article 15

[Legal proceedings arising from death, bankruptcy or a similar occurrence]

In any legal proceedings other than those mentioned in articles 13 and 14, including legal proceedings commenced upon the occurrence of:

(a) The death or incapacity of the debtor,

(b) The bankruptcy or any state of insolvency affecting the whole of the property of the debtor, or

(c) The dissolution or liquidation of a corporation, company, partnership, association or entity when it is the debtor,

the limitation period shall cease to run when the creditor asserts his claim in such proceedings for the purpose of obtaining satisfaction or recognition of the claim, subject to the law governing the proceedings.

Commentary

1. Article 15 governs the effect of commencing legal proceedings other than those mentioned in articles 13 and 14. Such proceedings include, *inter alia,* proceedings for the distribution of assets on death, bankruptcy, and the dissolution or liquidation of a corporation, as illustrated in subparagraphs *(a)* through *(c)* of article 15. It should be noted that the illustrations set forth in subparagraphs *(a)* through *(c)* do not limit the scope of the article, since it applies to "any legal proceedings other than those mentioned in articles 13 and 14". Thus, receivership proceedings or the re-organization of a corporation are also covered by this article. These proceedings often differ from ordinary judicial or arbitral proceedings in that they are not instituted by individual creditors; instead, creditors are given the opportunity to file claims in existing proceedings. Consequently, article 15 provides that the limitation period ceases to run "when the creditor *asserts* his claim in such proceedings for the purpose of obtaining satisfaction or recognition of the claim".

2. However, the rule of article 15 that the limitation period ceases to run when the creditor first asserts his claim in a legal proceeding covered by that article is "subject to the law governing the proceedings". As noted previously (para. 1 of the commentary to art. 13), the net effect in articles 13, 14 and 15, that the limitation period "shall cease to run" in the cases covered by these articles, is substantially the same as providing that claims may be exercised through legal proceedings if such proceedings are commenced before the limitation period established under this Convention has expired. Because of the peculiarly local nature and importance of the proceedings covered by article 15, it is necessary to respect fully the municipal law governing these proceedings. Creditors will often rely on that municipal law, particularly as to the time when claims should be filed, and might be misled if such law were not honoured. For this reason, the concluding phrase of this article provides that if the municipal law governing the proceedings prescribes different rules with regard to the necessary timing of claims for admissibility, these rules will prevail over this Convention.[39] This may be illustrated by the following examples:

Example 15A: The law of a forum requires that a claim be filed within a short specified period of time after the commencement of a bankruptcy proceeding and

---

[39]As has been noted (para. 3 of commentary on art. 1), this Convention applies only to the limitation period for claims between parties to a contract for the international sale of goods. In the proceedings covered by this article involving the distribution of assets (as in bankruptcy), the limitation period may affect the rights of third parties. The effect of the expiration of the limitation period established under this Convention on the rights of third parties is not regulated by this Convention but is left to the applicable national law.

provides that the claim is barred after the expiration of that period. If the creditor does not assert his claim within the specified period, he cannot assert his claim in that bankruptcy proceeding or otherwise even if the limitation period under this Convention has not expired.

Example 15B: The law of a forum directs the trustee in bankruptcy to recognize claims against the bankrupt which were enforceable at the time of the commencement of the bankruptcy proceedings. If the limitation period under this Convention had not expired at the time of the commencement of the bankruptcy proceeding, the creditor's claim is not time-barred even if the limitation period under this Convention already expired at the time he actually asserts his claim in the bankruptcy proceedings.

Example 15C: The law of a forum provides that the commencement of a bankruptcy proceeding shall suspend (cease) the running of the limitation period with regard to all claims which may be asserted in that proceeding. The net effect of this suspension is the same as the provision mentioned in Example 15C. Thus, if the limitation period under this Convention had not expired at the time of the commencement of the bankruptcy proceeding, the creditor's claim is not time-barred even if the limitation period under this Convention already expired at the time he actually asserts his claim in the bankruptcy proceeding.

Article 16
[Counterclaims]

For the purposes of articles 13, 14 and 15, any act performed by way of counterclaim shall be deemed to have been performed on the same date as the act performed in relation to the claim against which the counterclaim is raised, provided that both the claim and the counterclaim relate to the same contract or to several contracts concluded in the course of the same transaction.

Commentary

1. This article deals with the point in time when a counterclaim[40] is deemed to have been instituted for the purposes of articles 13, 14 and 15. This provision may be examined in terms of the following example:

Example 16A: The seller asserted his claim in a legal proceeding against the buyer on 1 March. In that same legal proceeding, the buyer interposed a counterclaim on 1 December. The limitation period governing the buyer's counterclaim would, in normal course, have expired on 1 June.

2. In the above example, the crucial question is whether the buyer's counterclaim shall be deemed to be instituted *(a)* on 1 March, the time when the seller asserted his claim or *(b)* on 1 December 1975, when the buyer's counterclaim was in fact interposed in the pending legal proceeding. Article 16 chooses alternative *(a)*.

3. Article 16 applies when the seller's claim and the buyer's counterclaim relate to the same contract or to several contracts concluded in the course of the same transaction.[41] The same benefit is not given to the buyer when his claim against the seller

---

[40]The meaning of "counterclaim" in this article may be derived from the reference in arts. 13 and 15 to proceedings employed "for the purpose of obtaining satisfaction or recognition" of a claim. A counterclaim can lead to affirmative recovery by the defendant against the plaintiff; the use of a claim "as a defence or for the purpose of set-off", after the limitation period for that claim has expired, is governed by art. 25 (2). (See para. 3 of commentary on art. 25.) The question whether a counterclaim is admissible on procedural grounds is, of course, left to the procedural rules of the forum.

[41]For example, if the plaintiff asserts a claim on the basis of a distributorship agreement and the defendant counterclaims based on an agreement to sell related to the distributorship agreement, these two claims might be regarded as arising "in the course of the same transaction".

92

arises from a different transaction than the one which provided the basis for the seller's claim against the buyer; in this latter case, the buyer must actually interpose his counterclaim before the expiration of the limitation period.

Article 17

[Proceedings not resulting in a decision on the merits of the claim]

1. Where a claim has been asserted in legal proceedings within the limitation period in accordance with articles 13, 14, 15 or 16, but such legal proceedings have ended without a decision binding on the merits of the claim, the limitation period shall be deemed to have continued to run.

2. If, at the time such legal proceedings ended, the limitation period has expired or has less than one year to run, the creditor shall be entitled to a period of one year from the date on which the legal proceedings ended.

Commentary

1. Article 17 is addressed to the problems that arise when the legal proceedings in which a creditor asserted his claim end without an adjudication on the merits of the claim. Under articles 13, 14 (1) and 15, when a creditor asserts his claim in legal proceedings for the purpose of satisfying his claim, the limitation period "shall cease to run"; when a creditor asserts his claim in legal proceedings before the expiration of the limitation period, in the absence of some further provision, the limitation period would never expire. Consequently, supplementary rules are required when such a proceeding does not lead to an adjudication on the merits of the claim. Legal proceedings may end without a decision binding on the merits of the claim for various reasons. A proceeding may be dismissed because it was brought in a tribunal lacking competence over the case; procedural defects may prevent adjudication on the merits; a higher authority within the same jurisdiction may declare that the lower court lacked competence to handle the case; arbitration may be stayed or the arbitral award may be set aside by a judicial authority within the same jurisdiction; moreover, a proceeding may not result in a decision binding on the merits of the claim because the creditor discontinues the proceedings or withdraws his claim. Article 17 covers all such instances where the "legal proceedings have ended without a decision binding on the merits of the claim". The general rule under paragraph 1 is that "the limitation period shall be deemed to have continued to run" and the cessation of the running of the limitation period under articles 13, 14, 15 or 16 is rendered inapplicable when such proceedings ended without a binding decision on the merits.

2. Paragraph 2 of this article, however, takes account of the possibility that, a substantial period of time after the creditor asserted his claim in a legal proceeding, that proceeding may be brought to an end without a decision on the merits because of lack of jurisdiction, a procedural defect, or some other reason. If this occurs after the expiration of the limitation period, the creditor would have no opportunity to institute a new legal proceeding; if this occurs shortly before the expiration of the limitation period the creditor may have insufficient time to institute a new legal proceeding.[42] To meet these problems, article 17 (2) provides that "If, at the time such legal proceedings ended, the limitation period has expired or has less than one year to run, the creditor shall be entitled to a period of one year from the date on which the legal proceedings ended".

Article 18

[Joint debtors: recourse actions]

1. Where legal proceedings have been commenced against one debtor, the limitation period prescribed in this Convention shall cease to run against any other

---

[42]The question whether a second legal proceeding pertaining to the same claim is admissible is, of course, left to the procedural law of the forum.

party jointly and severally liable with the debtor, provided that the creditor informs such party in writing within that period that the proceedings have been commenced.

2. Where legal proceedings have been commenced by a subpurchaser against the buyer, the limitation period prescribed in this Convention shall cease to run in relation to the buyer's claim over against the seller, if the buyer informs the seller in writing within that period that the proceedings have been commenced.

3. Where the legal proceedings referred to in paragraphs 1 and 2 of this article have ended, the limitation period in respect of the claim of the creditor or the buyer against the party jointly and severally liable or against the seller shall be deemed not to have ceased running by virtue of paragaphs 1 and 2 of this article, but the creditor or the buyer shall be entitled to an additional year from the date on which the legal proceedings ended, if at that time the limitation period had expired or had less than one year to run.

Commentary

I. *Effect of the institution of legal proceedings against a joint debtor, paragraph (1)*

1. The purpose of paragraph (1) of this article is to resolve questions that may arise in the following situation. Two persons (A and B) are jointly and severally responsible for the performance of a sales transaction. The other party (P) commences a legal proceeding against A within the limitation period. What is the effect of the legal proceeding commenced by P against A on the limitation period applicable to P's claim against B?

2. Under some national laws the institution of legal proceedings against A also stops the running of the limitation period applicable to P's claim against B. Under some other national laws the institution of legal proceedings against A has no effect on the running of the limitation period with regard to B. Consequently, the formulation of a uniform rule on this issue was considered desirable. A rule to the effect that the institution of legal proceedings against A has no effect on the running of the period against B would involve certain practical difficulties. Such a rule would make it advisable for the creditor (P) to institute legal proceedings against both A and B within the limitation period—at least in cases where there is some doubt concerning the financial ability of A to satisfy a judgement. Where A and B are in different jurisdictions, it may not be feasible to institute a single proceeding against them both, and instituting separate proceedings in different jurisdictions, merely to prevent the running of the limitation period against the second debtor (B), would involve expenses that turn out to have been incurred needlessly in all cases where A can and does satisfy the judgement.

3. Under article 18 (1), where legal proceedings have been commenced against A, the limitation period "shall cease to run" not only with respect to A but also with respect to B, the party jointly and severally liable with A. It will be noted that article 18 (1) becomes applicable only when the creditor informs B in writing within the limitation period that legal proceedings have been instituted against A. This written notice gives B the opportunity, if he chooses, to intervene or participate in the proceedings against A, provided such intervention by B is allowed under the procedural law of the forum. Whether or not B may intervene, the limitation period for the creditor's claim against joint debtor B ceases to run when the creditor institutes legal proceedings against joint debtor A, provided that the creditor gives the required notice to B.

II. *Recourse actions, paragraph (2)*

4. Paragraph (2) of this article deals with the following situation: A sells goods to B who resells the goods to a subpurchaser C. C commences legal proceedings against B on the ground that the goods are defective. In such a case, a recovery on C's claim against B may give rise to a claim by B against A for indemnification.

5. If C commences the legal proceedings against B only toward the end of the limitation period applicable to B's possible claim against A, B may not have sufficient time to institute legal proceedings against A, particularly if B wants to await the final adjudication of C's claim against him before commencing an action against A. In the absence of a rule in this Convention protecting B in such a case, B will be compelled to immediately institute legal proceedings against A, even though the need for indemnification is at that point speculative, and will arise only if C prevails in his claim against B. For this reason, article 18 (2) provides that where the subpurchaser C has commenced legal proceedings against the buyer B, the limitation period "shall cease to run" with respect to B's claim against the seller A.

6. It should be noted, however, that the limitation period applicable to B's claim against A shall "cease to run" only if B "informs [A] in writing within that period that the proceedings have been commenced". Hence, if C only commenced the legal proceedings against B[43] after the expiration of the limitation period applicable to B's claim against A under this Convention, B will not be protected under article 18 (2). It was felt necessary to so limit the operation of article 18 (2) in order to safeguard the original seller from being exposed, subsequent to the expiration of the limitation period provided under this Convention for claims against him, to possible claims that may arise as a consequence of a resale of the goods by the original buyer.[44]

III. *Time-limit for commencing legal proceedings against joint debtors or against the seller, paragraph (3)*

7. Paragraph (3) completes article 18 the same way as article 17 completes the operation of articles 13, 14, 15 and 16 where the legal proceedings covered by those articles ended without a decision binding on the merits of the claim. In the absence of paragraph (3), the limitation period for the claim referred to in paragraphs (1) and (2) of article 18 would never expire since they provide that "the limitation period prescribed in this Convention shall cease to run". Therefore, under paragraph (3) of article 18, where the legal proceedings referred to in paragraphs (1) and (2) of that article have *ended,* the limitation period for any claims by the creditor against other persons jointly and severally liable or by the buyer against the seller "shall be deemed not to have ceased running" at the time such legal proceedings were commenced. However, if at the time these legal proceedings ended, the limitation period for the claims referred to in paragraphs (1) and (2) had already expired or had less than one year to run, paragraph (3) provides an additional period (i.e., one year from the date on which those legal proceedings ended) within which the creditor or the buyer may institute legal proceedings.[45]

Article 19
[Recommencement of the period by service of notice]

Where the creditor performs, in the State in which the debtor has his place of business and before the expiration of the limitation period, any act, other than the acts described in articles 13, 14, 15 and 16, which under the law of that State has the effect of recommencing a limitation period, a new limitation period of four years shall commence on the date prescribed by that law.

---

[43]In many cases the sale by B to C will be a domestic sale for which no limitation period is prescribed by this Convention.

[44]In any case, claims based on the death or personal injury of any person, including the subpurchaser, are not covered by the Convention (see art. 5 *(a)* and accompanying commentary, para. 1).

[45]See also art. 23 for the over-all limitation for instituting legal proceedings.

Commentary

1. Under some national laws certain acts by the creditor such as a demand for performance may have the effect of recommencing the limitation period which is provided under the local law, even though these acts are not linked to the institution of legal proceedings. (In some jurisdictions a letter or even a verbal demand may suffice.) In other legal systems, such acts by the creditor would not recommence the limitation period, and the creditor would have to institute legal proceedings in order to stop the running of the period. Article 19 is a compromise between these two approaches. This article permits continued reliance on the special local procedure to which parties in some jurisdictions may have become accustomed; on the other hand, it assures that the creditor will not be allowed to take advantage of a local procedure for recommencing the limitation period with which the debtor may not be familiar. Thus, article 19 is applicable only when the creditor performs such act, pursuant to the special local procedure on recommencing the limitation period, "in the State in which the debtor has his place of business" before the expiration of the limitation period provided under this Convention. It may be noted that article 19 is applicable only if the act performed by the creditor would (in the absence of this Convention) have "the effect of *recommencing*" the local limitation period under the law of the State of the debtor. If the local rule only provides an additional shorter period after such act rather than "recommencing" the original limitation period, such local rule would not have the effect of bringing article 19 into operation.[46]

2. The effect given to such act under article 19 is that "a new limitation period of four years" commences to run afresh from the date on which the local limitation period would otherwise have recommenced in the absence of this Convention. It should be noted that this consequence differs from the effect of the institution of legal proceedings (arts. 13, 14, 15 and 16); on the institution of legal proceedings the period "shall cease to run" subject to the adjustments provided in articles 17 and 18.

Article 20
[Acknowledgement by debtor]

1. Where the debtor, before the expiration of the limitation period, acknowledges in writing his obligation to the creditor, a new limitation period of four years shall commence to run from the date of such acknowledgement.

2. Payment of interest or partial performance of an obligation by the debtor shall have the same effect as an acknowledgement under paragraph (1) of this article if it can reasonably be inferred from such payment or performance that the debtor acknowledges that obligation.

Commentary

1. The basic aims of the limitation period under this Convention are both to prevent the institution of legal proceedings at such a late date that the evidence is likely to be unreliable and to provide a degree of certainty in the legal relationships covered. An extension of the limitation period where the debtor acknowledges his obligation to the creditor before the expiration of the original limitation period is consistent with these aims. Consequently, under paragraph (1) of this article, when such acknowledgement occurs, a new limitation period of four years from the date of the acknowledgement will begin to run.

2. In view of the significant impact which this rule may have on the debtor's obligations, paragraph (1) requires that the acknowledgement be in writing. A writing by

---

[46]If, under the local law, "the effect of recommencing a limitation period" is given subject to certain conditions, the existence of such conditions under the local law will not interfere with the application of article 19.

96

a debtor confirming an earlier oral acknowledgement becomes an "acknowledgement" within the meaning of this article when the confirmation in writing is made.[47] The "acknowledgement" of the original debt will sometimes be similar to a transaction creating a new debt (sometimes called a "novation") which, under the applicable national law, may be deemed to be independent of the original obligation; in such cases the original transaction need not be proved to justify recovery under the new obligation. Applicable national law may not require that the "novation" be effected in writing. The rule of paragraph (1) of article 20, that an "acknowledgement" must be in writing, is not intended to interfere with the rules of the applicable national law on "novation".

3. Paragraph (2) deals with "payment of interest or partial performance of an obligation" when these acts imply an acknowledgement of the debt. In both cases, the new limitation period will commence to run afresh only with respect to the particular obligation acknowledged by such act. Partial payment of a debt is the typical instance of such partial performance, but the language of paragraph (2) is sufficiently broad to include other types of partial performance such as the partial repair by a seller of a defective machine. Whether there was an implied acknowledgement under the particular circumstances and if there was, the extent of the obligation so acknowledged, are questions that must be resolved on the basis of all relevant facts concerning the obligation and the act "acknowledging" the existence of the obligation.

Article 21
[Extension where institution of legal proceedings prevented]

Where, as a result of a circumstance which is beyond the control of the creditor and which he could neither avoid nor overcome, the creditor has been prevented from causing the limitation period to cease to run, the limitation period shall be extended so as not to expire before the expiration of one year from the date on which the relevant circumstance ceased to exist.

Commentary

1. This article provides for a limited extension of the limitation period when circumstances beyond the creditor's control prevent him from instituting legal proceedings.[48] This problem is often considered under the heading of *"force majeure"* or impossibility; however, this article does not employ those terms since they have different connotations in different legal systems. Instead, the basic test is whether the creditor "has been prevented" from taking appropriate action so as to stop the running of the limitation period. To avoid excessive liberality, no extension is permitted unless: (1) the preventing circumstance was *"beyond the control of the creditor"*, and (2) the creditor could not have avoided or overcome the occurrence of such circumstance.[49] There are many types of preventing circumstances that are *"beyond the control of the creditor"* and which therefore might provide a basis for an extension under this article. These may include: a state of war or the interruption of communications; the death or incapacity of the debtor where an administrator of the debtor's assets has not yet been

---

[47]The term "writing" is defined in art. 1 (3) *(g)* of this Convention.

[48]Under arts. 13, 14, 15 and 16, it is provided that the limitation period shall "cease to run" when a creditor asserts his claim in legal proceedings. The present article, in referring to circumstances preventing the creditor "from causing the limitation period to cease to run", refers to the actions described under those articles.

[49]It should be noted that even if these requirements were met with regard to a particular circumstance, if, in fact, the creditor had not been "prevented" from taking other appropriate action that would have stopped the running of the limitation period, this article would not permit the extension. Whether the creditor has been "prevented" from taking any action to stop the running of the limitation period is a question to be determined in the light of all the relevant facts surrounding the relationship between the creditor and the debtor. See art. 30 and accompanying commentary.

appointed (cf. art. 15); the debtor's misstatement or concealment of his identity or address which prevents the creditor from instituting legal proceedings; fraudulent concealment by the debtor of defects in the goods.[50]

2. There is no justification for extending the limitation period when the circumstance that prevented the institution of legal proceedings ceased to exist a substantial period in advance of the end of the normal limitation period under the Convention. Nor is there reason to extend the period for a longer period than is needed to institute legal proceedings to obtain satisfaction or recognition of the claim. For these reasons, the limitation period is extended only for one year from the date on which the preventing circumstance is removed. Thus, if, at the time the preventing circumstance ceased to exist, the limitation period had expired or had less than one year to run, the creditor is given one year from the date on which the preventing circumstance ceased to exist.[51]

MODIFICATION OF THE LIMITATION PERIOD BY THE PARTIES

Article 22
[Modification by the parties]

1. The limitation period cannot be modified or affected by any declaration or agreement between the parties, except in the cases provided for in paragraph (2) of this article.

2. The debtor may at any time during the running of the limitation period extend the period by a declaration in writing to the creditor. This declaration may be renewed.

3. The provisions of this article shall not affect the validity of a clause in the contract of sale which stipulates that arbitral proceedings shall be commenced within a shorter period of limitation than that prescribed by this Convention, provided that such clause is valid under the law applicable to the contract of sale.

Commentary

1. Paragraph (1) of article 22 establishes the general rule that this Convention does not allow parties to modify the limitation period. Exceptions to this rule, provided in paragraphs (2) and (3) of the article are explained below.

I. Extension of the limitation period

2. Paragraph (2) permits the debtor to extend the limitation period "by a declaration in writing to the creditor". While such an extension can be renewed by the debtor, the total period of permissible extension is subject to the over-all limitation provided under article 23. The extension can be accomplished by a unilateral declaration by the debtor; more often, the declaration by the debtor will be part of a wider agreement by the parties. As extension of the limitation period may have important consequences on the rights of the parties, only a declaration in writing can extend the period.

3. Under paragraph (2), a declaration by the debtor extending the limitation period is effective only if made "during the running of the limitation period". This restriction in the Convention would deny effect to possible attempts to extend the period by a declaration made at the time of contracting or at some other time before the claim accrues or the breach occurs.[52] Without this restriction a party with stronger bargaining

---

[50]As to the time when the limitation period commences to run with regard to claims based on fraud, see art. 10 (3).

[51]See also art. 23 on the over-all limitation for commencing legal proceedings.

[52]Under arts. 9 through 12, the limitation period does not commence to run unless the claim has accrued or the breach has occurred.

power might impose such extensions at the time of contracting; in addition, a clause extending the limitation period might be a part of a form contract to which the other party might not give sufficient attention. Similarly, a declaration by a debtor made after the expiration of the limitation period under this Convention will not be given effect, since it was not made "during the running of the limitation period".

4. Allowance of extension after the commencement of the limitation period, on the other hand, may be useful to prevent the hasty institution of legal proceedings close to the end of the period when the parties are still negotiating or are awaiting the outcome of similar proceedings in other forums.[53]

II. *Arbitration*

5. In order to give effect to contract clauses, often used in commodity trading, which provide that any dispute must be submitted to arbitration within a short period (e.g. within six months), paragraph (3) of article 22 makes an exception to the general rule of paragraph (1) by stating that this Convention does not render such clauses invalid. And, to guard against the possible abuse of such a provision, paragraph (3) concludes with the proviso that such clause must be valid under the law applicable to the sales contract. For example, the applicable national law may give courts the power, on the grounds of hardship to a party, to extend the short period provided for in the contract for the submission of disputes to arbitration; this Convention does not interfere with the continued exercise of this power by a court.

GENERAL LIMIT OF THE LIMITATION PERIOD

Article 23
[*Over-all limitation for bringing legal proceedings*]

Notwithstanding the provisions of this Convention, a limitation period shall in any event expire not later than 10 years from the date on which it commenced to run under articles 9, 10, 11 and 12 of this Convention.

Commentary

As already noted, this Convention contains provisions which permit the limitation period to be extended or modified in various situations (arts. 17 to 22). Thus, it is possible that the period will be extended, in some cases, for such a substantially prolonged period that the institution of the legal proceedings toward the end of that extended period would be no longer compatible with the purpose of this Convention of providing a definite limitation period. Moreover, as explained above (para. 1 of commentary on art. 17), under articles 13, 14, 15 and 16 of this Convention, when a creditor asserts his claim in legal proceedings, the limitation period "shall cease to run"; when a creditor asserts his claim in legal proceedings in one State before the expiration of the limitation period, in the absence of further provision,[54] the limitation period would never expire in that State or in other States. (See art. 30 and its accompanying commentary.) This article, therefore, sets forth an over-all cut-off point beyond which

---

[53]It may be noted that paragraph (1) of this article also precludes arrangements which would "affect" the limitation period. Thus, the effect of an agreement by the parties not to invoke prescription or limitation as a defence in legal proceedings is also regulated by this article because its effect of not allowing the assertion of the expiration of the limitation period is practically the same as extending the period. Cf. art. 24.

[54]E.g., see arts. 17 (1) and 18 (3).

no legal proceedings may be instituted under any circumstance. This cut-off point is the expiration of 10 years from the date on which the limitation period commenced to run under articles 9, 10, 11 and 12.[55]

CONSEQUENCES OF THE EXPIRATION OF THE LIMITATION PERIOD

Article 24
[Who can invoke limitation]

Expiration of the limitation period shall be taken into consideration in any legal proceedings only if invoked by a party to such proceedings.

Commentary

1.   Article 24 is addressed to the following question: if none of the parties to the legal proceedings chooses to assert that the claim is barred by the expiration of the limitation period under this Convention, may the tribunal hearing the claim raise the issue on its own *(suo officio)*? This article answers the above question in the negative: expiration of the limitation period is to be considered by a tribunal "only if invoked by a party to such proceedings". It may be stated in support of this result that many of the facts relevant to determining when the limitation period runs, ceases to run or expires, will be known only to the parties and will not ordinarily be disclosed when evidence is presented pertaining to the substance of the claim (e.g., facts relevant to possible prolongation of the limitation period under arts. 20 and 22). Under some legal systems, it would be deemed a departure from the customary neutral role of judges to require or even authorize them on their own to raise the issue and search out the facts relating to expiration of the limitation period. Moreover, this question is not of great practical importance because a party entitled to interpose this defence to the claim will rarely fail to do so. In addition, article 24 does not bar a tribunal from drawing the attention of the parties to the time that elapsed between the accrual of the claim and the commencement of the legal proceeding and from inquiring whether one of the parties wishes that the issue of the expiration of the limitation period be taken into consideration.[56] There may also be instances where a debtor prefers not to invoke the expiration of the limitation period as a defence because of his special business relationship with the creditor, while wanting an adjudication on the merits of the creditor's claim. For these reasons, article 24 provides that a tribunal shall consider the issue of expiration of the limitation period "only if invoked by a party to such proceedings".

2.   However, it was noted by several representatives at the Conference which adopted this Convention that limitation is a matter of public policy and should not be subjected to the parties' discretion; according to these representatives the tribunal should take the expiration of the limitation period into account *suo officio*. The tribunal can obtain the relevant facts from the parties without having to burden itself with the collection of evidence, and in any event the question of who has the burden of collecting evidence should not affect the issue of who may *invoke* limitation. Article 36 reflects this view by permitting a State to declare at the time of its ratification or accession to this Convention "that it shall not be compelled to apply the provisions of article 24 of this Convention".

---

[55]It may be noted that, under arts. 19 and 20, "a new limitation period" commences to run afresh under the circumstances specified in those articles. Such a new limitation period is technically not the same period which had commenced to run under art. 9, 10, 11 or 12. However, the over-all limitation provided under art. 23 is intended to apply to all forms of prolongation of the original limitation period, including the creation of a "new limitation period" under art. 19 or 20.

[56]Whether this would be proper judicial practice is a matter for decision under the procedural laws of the forum.

Article 25

[Effect of expiration of the period; set-off]

1. Subject to the provisions of paragraph (2) of this article and of article 24, no claim shall be recognized or enforced in any legal proceedings commenced after the expiration of the limitation period.

2. Notwithstanding the expiration of the limitation period, one party may rely on his claim as a defence or for the purpose of set-off against a claim asserted by the other party, provided that in the latter case this may only be done:

   (a) If both claims relate to the same contract or to several contracts concluded in the course of the same transaction; or

   (b) If the claims could have been set-off at any time before the expiration of the limitation period.

Commentary

I. Effect of expiration of the period, paragraph (1)

1. Paragraph (1) of article 25 emphasizes this Convention's basic aim of providing a limitation period within which the parties must commence legal proceedings for the exercise of their claims. (See para. 1 of commentary on art. 1.) Once the limitation period has expired, the claims can no longer be recognized or enforced in any legal proceedings.

2. It should be noted that paragraph (1) of this article is only concerned with the recognition or enforcement of claims "in any legal proceedings". This Convention does not attempt to resolve all possible questions that might be raised with respect to the effect of the expiration of the limitation period. For example, if collateral of the debtor remains in the possession of the creditor after the expiration of the period, questions may arise as to the right of the creditor to continue in possession of the collateral or to liquidate the collateral through sale. These issues may arise in a wide variety of factual settings and the results may vary due to differences in the security arrangements and in the national laws applicable to those arrangements. It may be expected, however, that the tribunals of Contracting States, when dealing with these problems, will give full effect to the basic policy of this Convention incorporated in article 25, which states that claims shall not be recognized or enforced in legal proceedings commenced after the expiration of the limitation period.[57]

II. Claim used as a defence or for the purpose of set-off, paragraph (2)

3. The rules of paragraph (2) can be illustrated by the following examples:

Example 25A: An international sales contract required A to deliver specified goods to B on 1 June of each year from 1975 through 1980. B claimed that the goods delivered in 1975 were defective. B did not pay for the goods delivered in 1980, and A instituted legal proceedings in 1981 to recover the price.

On these facts B may use his claim against A, based on defects of the goods delivered in 1975, as a set-off against A's claim. Such set-off is permitted under subparagraph (a) of article 25 (2), since both claims relate to the same contract;[58] the set-off by B is not barred even though the limitation period for B's claim expired in 1979, i.e. prior to his assertion of the claim in the legal proceedings and also prior to the accrual of the claim by A against B for the price of the goods delivered in 1980. It should also be noted that

---

[57]See also art. 5 (c). As to the effect of voluntary performance of an obligation after the expiration of the limitation period, see art. 26 and accompanying commentary.

[58]For an example where claims relate "to several contracts concluded in the course of the same transaction", see foot-note 41 in the commentary to art. 16.

under article 25 (2), B may rely on this claim "for the purpose of set-off". Thus, if A's claim is for $1,000 and B's claim is for $2,000, B's claim may extinguish A's claim but it may not be used as a basis for affirmative recovery against A for $1,000.[59]

Example 25B: On 1 June 1975, A delivered goods to B based on a contract of international sale of goods; B claimed the goods were defective. On 1 June 1978, under a different contract, B delivered goods to A; A claimed these goods were defective and in 1980 instituted legal proceedings against B based on this claim.

In these proceedings B may rely on his claim against A for the purpose of set-off even though B's claim arose in 1975—more than four years prior to the time when the claim was asserted in court as a set-off to A's claim. Under subparagraph *(b)* of article 25 (2), the claims "could have been set-off" before the date when the limitation period on B's claim expired—i.e. between 1 June 1978, the date on which A's claim accrued against B, and 1 June 1979.[60]

Article 26
[*Restitution of performance after the expiration of the period*]

Where the debtor performs his obligation after the expiration of the limitation period, he shall not on that ground be entitled in any way to claim restitution even if he did not know at the time when he performed his obligation that the limitation period had expired.

Commentary

1. As has been noted above (para. 1 of commentary on art. 25), expiration of the limitation period precludes the recognition or enforcement of the claims *in legal proceedings*. If a party obtains satisfaction of his claim in a manner other than through legal proceedings, this consequence is not initially the concern of the Convention. However, due to the existence of differences in theoretical approaches as to the nature of prescription or limitation under various national laws,[61] differing consequences may be attributed to an act by the debtor whereby he voluntarily performed his obligation only learning later that the limitation period for the creditor's claim against him had already expired. Article 26 aims to provide a uniform result where the debtor voluntarily performed his obligation after the expiration of the limitation period. Article 26 is included in the Convention not because this Convention adopts any particular theory as to the character of the limitation but because providing an answer to the problem will assist in eliminating unnecessary disputes and divergencies in interpretation.

2. The basic aims of the limitation period, i.e. to prevent the institution of legal proceedings at such a late date that the evidence is unreliable and to provide a degree of certainty in legal relationships, are not violated where the debtor voluntarily performs his obligation after the expiration of the limitation period. Article 26 accordingly provides that the debtor cannot claim restitution for any performance of his obligation to the creditor which he has voluntarily performed "even if he did not know" at the time of such performance that the limitation period had expired. It should be noted that this

---

[59]As to legal proceedings permitting affirmative recovery by the defendant against the plaintiff (i.e. counterclaims), see art. 16 and its accompanying commentary.

[60]This example assumes that the two claims could have been set-off *under the applicable national law*. This Convention does not affect the applicable law which regulates the permissibility of set-offs; the Convention only governs the limitation period for asserting claims, including claims asserted as set-offs.

[61]E.g., whether the claim itself is extinguished (prescription), or whether it is only the assertion of the claim in legal proceedings that is barred because of the expiry of the limitation period while the claim itself still exists. It has already been pointed out that this Convention governs limitation of legal proceedings regardless of the theoretical approach to the problem under national laws. See para. 1 of commentary on art. 1 and para. 5 of commentary on art. 3.

provision deals only with the effectiveness of claims for restitution based on the contention that the performance could not have been required because the limitation period had run.[62]

Article 27
[*Interest*]

The expiration of the limitation period with respect to a principal debt shall have the same effect with respect to an obligation to pay interest on that debt.

Commentary

To avoid divergent interpretations involving the theoretical question whether an obligation to pay interest is "independent" from the obligation to pay the principal debt, article 27 provides a uniform rule that "the expiration of the limitation period with respect to a principal debt shall have the same effect with respect to an obligation to pay interest on that debt". (Cf. art. 20 (2).)

CALCULATION OF THE PERIOD

Article 28
[*Basic rule*]

1.   The limitation period shall be calculated in such a way that it shall expire at the end of the day which corresponds to the date on which the period commenced to run. If there is no such corresponding date, the period shall expire at the end of the last day of the last month of the limitation period.

2.   The limitation period shall be calculated by reference to the date of the place where the legal proceedings are instituted.

Commentary

1.   One traditional formula for the calculation of the limitation period is to exclude the first day of the period and to include the last day. The concept of "inclusion" and "exclusion" of days, however, may be misunderstood by those who are not familiar with the application of this rule. For this reason, article 28 adopts a different formula to reach the same result. Under this article, where a limitation period begins on 1 June, the day when the period expires is the corresponding day of the later year, i.e., 1 June. The second sentence of article 28 (1) covers the situation which may occur in a leap year. (Thus, when the initial day is 29 February of a leap year, and the later year is not a leap year, the date on which the limitation period expires is "the last day of the last month of the limitation period", i.e., 28 February of the later year.)

2.   Paragraph (2) of article 28 is designed to overcome problems that may be encountered because of the existence of the international date line. If the date in State X is a day ahead of the date in State Y, the limitation period, which would commence on 1 May according to the date in State Y, will commence on 2 May in State X; therefore if the legal proceedings are instituted in State X, the last day for its commencement is 2 May in the relevant later year.

3.   Since a number of different calendars are used in different States, for uniformity "year" is defined to mean a year according to the Gregorian calendar for the purpose of

---

[62]Art. 26 does not deal with the question whether the creditor is entitled to apply a debtor's payment to the satisfaction of a time-barred claim where the creditor has many claims against the debtor some of which are time-barred and the debtor neither expressly nor impliedly indicated that the payment is for satisfaction of a particular debt. Solution of this question is left to the applicable national law.

this Convention (art. 1 (3) *(h)*). Under article 28, therefore, years shall always be calculated according to the Gregorian calendar, even if the place where the legal proceedings are instituted uses a different calendar.

Article 29
[*Effect of holiday*]

Where the last day of the limitation period falls on an official holiday or other *dies non juridicus* precluding the appropriate legal action in the jurisdiction where the creditor institutes legal proceedings or asserts a claim as envisaged in article 13, 14 or 15, the limitation period shall be extended so as not to expire until the end of the first day following that official holiday or *dies non juridicus* on which such proceedings could be instituted or on which such a claim could be asserted in that jurisdiction.

Commentary

1. This article deals with the problem that arises when the limitation period would end on a day when the courts and other tribunals are closed so that the creditor cannot take the steps prescribed in article 13, 14 or 15 to commence legal proceedings. This article provides for such cases by extending the limitation period "until the end of the first day following that official holiday or *dies non juridicus* on which such proceedings could be instituted or on which such a claim could be asserted in that jurisdiction".

2. It is recognized that the curtailment of the period that might result from the fact that the last day of the limitation period is a holiday is minor in relation to the total limitation period calculated in terms of years. However in many legal systems, such an extension is provided and local attorneys may rely on it. In addition, attorneys in one country might not know the legal holidays or "other *dies non juridicus*" in another country. The limited extension provided for in this article will avoid such difficulties.

3. It may be noted that the extension granted under this article is operative only in the jurisdiction where timely institution of legal proceedings was precluded due to such "official holiday or other *dies non juridicus*" (cf. art. 30).

INTERNATIONAL EFFECT

Article 30
[*Acts or circumstances to be given international effect*]

The acts and circumstances referred to in articles 13 through 19 which have taken place in one Contracting State shall have effect for the purposes of this Convention in another Contracting State, provided that the creditor has taken all reasonable steps to ensure that the debtor is informed of the relevant act or circumstances as soon as possible.

Commentary

1. Article 30 refers to the effect which Contracting States must give to "acts or circumstances" referred to in articles 13 through 19 that had taken place in other Contracting States. Those articles deal with the point which various types of legal proceedings must reach in order to extend the limitation period or to stop it from running. The purpose of article 30 is to ensure that the acts and circumstances referred to in articles 13 through 19, when occurring in one Contracting State, will be given the same effect of stopping or extending the limitation period in any other Contracting State. The problems to which this article is addressed may be illustrated by the following examples:

Example 30A: Buyer's claim against Seller arising from an international sale of goods accrued in 1975. In 1978 Buyer instituted a legal proceeding against Seller in

Contracting State X. In 1981 the proceeding in State X led to a decision on the merits of the claim in favour of Buyer and in 1982 Buyer sought its execution in Contracting State Y. Enforcement of the decision is refused by State Y. Since Buyer's claim accrued more than four years prior to 1981, Buyer's claim would be barred if he wished to institute a new legal proceeding in State Y *unless* the limitation period is regarded to have "ceased to run" also in State Y by virtue of the institution in 1978 of the legal proceeding in State X. Under article 30, stopping of the running of the period by the institution of a legal proceeding in State X has the same effect in State Y and Buyer may institute a new legal proceeding in State Y, subject to the over-all limitation under article 23 for bringing legal proceedings.

Example 30B: Buyer's claim against Seller arising from an international sale of goods accrued in 1975. In 1978 Buyer instituted a legal proceeding against Seller in Contracting State X. In 1981 the proceeding in State X led to a decision on the merits of the claim in favour of Buyer. Seller's assets are in Contracting State Y. State Y would recognize and enforce the decision of State X but the law of State Y does not preclude Buyer from asserting his original claim afresh in legal proceedings in State Y, provided that the limitation period with regard to the original claim had not expired. Buyer, finding it easier to sue again on the original claim than to involve himself in a complicated process of proving the validity of the first decision for its enforcement in State Y, decides to institute a new legal proceeding in State Y. Under article 30, stopping of the running of the limitation period by the institution of the legal proceeding in State X has the same effect in State Y and Buyer may institute a new legal proceeding in State Y, subject to the over-all limitation under article 23 for bringing legal proceedings.[63]

Example 30C: Buyer's claim against Seller arising from an international sale of goods accrued in 1975. In 1978 Buyer instituted a legal proceeding against Seller in Contracting State X. In 1980, while the proceeding in State X was still pending, Buyer instituted a legal proceeding in Contracting State Y based on the same claim. Since Buyer's claim arose more than four years prior to the institution of the proceeding in State Y, that proceeding would be barred unless the limitation period "ceased to run" when the legal proceeding was commenced in State X. Under article 30, Buyer's legal proceeding in State Y is not time-barred because State Y must recognize the cessation of the running of the limitation period that had taken place in State X by virtue of the institution of the legal proceeding in State X within the limitation period.[64]

2. Article 30 also refers to article 17, which deals with the effect on the running of the period of a legal proceeding that ends without a decision on the merits of the claim. To afford the creditor an opportunity to institute a further legal proceeding, in such cases the creditor is assured of a period of one year from the date on which the proceedings ended. Thus, in example 30C, if the proceeding in State X ended on 1 February 1980 without a decision on the merits of the claim, the limitation period "shall be deemed to have continued to run" but the period is extended to 1 February 1981.[65] Under article 30, if State X is a Contracting State, these events in State X must

---

[63]A creditor who received an unfavourable decision on the merits of his claim may also consider having his claim re-tried in another State provided that he is not precluded from asserting his original claim afresh in legal proceedings in that State. Legal rules such as *res judicata*, "merger" of the claim in the judgement, or the like, may prevent the assertion of the original claim after a decision on the merits of the claim in another State. This is a question to be answered according to the procedural law of the forum and is not covered by this Convention.

[64]Whether a legal proceeding may be instituted on a claim while another legal proceeding is pending in another State concerning the same claim will be resolved by the procedural law of the forum and is not covered by this Convention.

[65]The close relationship between the provisions of this Convention as to the circumstances when the limitation period "ceases to run" on the institution of legal proceedings (i.e., arts. 13, 14, 15 and 16) and the rules of art. 17 concerning the effect of proceedings not resulting in a decision on the merits of the claim is discussed in the commentary on art. 17.

be given "international" effect in Contracting State Y and a legal proceeding may be brought in State Y until 1 February 1981.[66]

3. Article 30 also prescribes the "international" effect of the recommencement of the limitation period which, under article 19, may occur in some jurisdictions as a result of acts such as the service of a demand notice. Attention is also drawn to the rules of article 18 concerning recourse actions and the effect of the institution of legal proceedings against a joint debtor. Under article 30, the effect given to the circumstances mentioned in articles 18 and 19 must also be given by other Contracting States.

4. The "international" effect of acts in one Contracting State (State X) in a second Contracting State (State Y) applies only with respect to acts covered by the articles listed in article 30. It may be noted that under this Convention the effectiveness of certain other acts does not depend on where they take place: e.g., acknowledgement of the debt (art. 20) and a declaration or agreement modifying the limitation period (art. 22) have the effect prescribed in those articles without regard to the place where the acknowledgement, declaration or agreement takes place.

5. An important requirement for the applicability of article 30 is that the creditor must take "all reasonable steps to ensure that the debtor is informed of the relevant act or circumstances as soon as possible". While in most instances commencement of a legal proceeding will require notification to the defendant-debtor, under some procedural rules this may not be necessary in certain cases. The above requirement was added to ensure that all reasonable steps were taken to apprise the debtor of the fact that due to certain acts of circumstances in one Contracting State, the limitation period has also been stopped or extended in all other Contracting States.

Part II. Implementation

Article 31
[Federal State; non-unitary State]

1. If a Contracting State has two or more territorial units in which, according to its constitution, different systems of law are applicable in relation to the matters dealt with in this Convention, it may, at the time of signature, ratification or accession, declare that this Convention shall extend to all its territorial units or only to one or more of them, and may amend its declaration by submitting another declaration at any time.

2. These declarations shall be notified to the Secretary-General of the United Nations and shall state expressly the territorial units to which the Convention applies.

3. If a Contracting State described in paragraph (1) of this article makes no declaration at the time of signature, ratification or accession, the Convention shall have effect within all territorial units of that State.

Commentary

1. Where a Contracting State to this Convention is a federal or non-unitary State, the federal authority may not have the power to implement certain provisions of this Convention in its constituent states or provinces because those provisions may relate to matters that are within the legislative jurisdiction of such constituent states or provinces. On the other hand, adoption by a State of this Convention obligates that State to take the necessary implementing steps that would give the provisions of part I of this

---

[66]Art. 30 does not bar a Contracting State from giving comparable effect to acts occurring in non-Contracting States; but this Convention does not require that such "international" effect be given to circumstances that took place in non-Contracting States.

Convention (subject to the reservations permitted under part III) the force of law within that State. Yet, a federal or non-unitary State may not be able to so implement this Convention unless each of its constituent states or provinces passes appropriate legislation. Article 31 is designed to enable a federal or non-unitary State to adopt this Convention even if that State could not absolutely ensure that *all* of its constituent states or provinces will take the legislative steps necessary to implement the provisions of this Convention. Thus, under article 31 (1), a federal or non-unitary State may, "at the time of signature, ratification or accession, declare that this Convention shall extend to all its territorial units or only to one or more of them". Under article 31 (2), a State making such a declaration must state "expressly the territorial units to which the Convention applies" at the time of the notification of the declaration to the Secretary-General of the United Nations. The important qualification under article 31 (1) is that the different systems of law applicable in the various territorial units must be *based on the constitution* of the federal or non-unitary State making such a declaration.

2.   It may be noted that article 31 (1) further provides that the declaration thereunder may be amended *at any time* by submitting another declaration. Such an amendment should technically be regarded as a combination of a new declaration and a withdrawal of the original declaration; article 40 governs the point in time when such an amended declaration will take effect.

3.   Paragraph (3) of article 31 reflects the *basic* obligation of a State adopting this Convention to implement the provisions of the Convention within the whole territory of that State: in the absence of any declaration permitted under this article "at the time of signature, ratification or accession" by a federal or non-unitary State, this Convention shall have effect "within *all* territorial units of that State".

Article 32
[Determination of the proper law when federal or a non-unitary State is involved]

Where in this Convention reference is made to the law of a State in which different systems of law apply such reference shall be construed to mean the law of the particular legal system concerned.

Commentary

In this Convention, several references have been made to the law of a State. For example, articles 12 and 22 (3) refer to "the law *applicable* to the contract"; article 14 (1) refers to "the law *applicable* to [arbitral] proceedings"; and article 15 refers to "the law *governing* the proceedings". In such cases, the determination as to the proper law to govern each situation will be made in accordance with the private international law rules of the forum. Article 32 is intended to clarify that the same approach should be pursued in arriving at the proper law where different systems of law exist in the State whose law is chosen as applicable by the conflict-of-laws rules of the forum.[67]

Article 33
[Non-applicability to prior contracts]

Each Contracting State shall apply the provisions of this Convention to contracts concluded on or after the date of the entry into force of this Convention.

Commentary

1.   This article serves to clarify the application of the principle prescribed in article 3 (1) by providing a definite rule as to the contracts to which this Convention applies: a

---

[67]Cf. art. 13, where the reference is to "the law of the court".

Contracting State is bound to apply the provisions of the Convention to contracts that are concluded on or *after* the date of *the entry into force* of this Convention in the State concerned.

2. The date of the entry into force of this Convention is dealt with in article 44 of this Convention (see also art. 3 (3)).

Part III. Declarations and reservations

Article 34
[Declarations limiting the application of the Convention]

Two or more Contracting States may at any time declare that contracts of sale between a seller having a place of business in one of these States and a buyer having a place of business in another of these States shall not be governed by this Convention, because they apply to the matters governed by this Convention the same or closely related legal rules.

Commentary

1. Some States, in the absence of this Convention, apply the same or closely related rules to the subject-matter governed by this Convention, *i.e.*, limitation (prescription) of claims based on a contract of international sale of goods. Under article 34 these States are permitted, if they so choose, to apply their common or closely related rules to claims arising from transaction involving buyers and sellers in such States, and yet adhere to the Convention.

2. This article enables two or more Contracting States to make a joint declaration, *at any time,* that contracts of sale entered into by a seller having a place of business in one of these States and a buyer having a place of business in another of these States, *"shall not be governed by this Convention"*. The over-all effect is that such contracts are *excluded from the scope* of application of the Convention by virtue of such a declaration. It should be noted that a declaration under article 34 may be made well after the time these States have ratified this Convention. (See also art. 40 and accompanying commentary, para. 2.)[68]

Article 35
[Reservation with respect to actions for annulment of the contract]

A Contracting State may declare, at the time of the deposit of its instrument of ratification or accession, that it will not apply the provisions of this Convention to actions for annulment of the contract.

Commentary

As has already been noted, this Convention governs the limitation period for bringing an "action for annulment" in those legal systems which require that the nullity of a contract be first established by way of a legal proceeding instituted for that purpose.[69] However, in the States which require an initial judicial determination of the contract's invalidity, the limitation period for bringing such actions may be different from the normal period for the exercise of claims based on the contract. This article permits a State to declare that it will not apply the provisions of this Convention to actions for

---

[68]As to the situations where the same limitation rules are applied among several States because these States are parties to conventions containing limitation provisions in respect of international sales, see art. 37.

[69]See foot-note 3 in commentary on art. 1 and its accompanying text.

annulment of the contract. Consequently, the State which has made a reservation under this article may continue to apply its particular local rules (including its rules of private international law) to actions for annulment of contracts. It may be noted that reservations under this article may also be made by States which adhere to legal systems where termination or invalidity of a contract need not first be established by way of a legal proceeding brought for this purpose.

Article 36
[Reservation with respect to who can invoke limitation]

Any State may declare, at the time of the deposit of its instrument of ratification or accession, that it shall not be compelled to apply the provisions of article 24 of this Convention.

Commentary

This article permits a Contracting State to make a reservation with regard to the application of the rule of article 24 which provides that a tribunal shall take into consideration the expiration of the limitation period only if a party invokes it. (The need for this reservation has already been noted in para. 2 of commentary on art. 24.)

Article 37
[Relationship with conventions containing limitation provisions in respect of international sale of goods]

This Convention shall not prevail over conventions already entered into or which may be entered into, and which contain provisions concerning the matters covered by this Convention, provided that the seller and buyer have their places of business in States parties to such a convention.

Commentary

1. This article provides that this Convention shall not prevail over present or future conventions which contain provisions concerning the limitation or prescription of claims based on the international sale of goods. In case of conflict, therefore, the rules of those other conventions shall be applied to the limitation or prescription of claims, rather than the rules of this Convention.

2. Such situations could occur in regard to conventions that deal with the international sale of a particular commodity, or a special group of commodities. In addition, it has been suggested that article 49 of the 1964 ULIS may conflict with some of the provisions of part I of this Convention. A conflicting provision may also be contained in conventions concluded on the regional level, such as the General Conditions of Delivery of Goods between Organizations of the Member Countries of the Council for Mutual Economic Assistance, 1968. Article 37 permits States parties to such a convention to apply its conflicting provision only when both the seller and the buyer have their places of business in States which have ratified that convention.

3. It may be noted that the rule in this article operates automatically, without requiring any advance declaration by the States who are parties to the convention containing a conflicting provision as to the limitation or prescription of claims (cf. art. 34).

Article 38
[Reservations with respect to the definition of a contract of international sale]

1. A Contracting State which is a party to an existing convention relating to the international sale of goods may declare, at the time of the deposit of its instrument of ratification or accession, that it will apply this Convention exclusively to contracts of international sale of goods as defined in such existing convention.

2. Such declaration shall cease to be effective on the first day of the month following the expiration of 12 months after a new convention on the international sale of goods, concluded under the auspices of the United Nations, shall have entered into force.

Commentary

1. Article 2 of this Convention deals with the degree of internationality which makes a contract for sale of goods an "international" one for the purposes of this Convention. Article 3 (1) sets the obligation of Contracting States to apply the provisions of this Convention to contracts of international sale of goods. Article 38 is designed to facilitate adoption of this Convention by States which are already parties to an existing convention on the international sale of goods (such as ULIS) which contains a definition of "international" sale different from article 2 of this Convention. Article 38 permits such a State to exclude the application of article 2 with regard to the definition of "international" sale by making a declaration that it will apply this Convention only to international sales of goods as defined in such an existing convention. The net effect of such a declaration is to obligate the declaring State to apply the provisions of this Convention *only* to those contracts which fall within *the definition* of a contract of international sale of goods *under the other existing convention* when a legal proceeding is commenced within the jurisdiction of that State.[70]

2. Article 38 (2), however, makes it clear that reservations permitted under article 38 (1) is a temporary expedient; it also reflects the general expectations of the Conference which adopted this Convention that the definition of "international" sale of goods be ultimately brought into line with the definition in a new convention on the international sale of goods the draft of which is presently under study by the United Nations Commission on International Trade Law.

Article 39
[No other reservations permitted]

No reservation other than those made in accordance with articles 34, 35, 36, and 38 shall be permitted.

Commentary

This article provides a basis for uniformity in application of the Convention by prohibiting Contracting States from making any reservation other than those specifically permitted under this Convention.[71]

Article 40
[When declarations and reservations take effect; withdrawal]

1. Declarations made under this Convention shall be addressed to the Secretary-General of the United Nations and shall take effect simultaneously with the entry of this Convention into force in respect of the State concerned, except declarations made thereafter. The latter declarations shall take effect on the first day of the month following the expiration of six months after the date of their receipt by the Secretary-General of the United Nations.

---

[70]See e.g., ULIS art. 1. It is expected, however, that the difference in the applicable scope, because of a reservation under art. 38, will not be so great as might first appear from the comparison of art. 1 of ULIS and art. 2 of this Convention. Cf. art. 2 *(b) (c)*.

[71]The 1969 Vienna Convention on the Law of Treaties provides, *inter alia,* that a State may make a reservation, when ratifying or acceding to a Convention, unless the treaty provides that only specified reservations, which do not include the reservation in question, may be made (art. 19).

2. Any State which has made a declaration under this Convention may withdraw it at any time by a notification addressed to the Secretary-General of the United Nations. Such withdrawal shall take effect on the first day of the month following the expiration of six months after the date of the receipt of the notification by the Secretary-General of the United Nations. In the case of a declaration made under article 34 of this Convention, such withdrawal shall also render inoperative, as from the date on which the withdrawal takes effect, any reciprocal declaration made by another State under that article.

Commentary

1. Paragraph (1) of this article provides the manner in which declarations under articles 31, 34, 35, 36 and 38 must be made and specifies the point in time when such declarations take effect. Article 40 (2) permits withdrawal of such declarations and provides both the manner in which such withdrawal may be made and the point in time when it becomes effective.

2. It may be noted that, under the last sentence of article 40 (2), a joint declaration made under article 34 becomes inoperative when one of the parties to that joint declaration withdraws therefrom. Even where a joint declaration has been made by *more than two* States, a notification of withdrawal to the Secretary-General of the United Nations by one of those States will render the joint declaration inoperative in respect of the remaining States on the first day of the month following the expiration of six months after that notification. Thus, if the other remaining States still wish to maintain the joint declaration under article 34 among themselves, they will have to make a new declaration in accordance with article 40 (1).

Part IV. Final clauses

Article 41

This Convention shall be open until 31 December 1975 for signature by all States at the Headquarters of the United Nations.

Article 42

This Convention is subject to ratification. The instruments of ratification shall be deposited with the Secretary-General of the United Nations.

Article 43

This Convention shall remain open for accession by any State. The instrument of accession shall be deposited with the Secretary-General of the United Nations.

Article 44

1. This Convention shall enter into force on the first day of the month following the expiration of six months after the date of the deposit of the tenth instrument of ratification or accession.

2. For each State ratifying or acceding to this Convention after the deposit of the tenth instrument of ratification or accession, this Convention shall enter into force on the first day of the month following the expiration of six months after the date of the deposit of its instrument of ratification or accession.

Article 45

1. Any Contracting State may denounce this Convention by notifying the Secretary-General of the United Nations to that effect.

2.   The denunciation shall take effect on the first day of the month following the expiration of 12 months after receipt of the notification by the Secretary-General of the United Nations.

Article 46

The original of this Convention, of which the Chinese, English, French, Russian and Spanish texts are equally authentic, shall be deposited with the Secretary-General of the United Nations.

C.   General Assembly resolution 3317 (XXIX) of 14 December 1974

3317 (XXIX).   UNITED NATIONS CONFERENCE ON PRESCRIPTION (LIMITATION) IN THE INTERNATIONAL SALE OF GOODS

The General Assembly,

Recalling its resolutions 2929 (XXVII) of 28 November 1972 and 3104 (XXVIII) of 12 December 1973 on the convening of a United Nations Conference on Prescription (Limitation) in the International Sale of Goods,

Noting that the United Nations Conference on Prescription (Limitation) in the International Sale of Goods was held at United Nations Headquarters, from 20 May to 14 June 1974 and that the Conference adopted, on 12 June 1974, a Convention on the Limitation Period in the International Sale of Goods,[1]

Noting further that the Convention was opened for signature by all States on 14 June 1974 and will remain open until 31 December 1975, in accordance with its provisions, at United Nations Headquarters, and was also opened for accession in accordance with its provisions,

Reaffirming the conviction, expressed in the foregoing resolutions, that the harmonization and unification of national rules governing prescription (limitation) in the international sale of goods would contribute to the removal of obstacles to the development of world trade,

Invites all States which have not yet done so to consider the possibility of signing, ratifying or acceding to the Convention on the Limitation Period in the International Sale of Goods.

2319th plenary meeting,
14 December 1974

D.   Protocol amending the Convention on the Limitation Period in the International Sale of Goods

The States Parties to this Protocol,

Considering that international trade is an important factor in the promotion of friendly relations amongst States,

---

[1]See *Official Records of the United Nations Conference on Prescription (Limitation) in the International Sale of Goods* (United Nations publication, Sales No. E.74.V.8), p. 101 (document A/CONF.63/15).

Believing that the adoption of uniform rules governing the limitation period in the international sale of goods would facilitate the development of world trade,

Considering that amending the Convention on the Limitation Period in the International Sale of Goods, concluded at New York on 14 June 1974 (the 1974 Limitation Convention), to conform to the United Nations Convention on Contracts for the International Sale of Goods, concluded at Vienna on 11 April 1980 (the 1980 Sales Convention), would promote the adoption of the uniform rules governing the limitation period contained in the 1974 Limitation Convention,

Have agreed to amend the 1974 Limitation Convention as follows:

Article I

(1) Paragraph 1 of article 3 is replaced by the following provisions:

"1. This Convention shall apply only

(a) if, at the time of the conclusion of the contract, the places of business of the parties to a contract of international sale of goods are in Contracting States; or

(b) if the rules of private international law make the law of a Contracting State applicable to the contract of sale."

(2) Paragraph 2 of article 3 is deleted.

(3) Paragraph 3 of article 3 is renumbered as paragraph 2.

Article II

(1) Subparagraph *(a)* of article 4 is deleted and replaced by the following provision:

"*(a)* of goods bought for personal, family or household use, unless the seller, at any time before or at the conclusion of the contract, neither knew nor ought to have known that the goods were bought for any such use;"

(2) Subparagraph *(e)* of article 4 is deleted and is replaced by the following provision:

"*(e)* of ships, vessels, hovercraft or aircraft;"

Article III

A new paragraph 4 is added to article 31 reading as follows:

"(4) If, by virtue of a declaration under this article, this Convention extends to one or more but not all of the territorial units of a Contracting State, and if the place of business of a party to a contract is located in that State, this place of business shall, for the purposes of this Convention, be considered not to be in a Contracting State unless it is in a territorial unit to which the Convention extends."

Article IV

The provisions of article 34 are deleted and are replaced by the following provisions:

"1. Two or more Contracting States which have the same or closely related legal rules on matters governed by this Convention may at any time declare that the Convention shall not apply to contracts of international sale of goods where the parties have their places of business in those States. Such declarations may be made jointly or by reciprocal unilateral declarations.

2. A Contracting State which has the same or closely related legal rules on matters governed by this Convention as one or more non-Contracting States may at any time declare that the Convention shall not apply to contracts of international sale of goods where the parties have their places of business in those States.

3. If a State which is the object of a declaration under paragraph (2) of this article subsequently becomes a Contracting State, the declaration made shall, as from the date on which this Convention enters into force in respect of the new Contracting State, have the effect of a declaration made under paragraph (1), provided that the new Contracting State joins in such declaration or makes a reciprocal unilateral declaration."

Article V

The provisions of article 37 are deleted and are replaced by the following provisions:

"This Convention shall not prevail over any international agreement which has already been or may be entered into and which contains provisions concerning the matters governed by this Convention, provided that the seller and buyer have their places of business in States parties to such agreement."

Article VI

At the end of paragraph 1 of article 40, the following provision is added:

"Reciprocal unilateral declarations under article 34 shall take effect on the first day of the month following the expiration of six months after the receipt of the latest declaration by the Secretary-General of the United Nations."

FINAL PROVISIONS

Article VII

The Secretary-General of the United Nations is hereby designated as the depositary for this Protocol.

Article VIII

(1) This Protocol shall be open for accession by all States.

(2) Accession to this Protocol by any State which is not a Contracting Party to the 1974 Limitation Convention shall have the effect of accession to that Convention as amended by this Protocol, subject to the provisions of article XI.

(3) Instruments of accession shall be deposited with the Secretary-General of the United Nations.

Article IX

(1) This Protocol shall enter into force on the first day of the sixth month following the deposit of the second instrument of accession, provided that on that date:

(a) the 1974 Limitation Convention is itself in force; and

(b) the 1980 Sales Convention is also in force.

If these Conventions are not both in force on that date, this Protocol shall enter into force on the first day on which both Conventions are in force.

(2) For each State acceding to this Protocol after the second instrument of accession has been deposited, this Protocol shall enter into force on the first day of the sixth month following the deposit of its instrument of accession, if by that date the Protocol is itself in force. If by that date the Protocol itself is not yet in force, the Protocol shall enter into force for that State on the date the Protocol itself enters into force.

Article X

If a State ratifies or accedes to the 1974 Limitation Convention after the entry into force of this Protocol, the ratification or accession shall also constitute an accession to this Protocol if the State notifies the depositary accordingly.

Article XI

Any State which becomes a Contracting Party to the 1974 Limitation Convention, as amended by this Protocol, by virtue of articles VIII, IX or X of this Protocol shall, unless it notifies the depositary to the contrary, be considered to be also a Contracting Party to the Convention not yet a Contracting Party to this Protocol.

Article XII

Any State may declare at the time of the deposit of its instrument of accession or its notification under article X that it will not be bound by article I of the Protocol. A declaration made under this article shall be in writing and be formally notified to the depositary.

Article XIII

(1) A Contracting State may denounce this Protocol by notifying the depositary to that effect.

(2) The denunciation shall take effect on the first day of the month following the expiration of twelve months after receipt of the notification by the depositary.

(3) Any Contracting State in respect of which this Protocol ceases to have effect by the application of paragraphs (1) and (2) of this article shall remain a Contracting Party to the 1974 Limitation Convention, unamended, unless it denounces the unamended Convention in accordance with article 45 of that Convention.

Article XIV

(1) The depositary shall transmit certified true copies of this Protocol to all States.

(2) When this Protocol enters into force in accordance with article IX, the depositary shall prepare a text of the 1974 Limitation Convention, as amended by this Protocol, and shall transmit certified true copies to all States Parties to that Convention, as amended by this Protocol.

DONE at Vienna, this day of 11 April 1980, in a single original, of which the Arabic, Chinese, English, French, Russian and Spanish texts are equally authentic.

ANNEX III. INTERNATIONAL SALE OF GOODS: CONTRACTS

United Nations Convention on Contracts for the International Sale of Goods (Vienna, 1980)

The States Parties to this Convention,

Bearing in mind the broad objectives in the resolutions adopted by the sixth special session of the General Assembly of the United Nations on the establishment of a New International Economic Order,

Considering that the development of international trade on the basis of equality and mutual benefit is an important element in promoting friendly relations among States,

Being of the opinion that the adoption of uniform rules which govern contracts for the international sale of goods and take into account the different social, economic and legal systems would contribute to the removal of legal barriers in international trade and promote the development of international trade,

Have agreed as follows:

Part I. Sphere of application and general provisions

CHAPTER I. SPHERE OF APPLICATION

Article 1

(1) This Convention applies to contracts of sale of goods between parties whose places of business are in different States:

(a) when the States are Contracting States; or

(b) when the rules of private international law lead to the application of the law of a Contracting State.

(2) The fact that the parties have their places of business in different States is to be disregarded whenever this fact does not appear either from the contract or from any dealings between, or from information disclosed by, the parties at any time before or at the conclusion of the contract.

(3) Neither the nationality of the parties nor the civil or commercial character of the parties or of the contract is to be taken into consideration in determining the application of this Convention.

Article 2

This Convention does not apply to sales:

(a) of goods bought for personal, family or household use, unless the seller, at any time before or at the conclusion of the contract, neither knew nor ought to have known that the goods were bought for any such use;

(b) by auction;

(c) on execution or otherwise by authority of law;

(d) of stocks, shares, investment securities, negotiable instruments or money;

(e) of ships, vessels, hovercraft or aircraft;

(f) of electricity.

Article 3

(1) Contracts for the supply of goods to be manufactured or produced are to be considered sales unless the party who orders the goods undertakes to supply a substantial part of the materials necessary for such manufacture or production.

(2) This Convention does not apply to contracts in which the preponderant part of the obligations of the party who furnishes the goods consists in the supply of labour or other services.

Article 4

This Convention governs only the formation of the contract of sale and the rights and obligations of the seller and the buyer arising from such a contract. In particular, except as otherwise expressly provided in this Convention, it is not concerned with:

(a) the validity of the contract or of any of its provisions or of any usage;

(b) the effect which the contract may have on the property in the goods sold.

Article 5

This Convention does not apply to the liability of the seller for death or personal injury caused by the goods to any person.

Article 6

The parties may exclude the application of this Convention or, subject to article 12, derogate from or vary the effect of any of its provisions.

CHAPTER II.   GENERAL PROVISIONS

Article 7

(1) In the interpretation of this Convention, regard is to be had to its international character and to the need to promote uniformity in its application and the observance of good faith in international trade.

(2) Questions concerning matters governed by this Convention which are not expressly settled in it are to be settled in conformity with the general principles on which it is based or, in the absence of such principles, in conformity with the law applicable by virtue of the rules of private international law.

Article 8

(1) For the purposes of this Convention statements made by and other conduct of a party are to be interpreted according to his intent where the other party knew or could not have been unaware what that intent was.

(2) If the preceding paragraph is not applicable, statements made by and other conduct of a party are to be interpreted according to the understanding that a reasonable person of the same kind as the other party would have had in the same circumstances.

(3) In determining the intent of a party or the understanding a reasonable person would have had, due consideration is to be given to all relevant circumstances of the case including the negotiations, any practices which the parties have established between themselves, usages and any subsequent conduct of the parties.

Article 9

(1)   The parties are bound by any usage to which they have agreed and by any practices which they have established between themselves.

(2)   The parties are considered, unless otherwise agreed, to have impliedly made applicable to their contract or its formation a usage of which the parties knew or ought to have known and which in international trade is widely known to, and regularly observed by, parties to contracts of the type involved in the particular trade concerned.

Article 10

For the purposes of this Convention:

(a)   if a party has more than one place of business, the place of business is that which has the closest relationship to the contract and its performance, having regard to the circumstances known to or contemplated by the parties at any time before or at the conclusion of the contract;

(b)   if a party does not have a place of business, reference is to be made to his habitual residence.

Article 11

A contract of sale need not be concluded in or evidenced by writing and is not subject to any other requirement as to form. It may be proved by any means, including witnesses.

Article 12

Any provision of article 11, article 29 or Part II of this Convention that allows a contract of sale or its modification or termination by agreement or any offer, acceptance or other indication of intention to be made in any form other than in writing does not apply where any party has his place of business in a Contracting State which has made a declaration under article 96 of this Convention. The parties may not derogate from or vary the effect of this article.

Article 13

For the purposes of this Convention "writing" includes telegram and telex.

Part II.   Formation of the contract

Article 14

(1)   A proposal for concluding a contract addressed to one or more specific persons constitutes an offer if it is sufficiently definite and indicates the intention of the offeror to be bound in case of acceptance. A proposal is sufficiently definite if it indicates the goods and expressly or implicitly fixes or makes provision for determining the quantity and the price.

(2)   A proposal other than one addressed to one or more specific persons is to be considered merely as an invitation to make offers, unless the contrary is clearly indicated by the person making the proposal.

Article 15

(1)   An offer becomes effective when it reaches the offeree.

(2)   An offer, even if it is irrevocable, may be withdrawn if the withdrawal reaches the offeree before or at the same time as the offer.

118

Article 16

(1)   Until a contract is concluded an offer may be revoked if the revocation reaches the offeree before he has dispatched an acceptance.

(2)   However, an offer cannot be revoked:

(a)   if it indicates, whether by stating a fixed time for acceptance or otherwise, that it is irrevocable; or

(b)   if it was reasonable for the offeree to rely on the offer as being irrevocable and the offeree has acted in reliance on the offer.

Article 17

An offer, even if it is irrevocable, is terminated when a rejection reaches the offeror.

Article 18

(1)   A statement made by or other conduct of the offeree indicating assent to an offer is an acceptance. Silence or inactivity does not in itself amount to acceptance.

(2)   An acceptance of an offer becomes effective at the moment the indication of assent reaches the offeror. An acceptance is not effective if the indication of assent does not reach the offeror within the time he has fixed or, if no time is fixed, within a reasonable time, due account being taken of the circumstances of the transaction, including the rapidity of the means of communication employed by the offeror. An oral offer must be accepted immediately unless the circumstances indicate otherwise.

(3)   However, if, by virtue of the offer or as a result of practices which the parties have established between themselves or of usage, the offeree may indicate assent by performing an act, such as one relating to the dispatch of the goods or payment of the price, without notice to the offeror, the acceptance is effective at the moment the act is performed, provided that the act is performed within the period of time laid down in the preceding paragraph.

Article 19

(1)   A reply to an offer which purports to be an acceptance but contains additions, limitations or other modifications is a rejection of the offer and constitutes a counter-offer.

(2)   However, a reply to an offer which purports to be an acceptance but contains additional or different terms which do not materially alter the terms of the offer constitutes an acceptance, unless the offeror, without undue delay, objects orally to the discrepancy or dispatches a notice to that effect. If he does not so object, the terms of the contract are the terms of the offer with the modifications contained in the acceptance.

(3)   Additional or different terms relating, among other things, to the price, payment, quality and quantity of the goods, place and time of delivery, extent of one party's liability to the other or the settlement of disputes are considered to alter the terms of the offer materially.

Article 20

(1)   A period of time of acceptance fixed by the offeror in a telegram or a letter begins to run from the moment the telegram is handed in for dispatch or from the date shown on the letter or, if no such date is shown, from the date shown on the envelope. A period of time for acceptance fixed by the offeror by telephone, telex or other means of instantaneous communication, begins to run from the moment that the offer reaches the offeree.

(2) Official holidays or non-business days occurring during the period for acceptance are included in calculating the period. However, if a notice of acceptance cannot be delivered at the address of the offeror on the last day of the period because that day falls on an official holiday or a non-business day at the place of business of the offeror, the period is extended until the first business day which follows.

Article 21

(1) A late acceptance is nevertheless effective as an acceptance if without delay the offeror orally so informs the offeree or dispatches a notice to that effect.

(2) If a letter or other writing containing a late acceptance shows that it has been sent in such circumstances that if its transmission had been normal it would have reached the offeror in due time, the late acceptance is effective as an acceptance unless, without delay, the offeror orally informs the offeree that he considers his offer as having lapsed or dispatches a notice to that effect.

Article 22

An acceptance may be withdrawn if the withdrawal reaches the offeror before or at the same time as the acceptance would have become effective.

Article 23

A contract is concluded at the moment when an acceptance of an offer becomes effective in accordance with the provisions of this Convention.

Article 24

For the purposes of this Part of the Convention, an offer, declaration of acceptance or any other indication of intention "reaches" the addressee when it is made orally to him or delivered by any other means to him personally, to his place of business or mailing address or, if he does not have a place of business or mailing address, to his habitual residence.

Part III. Sale of goods

CHAPTER I. GENERAL PROVISIONS

Article 25

A breach of contract committed by one of the parties is fundamental if it results in such detriment to the other party as substantially to deprive him of what he is entitled to expect under the contract, unless the party in breach did not foresee and a reasonable person of the same kind in the same circumstances would not have foreseen such a result.

Article 26

A declaration of avoidance of the contract is effective only if made by notice to the other party.

Article 27

Unless otherwise expressly provided in this Part of the Convention, if any notice, request or other communication is given or made by a party in accordance with this Part and by means appropriate in the circumstances, a delay or error in the transmission of the communication or its failure to arrive does not deprive that party of the right to rely on the communication.

Article 28

If, in accordance with the provisions of this Convention, one party is entitled to require performance of any obligation by the other party, a court is not bound to enter a judgement for specific performance unless the court would do so under its own law in respect of similar contracts of sale not governed by this Convention.

Article 29

(1) A contract may be modified or terminated by the mere agreement of the parties.

(2) A contract in writing which contains a provision requiring any modification or termination by agreement to be in writing may not be otherwise modified or terminated by agreement. However, a party may be precluded by his conduct from asserting such a provision to the extent that the other party has relied on that conduct.

CHAPTER II. OBLIGATIONS OF THE SELLER

Article 30

The seller must deliver the goods, hand over any documents relating to them and transfer the property in the goods, as required by the contract and this Convention.

Section I. *Delivery of the goods and handing over of documents*

Article 31

If the seller is not bound to deliver the goods at any other particular place, his obligation to deliver consists:

(a) if the contract of sale involves carriage of the goods—in handing the goods over to the first carrier for transmission to the buyer;

(b) if, in cases not within the preceding subparagraph, the contract relates to specific goods, or unidentified goods to be drawn from a specific stock or to be manufactured or produced, and at the time of the conclusion of the contract the parties knew that the goods were at, or were to be manufactured or produced at, a particular place—in placing the goods at the buyer's disposal at that place;

(c) in other cases—in placing the goods at the buyer's disposal at the place where the seller had his place of business at the time of the conclusion of the contract.

Article 32

(1) If the seller, in accordance with the contract or this Convention, hands the goods over to a carrier and if the goods are not clearly identified to the contract by markings on the goods, by shipping documents or otherwise, the seller must give the buyer notice of the consignment specifying the goods.

(2) If the seller is bound to arrange for carriage of the goods, he must make such contracts as are necessary for carriage to the place fixed by means of transportation appropriate in the circumstances and according to the usual terms for such transportation.

(3) If the seller is not bound to effect insurance in respect of the carriage of the goods, he must, at the buyer's request, provide him with all available information necessary to enable him to effect such insurance.

Article 33

The seller must deliver the goods:

(a) if a date is fixed by or determinable from the contract, on that date;

(b) if a period of time is fixed by or determinable from the contract, at any time within that period unless circumstances indicate that the buyer is to choose a date; or

(c) in any other case, within a reasonable time after the conclusion of the contract.

Article 34

If the seller is bound to hand over documents relating to the goods, he must hand them over at the time and place and in the form required by the contract. If the seller has handed over documents before that time, he may, up to that time, cure any lack of conformity in the documents, if the exercise of this right does not cause the buyer unreasonable inconvenience or unreasonable expense. However, the buyer retains any right to claim damages as provided for in this Convention.

Section II. *Conformity of the goods and third party claims*

Article 35

(1) The seller must deliver goods which are of the quantity, quality and description required by the contract and which are contained or packaged in the manner required by the contract.

(2) Except where the parties have agreed otherwise, the goods do not conform with the contract unless they:

(a) are fit for the purposes for which goods of the same description would ordinarily be used;

(b) are fit for any particular purpose expressly or impliedly made known to the seller at the time of the conclusion of the contract, except where the circumstances show that the buyer did not rely, or that it was unreasonable for him to rely, on the seller's skill and judgement;

(c) possess the qualities of goods which the seller has held out to the buyer as a sample or model;

(d) are contained or packaged in the manner usual for such goods or, where there is no such manner, in a manner adequate to preserve and protect the goods.

(3) The seller is not liable under subparagraphs *(a)* to *(d)* of the preceding paragraph for any lack of conformity of the goods if at the time of the conclusion of the contract the buyer knew or could not have been unaware of such lack of conformity.

Article 36

(1) The seller is liable in accordance with the contract and this Convention for any lack of conformity which exists at the time when the risk passes to the buyer, even though the lack of conformity becomes apparent only after that time.

(2) The seller is also liable for any lack of conformity which occurs after the time indicated in the preceding paragraph and which is due to a breach of any of his obligations, including a breach of any guarantee that for a period of time the goods will remain fit for their ordinary purpose or for some particular purpose or will retain specified qualities or characteristics.

Article 37

If the seller has delivered goods before the date for delivery, he may, up to that date, deliver any missing part or make up any deficiency in the quantity of the goods

122

delivered, or deliver goods in replacement of any non-conforming goods delivered or remedy any lack of conformity in the goods delivered, provided that the exercise of this right does not cause the buyer unreasonable inconvenience or unreasonable expense. However, the buyer retains any right to claim damages as provided for in this Convention.

Article 38

(1)   The buyer must examine the goods, or cause them to be examined, within as short a period as is practicable in the circumstances.

(2)   If the contract involves carriage of the goods, examination may be deferred until after the goods have arrived at their destination.

(3)   If the goods are redirected in transit or redispatched by the buyer without a reasonable opportunity for examination by him and at the time of the conclusion of the contract the seller knew or ought to have known of the possibility of such redirection or redispatch, examination may be deferred until after the goods have arrived at the new destination.

Article 39

(1)   The buyer loses the right to rely on a lack of conformity of the goods if he does not give notice to the seller specifying the nature of the lack of conformity within a reasonable time after he has discovered it or ought to have discovered it.

(2)   In any event, the buyer loses the right to rely on a lack of conformity of the goods if he does not give the seller notice thereof at the latest within a period of two years from the date on which the goods were actually handed over to the buyer, unless this time-limit is inconsistent with a contractual period of guarantee.

Article 40

The seller is not entitled to rely on the provisions of articles 38 and 39 if the lack of conformity relates to facts of which he knew or could not have been unaware and which he did not disclose to the buyer.

Article 41

The seller must deliver goods which are free from any right or claim of a third party, unless the buyer agreed to take the goods subject to that right or claim. However, if such right or claim is based on industrial property or other intellectual property, the seller's obligation is governed by article 42.

Article 42

(1)   The seller must deliver goods which are free from any right or claim of a third party based on industrial property or other intellectual property, of which at the time of the conclusion of the contract the seller knew or could not have been unaware, provided that the right or claim is based on industrial property or other intellectual property:

(a)   under the law of the State where the goods will be resold or otherwise used, if it was contemplated by the parties at the time of the conclusion of the contract that the goods would be resold or otherwise used in that State; or

(b)   in any other case, under the law of the State where the buyer has his place of business.

(2)   The obligation of the seller under the preceding paragraph does not extend to cases where:

(a)   at the time of the conclusion of the contract the buyer knew or could not have been unaware of the right or claim; or

(b)   the right or claim results from the seller's compliance with technical drawings, designs, formulae or other such specifications furnished by the buyer.

Article 43

(1) The buyer loses the right to rely on the provisions of article 41 or article 42 if he does not give notice to the seller specifying the nature of the right or claim of the third party within a reasonable time after he has become aware or ought to have become aware of the right or claim.

(2) The seller is not entitled to rely on the provisions of the preceding paragraph if he knew of the right or claim of the third party and the nature of it.

Article 44

Notwithstanding the provisions of paragraph (1) of article 39 and paragraph (1) of article 43, the buyer may reduce the price in accordance with article 50 or claim damages, except for loss of profit, if he has a reasonable excuse for his failure to give the required notice.

Section III. *Remedies for breach of contract by the seller*

Article 45

(1) If the seller fails to perform any of his obligations under the contract or this Convention, the buyer may:

(a) exercise the rights provided in articles 46 to 52;

(b) claim damages as provided in articles 74 to 77.

(2) The buyer is not deprived of any right he may have to claim damages by exercising his right to other remedies.

(3) No period of grace may be granted to the seller by a court or arbitral tribunal when the buyer resorts to a remedy for breach of contract.

Article 46

(1) The buyer may require performance by the seller of his obligations unless the buyer has resorted to a remedy which is inconsistent with this requirement.

(2) If the goods do not conform with the contract, the buyer may require delivery of substitute goods only if the lack of conformity constitutes a fundamental breach of contract and a request for substitute goods is made either in conjunction with notice given under article 39 or within a reasonable time thereafter.

(3) If the goods do not conform with the contract, the buyer may require the seller to remedy the lack of conformity by repair, unless this is unreasonable having regard to all the circumstances. A request for repair must be made either in conjunction with notice given under article 39 or within a reasonable time thereafter.

Article 47

(1) The buyer may fix an additional period of time of reasonable length for performance by the seller of his obligations.

(2) Unless the buyer has received notice from the seller that he will not perform within the period so fixed, the buyer may not, during that period, resort to any remedy for breach of contract. However, the buyer is not deprived thereby of any right he may have to claim damages for delay in performance.

Article 48

(1) Subject to article 49, the seller may, even after the date for delivery, remedy at his own expense any failure to perform his obligations, if he can do so without

unreasonable delay and without causing the buyer unreasonable inconvenience or uncertainty of reimbursement by the seller of expenses advanced by the buyer. However, the buyer retains any right to claim damages as provided for in this Convention.

(2) If the seller requests the buyer to make known whether he will accept performance and the buyer does not comply with the request within a reasonable time, the seller may perform within the time indicated in his request. The buyer may not, during that period of time, resort to any remedy which is inconsistent with performance by the seller.

(3) A notice by the seller that he will perform within a specified period of time is assumed to include a request, under the preceding paragraph, that the buyer make known his decision.

(4) A request or notice by the seller under paragraph (2) or (3) of this article is not effective unless received by the buyer.

Article 49

(1) The buyer may declare the contract avoided:

(a) if the failure by the seller to perform any of his obligations under the contract or this Convention amounts to a fundamental breach of contract; or

(b) in case of non-delivery, if the seller does not deliver the goods within the additional period of time fixed by the buyer in accordance with paragraph (1) of article 47 or declares that he will not deliver within the period so fixed.

(2) However, in cases where the seller has delivered the goods, the buyer loses the right to declare the contract avoided unless he does so:

(a) in respect of late delivery, within a reasonable time after he has become aware that delivery has been made;

(b) in respect of any breach other than late delivery, within a reasonable time:

(i) after he knew or ought to have known of the breach;

(ii) after the expiration of any additional period of time fixed by the buyer in accordance with paragraph (1) of article 47, or after the seller has declared that he will not perform his obligations within such an additional period; or

(iii) after the expiration of any additional period of time indicated by the seller in accordance with paragraph (2) of article 48, or after the buyer has declared that he will not accept performances.

Article 50

If the goods do not conform with the contract and whether or not the price has already been paid, the buyer may reduce the price in the same proportion as the value that the goods actually delivered had at the time of the delivery bears to the value that conforming goods would have had at that time. However, if the seller remedies any failure to perform his obligations in accordance with article 37 or article 48 or if the buyer refuses to accept performance by the seller in accordance with those articles, the buyer may not reduce the price.

Article 51

(1) If the seller delivers only a part of the goods or if only a part of the goods delivered is in conformity with the contract, articles 46 to 50 apply in respect of the part which is missing or which does not conform.

(2) The buyer may declare the contract avoided in its entirety only if the failure to make delivery completely or in conformity with the contract amounts to a fundamental breach of the contract.

Article 52

(1)   If the seller delivers the goods before the date fixed, the buyer may take delivery or refuse to take delivery.

(2)   If the seller delivers a quantity of goods greater than that provided for in the contract, the buyer may take delivery or refuse to take delivery of the excess quantity. If the buyer takes delivery of all or part of the excess quantity, he must pay for it at the contract rate.

CHAPTER III.   OBLIGATIONS OF THE BUYER

Article 53

The buyer must pay the price for the goods and take delivery of them as required by the contract and this Convention.

Section I.   *Payment of the price*

Article 54

The buyer's obligation to pay the price includes taking such steps and complying with such formalities as may be required under the contract or any laws and regulations to enable payment to be made.

Article 55

Where a contract has been validly concluded but does not expressly or implicitly fix or make provision for determining the price, the parties are considered, in the absence of any indication to the contrary, to have impliedly made reference to the price generally charged at the time of the conclusion of the contract for such goods sold under comparable circumstances in the trade concerned.

Article 56

If the price is fixed according to the weight of the goods, in case of doubt it is to be determined by the net weight.

Article 57

(1)   If the buyer is not bound to pay the price at any other particular place, he must pay it to the seller:

(a)   at the seller's place of business; or

(b)   if the payment is to be made against the handing over of the goods or of documents, at the place where the handing over takes place.

(2)   The seller must bear any increase in the expenses incidental to payment which is caused by a change in his place of business subsequent to the conclusion of the contract.

Article 58

(1)   If the buyer is not bound to pay the price at any other specific time he must pay it when the seller places either the goods or documents controlling their disposition at the buyer's disposal in accordance with the contract and this Convention. The seller may make such payment a condition for handing over the goods or documents.

(2)   If the contract involves carriage of the goods, the seller may dispatch the goods on terms whereby the goods, or documents controlling their disposition, will not be handed over to the buyer except against payment of the price.

(3)   The buyer is not bound to pay the price until he has had an opportunity to examine the goods, unless the procedures for delivery or payment agreed upon by the parties are inconsistent with his having such an opportunity.

Article 59

The buyer must pay the price on the date fixed by or determinable from the contract and this Convention without the need for any request or compliance with any formality on the part of the seller.

Section II.   *Taking delivery*

Article 60

The buyer's obligation to take delivery consists:

(a)   in doing all the acts which could reasonably be expected of him in order to enable the seller to make delivery; and

(b)   in taking over the goods.

Section III.   *Remedies for breach of contract by the buyer*

Article 61

(1)   If the buyer fails to perform any of his obligations under the contract or this Convention, the seller may:

(a)   exercise the rights provided in articles 62 to 65;

(b)   claim damages as provided in articles 74 to 77.

(2)   The seller is not deprived of any right he may have to claim damages by exercising his right to other remedies.

(3)   No period of grace may be granted to the buyer by a court or arbitral tribunal when the seller resorts to a remedy for breach of contract.

Article 62

The seller may require the buyer to pay the price, take delivery or perform his other obligations, unless the seller has resorted to a remedy which is inconsistent with this requirement.

Article 63

(1)   The seller may fix an additional period of time of reasonable length for performance by the buyer of his obligations.

(2)   Unless the seller has received notice from the buyer that he will not perform within the period so fixed, the seller may not, during that period, resort to any remedy for breach of contract. However, the seller is not deprived thereby of any right he may have to claim damages for delay in performance.

Article 64

(1)   The seller may declare the contract avoided:

(a)   if the failure by the buyer to perform any of his obligations under the contract or this Convention amounts to a fundamental breach of contract; or

(b)   if the buyer does not, within the additional period of time fixed by the seller in accordance with paragraph (1) of article 63, perform his obligation to pay the price or

take delivery of the goods, or if he declares that he will not do so within the period so fixed.

(2) However, in cases where the buyer has paid the price, the seller loses the right to declare the contract avoided unless he does so:

(a) in respect of late performance by the buyer, before the seller has become aware that performance has been rendered; or

(b) in respect of any breach other than late performance by the buyer, within a reasonable time:

    (i) after the seller knew or ought to have known of the breach; or

    (ii) after the expiration of any additional period of time fixed by the seller in accordance with paragraph (1) of article 63, or after the buyer has declared that he will not perform his obligations within such an additional period.

Article 65

(1) If under the contract the buyer is to specify the form, measurement or other features of the goods and he fails to make such specification either on the date agreed upon or within a reasonable time after receipt of a request from the seller, the seller may, without prejudice to any other rights he may have, make the specification himself in accordance with the requirements of the buyer that may be known to him.

(2) If the seller makes the specification himself, he must inform the buyer of the details thereof and must fix a reasonable time within which the buyer may make a different specification. If, after receipt of such a communication, the buyer fails to do so within the time so fixed, the specification made by the seller is binding.

CHAPTER IV. PASSING OF RISK

Article 66

Loss of or damage to the goods after the risk has passed to the buyer does not discharge him from his obligation to pay the price, unless the loss or damage is due to an act or omission of the seller.

Article 67

(1) If the contract of sale involves carriage of the goods and the seller is not bound to hand them over at a particular place, the risk passes to the buyer when the goods are handed over to the first carrier for transmission to the buyer in accordance with the contract of sale. If the seller is bound to hand the goods over to a carrier at a particular place, the risk does not pass to the buyer until the goods are handed over to the carrier at that place. The fact that the seller is authorized to retain documents controlling the disposition of the goods does not affect the passage of the risk.

(2) Nevertheless, the risk does not pass to the buyer until the goods are clearly identified to the contract, whether by markings on the goods, by shipping documents, by notice given to the buyer or otherwise.

Article 68

The risk in respect of goods sold in transit passes to the buyer from the time of the conclusion of the contract. However, if the circumstances so indicate, the risk is assumed by the buyer from the time the goods were handed over to the carrier who issued the documents embodying the contract of carriage. Nevertheless, if at the time of the conclusion of the contract of sale the seller knew or ought to have known that the goods had been lost or damaged and did not disclose this to the buyer, the loss or damage is at the risk of the seller.

Article 69

(1)   In cases not within articles 67 and 68, the risk passes to the buyer when he takes over the goods or, if he does not do so in due time, from the time when the goods are placed at his disposal and he commits a breach of contract by failing to take delivery.

(2)   However, if the buyer is bound to take over the goods at a place other than a place of business of the seller, the risk passes when delivery is due and the buyer is aware of the fact that the goods are placed at his disposal at that place.

(3)   If the contract relates to goods not then identified, the goods are considered not to be placed at the disposal of the buyer until they are clearly identified to the contract.

Article 70

If the seller has committed a fundamental breach of contract, articles 67, 68 and 69 do not impair the remedies available to the buyer on account of the breach.

CHAPTER V.   PROVISIONS COMMON TO THE OBLIGATIONS OF THE SELLER
AND OF THE BUYER

Section I.   *Anticipatory breach and instalment contracts*

Article 71

(1)   A party may suspend the performance of his obligations if, after the conclusion of the contract, it becomes apparent that the other party will not perform a substantial part of his obligations as a result of:

   (a)   a serious deficiency in his ability of perform or in his creditworthiness; or

   (b)   his conduct in preparing to perform or in performing the contract.

(2)   If the seller has already dispatched the goods before the grounds described in the preceding paragraph become evident, he may prevent the handing over of the goods to the buyer even though the buyer holds a document which entitles him to obtain them. The present paragraph relates only to the rights in the goods as between the buyer and the seller.

(3)   A party suspending performance, whether before or after dispatch of the goods, must immediately give notice of the suspension to the other party and must continue with performance if the other party provides adequate assurance of his performance.

Article 72

(1)   If prior to the date for performance of the contract it is clear that one of the parties will commit a fundamental breach of contract, the other party may declare the contract avoided.

(2)   If time allows, the party intending to declare the contract avoided must give reasonable notice to the other party in order to permit him to provide adequate assurance of his performance.

(3)   The requirements of the preceding paragraph do not apply if the other party has declared that he will not perform his obligations.

Article 73

(1)   In the case of a contract for delivery of goods by instalments, if the failure of one party to perform any of his obligations in respect of any instalment constitutes a fundamental breach of contract with respect to that instalment, the other party may declare the contract avoided with respect to that instalment.

(2) If one party's failure to perform any of his obligations in respect of any instalment gives the other party good grounds to conclude that a fundamental breach of contract will occur with respect to future instalments, he may declare the contract avoided for the future, provided that he does so within a reasonable time.

(3) A buyer who declares the contract avoided in respect of any delivery may, at the same time, declare it avoided in respect of deliveries already made or of future deliveries if, by reason of their interdependence, those deliveries could not be used for the purpose contemplated by the parties at the time of the conclusion of the contract.

Section II. *Damages*

Article 74

Damages for breach of contract by one party consist of a sum equal to the loss, including loss of profit, suffered by the other party as a consequence of the breach. Such damages may not exceed the loss which the party in breach foresaw or ought to have foreseen at the time of the conclusion of the contract, in the light of the facts and matters of which he then knew or ought to have known, as a possible consequence of the breach of contract.

Article 75

If the contract is avoided and if, in a reasonable manner and within a reasonable time after avoidance, the buyer has bought goods in replacement or the seller has resold the goods, the party claiming damages may recover the difference between the contract price and the price in the substitute transaction as well as any further damages recoverable under article 74.

Article 76

(1) If the contract is avoided and there is a current price for the goods, the party claiming damages may, if he has not made a purchase or resale under article 75, recover the difference between the price fixed by the contract and the current price at the time of avoidance as well as any further damages recoverable under article 74. If, however, the party claiming damages has avoided the contract after taking over the goods, the current price at the time of such taking over shall be applied instead of the current price at the time of avoidance.

(2) For the purposes of the preceding paragraph, the current price is the price prevailing at the place where delivery of the goods should have been made or, if there is no current price at that place, the price at such other place as serves as a reasonable substitute, making due allowance for differences in the cost of transporting the goods.

Article 77

A party who relies on a breach of contract must take such measures as are reasonable in the circumstances to mitigate the loss, including loss of profit, resulting from the breach. If he fails to take such measures, the party in breach may claim a reduction in the damages in the amount by which the loss should have been mitigated.

Section III. *Interest*

Article 78

If a party fails to pay the price or any other sum that is in arrears, the other party is entitled to interest on it, without prejudice to any claim for damages recoverable under article 74.

Section IV. *Exemption*

Article 79

(1)   A party is not liable for a failure to perform any of his obligations if he proves that the failure was due to an impediment beyond his control and that he could not reasonably be expected to have taken the impediment into account at the time of the conclusion of the contract or to have avoided or overcome it or its consequences.

(2)   If the party's failure is due to the failure by a third person whom he has engaged to perform the whole or a part of the contract, that party is exempt from liability only if:

(a)   he is exempt under the preceding paragraph; and

(b)   the person whom he has so engaged would be so exempt if the provisions of that paragraph were applied to him.

(3)   The exemption provided by this article has effect for the period during which the impediment exists.

(4)   The party who fails to perform must give notice to the other party of the impediment and its effect on his ability to perform. If the notice is not received by the other party within a reasonable time after the party who fails to perform knew or ought to have known of the impediment, he is liable for damages resulting from such non-receipt.

(5)   Nothing in this article prevents either party from exercising any right other than to claim damages under this Convention.

Article 80

A party may not rely on a failure of the other party to perform, to the extent that such failure was caused by the first party's act or omission.

Section V. *Effects of avoidance*

Article 81

(1)   Avoidance of the contract releases both parties from their obligations under it, subject to any damages which may be due. Avoidance does not affect any provision of the contract for the settlement of disputes or any other provision of the contract governing the rights and obligations of the parties consequent upon the avoidance of the contract.

(2)   A party who has performed the contract either wholly or in part may claim restitution from the other party of whatever the first party has supplied or paid under the contract. If both parties are bound to make restitution, they must do so concurrently.

Article 82

(1)   The buyer loses the right to declare the contract avoided or to require the seller to deliver substitute goods if it is impossible for him to make restitution of the goods substantially in the condition in which be received them.

(2)   The preceding paragraph does not apply:

(a)   if the impossibility of making restitution of the goods or of making restitution of the goods substantially in the condition in which the buyer received them is not due to his act or omission;

(b)   if the goods or part of the goods have perished or deteriorated as a result of the examination provided for in article 38; or

(c) if the goods or part of the goods have been sold in the normal course of business or have been consumed or transformed by the buyer in the course of normal use before he discovered or ought to have discovered the lack of conformity.

Article 83

A buyer who has lost the right to declare the contract avoided or to require the seller to deliver substitute goods in accordance with article 82 retains all other remedies under the contract and this Convention.

Article 84

(1) If the seller is bound to refund the price, he must also pay interest on it, from the date on which the price was paid.

(2) The buyer must account to the seller for all benefits which he has derived from the goods or part of them:

(a) if he must make restitution of the goods or part of them; or

(b) if it is impossible for him to make restitution of all or part of the goods or to make restitution of all or part of the goods substantially in the condition in which he received them, but he has nevertheless declared the contract avoided or required the seller to deliver substitute goods.

Section VI. *Preservation of the goods*

Article 85

If the buyer is in delay in taking delivery of the goods or, where payment of the price and delivery of the goods are to be made concurrently, if he fails to pay the price, and the seller is either in possession of the goods or otherwise able to control their disposition, the seller must take such steps as are reasonable in the circumstances to preserve them. He is entitled to retain them until he has been reimbursed his reasonable expenses by the buyer.

Article 86

(1) If the buyer has received the goods and intends to exercise any right under the contract or this Convention to reject them, he must take such steps to preserve them as are reasonable in the circumstances. He is entitled to retain them until he has been reimbursed his reasonable expenses by the seller.

(2) If goods dispatched to the buyer have been placed at his disposal at their destination and he exercises the right to reject them, he must take possession of them on behalf of the seller, provided that this can be done without payment of the price and without unreasonable inconvenience or unreasonable expense. This provision does not apply if the seller or a person authorized to take charge of the goods on his behalf is present at the destination. If the buyer takes possession of the goods under this paragraph, his rights and obligations are governed by the preceding paragraph.

Article 87

A party who is bound to take steps to preserve the goods may deposit them in a warehouse of a third person at the expense of the other party provided that the expense incurred is not unreasonable.

Article 88

(1) A party who is bound to preserve the goods in accordance with article 85 or 86 may sell them by any appropriate means if there has been an unreasonable delay by the

other party in taking possession of the goods or in taking them back or in paying the price or the cost of preservation, provided that reasonable notice of the intention to sell has been given to the other party.

(2) If the goods are subject to rapid deterioration or their preservation would involve unreasonable expense, a party who is bound to preserve the goods in accordance with article 85 or 86 must take reasonable measures to sell them. To the extent possible he must give notice to the other party of his intention to sell.

(3) A party selling the goods has the right to retain out of the proceeds of sale an amount equal to the reasonable expenses of preserving the goods and of selling them. He must account to the other party for the balance.

Part IV. Final provisions

Article 89

The Secretary-General of the United Nations is hereby designated as the depositary for this Convention.

Article 90

This Convention does not prevail over any international agreement which has already been or may be entered into and which contains provisions concerning the matters governed by this Convention, provided that the parties have their places of business in States parties to such agreement.

Article 91

(1) This Convention is open for signature at the concluding meeting of the United Nations Conference on Contracts for the International Sale of Goods and will remain open for signature by all States at the Headquarters of the United Nations, New York until 30 September 1981.

(2) This Convention is subject to ratification, acceptance or approval by the signatory States.

(3) This Convention is open for accession by all States which are not signatory States as from the date it is open for signature.

(4) Instruments of ratification, acceptance, approval and accession are to be deposited with the Secretary-General of the United Nations.

Article 92

(1) A Contracting State may declare at the time of signature, ratification, acceptance, approval or accession that it will not be bound by Part II of this Convention or that it will not be bound by Part III of this Convention.

(2) A Contracting State which makes a declaration in accordance with the preceding paragraph in respect of Part II or Part III of this Convention is not to be considered a Contracting State within paragraph (1) of article 1 of this Convention in respect of matters governed by the Part to which the declaration applies.

Article 93

(1) If a Contracting State has two or more territorial units in which, according to its constitution, different systems of law are applicable in relation to the matters dealt with in this Convention, it may, at the time of signature, ratification, acceptance, approval or

accession, declare that this Convention is to extend to all its territorial units or only to one or more of them, and may amend its declaration by submitting another declaration at any time.

(2)   These declarations are to be notified to the depositary and are to state expressly the territorial units to which the Convention extends.

(3)   If, by virtue of a declaration under this article, this Convention extends to one or more but not all of the territorial units of a Contracting State, and if the place of business of a party is located in that State, this place of business, for the purposes of this Convention, is considered not to be in a Contracting State, unless it is in a territorial unit to which the Convention extends.

(4)   If a Contracting State makes no declaration under paragraph (1) of this article, the Convention is to extend to all territorial units of that State.

Article 94

(1)   Two or more Contracting States which have the same or closely related legal rules on matters governed by this Convention may at any time declare that the Convention is not to apply to contracts of sale or to their formation where the parties have their places of business in those States. Such declarations may be made jointly or by reciprocal unilateral declarations.

(2)   A Contracting State which has the same or closely related legal rules on matters governed by this Convention as one or more non-Contracting States may at any time declare that the Convention is not to apply to contracts of sale or to their formation where the parties have their places of business in those States.

(3)   If a State which is the object of a declaration under the preceding paragraph subsequently becomes a Contracting State, the declaration made will, as from the date on which the Convention enters into force in respect of the new Contracting State, have the effect of a declaration made under paragraph (1), provided that the new Contracting State joins in such declaration or makes a reciprocal unilateral declaration.

Article 95

Any State may declare at the time of the deposit of its instrument of ratification, acceptance, approval or accession that it will not be bound by subparagraph (1) *(b)* of article 1 of this Convention.

Article 96

A Contracting State whose legislation requires contracts of sale to be concluded in or evidenced by writing may at any time make a declaration in accordance with article 12 that any provision of article 11, article 29, or Part II of this Convention, that allows a contract of sale or its modification or termination by agreement or any offer, acceptance, or other indication of intention to be made in any form other than in writing, does not apply where any party has his place of business in that State.

Article 97

(1)   Declarations made under this Convention at the time of signature are subject to confirmation upon ratification, acceptance or approval.

(2)   Declarations and confirmations of declarations are to be in writing and be formally notified to the depositary.

(3)   A declaration takes effect simultaneously with the entry into force of this Convention in respect of the State concerned. However, a declaration of which the depositary receives formal notification after such entry into force takes effect on the first day of the month following the expiration of six months after the date of its receipt by

the depositary. Reciprocal unilateral declarations under article 94 take effect on the first day of the month following the expiration of six months after the receipt of the latest declaration by the depositary.

(4)   Any State which makes a declaration under this Convention may withdraw it at any time by a formal notification in writing addressed to the depositary. Such withdrawal is to take effect on the first day of the month following the expiration of six months after the date of the receipt of the notification by the depositary.

(5)   A withdrawal of a declaration made under article 94 renders inoperative, as from the date on which the withdrawal takes effect, any reciprocal declaration made by another State under that article.

Article 98

No reservations are permitted except those expressly authorized in this Convention.

Article 99

(1)   This Convention enters into force, subject to the provisions of paragraph (6) of this article, on the first day of the month following the expiration of twelve months after the date of deposit of the tenth instrument of ratification, acceptance, approval or accession, including an instrument which contains a declaration made under article 92.

(2)   When a State ratifies, accepts, approves or accedes to this Convention after the deposit of the tenth instrument of ratification, acceptance, approval or accession, this Convention, with the exception of the Part excluded, enters into force in respect of that State, subject to the provisions of paragraph (6) of this article, on the first day of the month following the expiration of twelve months after the date of the deposit of its instrument of ratification, acceptance, approval or accession.

(3)   A State which ratifies, accepts, approves or accedes to this Convention and is a party to either or both the Convention relating to a Uniform Law on the Formation of Contracts for the International Sale of Goods done at The Hague on 1 July 1964 (1964 Hague Formation Convention) and the Convention relating to a Uniform Law on the International Sale of Goods done at The Hague on 1 July 1964 (1964 Hague Sales Convention) shall at the same time denounce, as the case may be, either or both the 1964 Hague Sales Convention and the 1964 Hague Formation Convention by notifying the Government of the Netherlands to that effect.

(4)   A State party to the 1964 Hague Sales Convention which ratifies, accepts, approves or accedes to the present Convention and declares or has declared under article 92 that it will not be bound by Part II of this Convention shall at the time of ratification, acceptance, approval or accession denounce the 1964 Hague Sales Convention by notifying the Government of the Netherlands to that effect.

(5)   A State party to the 1964 Hague Formation Convention which ratifies, accepts, approves or accedes to the present Convention and declares or has declared under article 92 that it will not be bound by Part III of this Convention shall at the time of ratification, acceptance, approval or accession denounce the 1964 Hague Formation Convention by notifying the Government of the Netherlands to that effect.

(6)   For the purpose of this article, ratifications, acceptances, approvals and accessions in respect of this Convention by States parties to the 1964 Hague Formation Convention or to the 1964 Hague Sales Convention shall not be effective until such denunciations as may be required on the part of those States in respect of the latter two Conventions have themselves become effective. The depositary of this Convention shall consult with the Government of the Netherlands, as the depositary of the 1964 Conventions, so as to ensure necessary co-ordination in this respect.

Article 100

(1) This Convention applies to the formation of a contract only when the proposal for concluding the contract is made on or after the date when the Convention enters into force in respect of the Contracting States referred to in subparagraph (1) *(a)* or the Contracting State referred to in subparagraph (1) *(b)* of article 1.

(2) This Convention applies only to contracts concluded on or after the date when the Convention enters into force in respect of the Contracting States referred to in subparagraph (1) *(a)* or the Contracting State referred to in subparagraph (1) *(b)* of article 1.

Article 101

(1) A Contracting State may denounce this Convention, or Part II or Part III of the Convention, by a formal notification in writing addressed to the depositary.

(2) The denunciation takes effect on the first day of the month following the expiration of twelve months after the notification is received by the depositary. Where a longer period for the denunciation to take effect is specified in the notification, the denunciation takes effect upon the expiration of such longer period after the notification is received by the depositary.

DONE at Vienna, this day of eleventh day of April, one thousand nine hundred and eighty, in a single original, of which the Arabic, Chinese, English, French, Russian and Spanish texts are equally authentic.

IN WITNESS WHEREOF the undersigned plenipotentiaries, being duly authorized by their respective Governments, have signed this Convention.

ANNEX IV.   RULES OF ARBITRAL PROCEDURE

A.   UNCITRAL Arbitration Rules

Section I.   Introductory rules

Article 1

1.   Where the parties to a contract have agreed in writing* that disputes in relation to that contract shall be referred to arbitration under the UNCITRAL Arbitration Rules, then such disputes shall be settled in accordance with these Rules subject to such modification as the parties may agree in writing.

2.   These Rules shall govern the arbitration except that where any of these Rules is in conflict with a provision of the law applicable to the arbitration from which the parties cannot derogate, that provision shall prevail.

NOTICE, CALCULATION OF PERIODS OF TIME

Article 2

1.   For the purposes of these Rules, any notice, including a notification, communication or proposal, is deemed to have been received if it is physically delivered to the addressee or if it is delivered at his habitual residence, place of business or mailing address, or, if none of these can be found after making reasonable inquiry, then at the addressee's last known residence or place of business. Notice shall be deemed to have been received on the day it is so delivered.

2.   For the purposes of calculating a period of time under these Rules, such period shall begin to run on the day following the day when a notice, notification, communication or proposal is received. If the last day of such period is an official holiday or a non-business day at the residence or place of business of the addressee, the period is extended until the first business day which follows. Official holidays or non-business days occurring during the running of the period of time are included in calculating the period.

---

*Model Arbitration Clause.

Any dispute, controversy or claim arising out of or relating to this contract, or the breach, termination or invalidity thereof, shall be settled by arbitration in accordance with the UNCITRAL Arbitration Rules as at present in force.

Note—Parties may wish to consider adding:
  (a)   The appointing authority shall be . . . (name of institution or person);
  (b)   The number of arbitrators shall be . . . (one or three);
  (c)   The place of arbitration shall be . . . (town or country);
  (d)   The language(s) to be used in the arbitral proceedings shall be . . ..

Article 3

1. The party initiating recourse to arbitration (hereinafter called the "claimant") shall give to the other party (hereinafter called the "respondent") a notice of arbitration.

2. Arbitral proceedings shall be deemed to commence on the date on which the notice of arbitration is received by the respondent.

3. The notice of arbitration shall include the following:

(a) A demand that the dispute be referred to arbitration;

(b) The names and addresses of the parties;

(c) A reference to the arbitration clause or the separate arbitration agreement that is invoked;

(d) A reference to the contract out of or in relation to which the dispute arises;

(e) The general nature of the claim and an indication of the amount involved, if any;

(f) The relief or remedy sought;

(g) A proposal as to the number of arbitrators (i.e. one or three), if the parties have not previously agreed thereon.

4. The notice of arbitration may also include:

(a) The proposals for the appointments of a sole arbitrator and an appointing authority referred to in article 6, paragraph 1;

(b) The notification of the appointment of an arbitrator referred to in article 7;

(c) The statement of claim referred to in article 18.

Representation and assistance

Article 4

The parties may be represented or assisted by persons of their choice. The names and addresses of such persons must be communicated in writing to the other party; such communication must specify whether the appointment is being made for purposes of representation or assistance.

Section II.   Composition of the arbitral tribunal

Number of arbitrators

Article 5

If the parties have not previously agreed on the number of arbitrators (i.e. one or three), and if within 15 days after the receipt by the respondent of the notice of arbitration the parties have not agreed that there shall be only one arbitrator, three arbitrators shall be appointed.

Appointment of arbitrators (articles 6 to 8)

Article 6

1. If a sole arbitrator is to be appointed, either party may propose to the other:

(a) The names of one or more persons, one of whom would serve as the sole arbitrator; and

(b) If no appointing authority has been agreed upon by the parties, the name or names of one or more institutions or persons, one of whom would serve as appointing authority.

2. If within 30 days after receipt by a party of a proposal made in accordance with paragraph 1 the parties have not reached agreement on the choice of a sole arbitrator, the sole arbitrator shall be appointed by the appointing authority agreed upon by the parties. If no appointing authority has been agreed upon by the parties, or if the appointing authority agreed upon refuses to act or fails to appoint the arbitrator within 60 days of the receipt of a party's request therefor, either party may request the Secretary-General of the Permanent Court of Arbitration at The Hague to designate an appointing authority.

3. The appointing authority shall, at the request of one of the parties, appoint the sole arbitrator as promptly as possible. In making the appointment the appointing authority shall use the following list-procedure, unless both parties agree that the list-procedure should not be used or unless the appointing authority determines in its discretion that the use of the list-procedure is not appropriate for the case:

(a) At the request of one of the parties the appointing authority shall communicate to both parties an identical list containing at least three names;

(b) Within 15 days after the receipt of this list, each party may return the list to the appointing authority after having deleted the name or names to which he objects and numbered the remaining names on the list in the order of his preference;

(c) After the expiration of the above period of time the appointing authority shall appoint the sole arbitrator from among the names approved on the lists returned to it and in accordance with the order of preference indicated by the parties;

(d) If for any reason the appointment cannot be made according to this procedure, the appointing authority may exercise its discretion in appointing the sole arbitrator.

4. In making the appointment, the appointing authority shall have regard to such considerations as are likely to secure the appointment of an independent and impartial arbitrator and shall take into account as well the advisability of appointing an arbitrator of a nationality other than the nationalities of the parties.

Article 7

1. If three arbitrators are to be appointed, each party shall appoint one arbitrator. The two arbitrators thus appointed shall choose the third arbitrator who will act as the presiding arbitrator of the tribunal.

2. If within 30 days after the receipt of a party's notification of the appointment of an arbitrator the other party has not notified the first party of the arbitrator he has appointed:

(a) The first party may request the appointing authority previously designated by the parties to appoint the second arbitrator; or

(b) If no such authority has been previously designated by the parties, or if the appointing authority previously designated refuses to act or fails to appoint the arbitrator within 30 days after receipt of a party's request therefor, the first party may request the Secretary-General of the Permanent Court of Arbitration at The Hague to designate the appointing authority. The first party may then request the appointing authority so designated to appoint the second arbitrator. In either case, the appointing authority may exercise its discretion in appointing the arbitrator.

3. If within 30 days after the appointment of the second arbitrator the two arbitrators have not agreed on the choice of the presiding arbitrator, the presiding arbitrator shall be appointed by an appointing authority in the same way as a sole arbitrator would be appointed under article 6.

Article 8

1. When an appointing authority is requested to appoint an arbitrator pursuant to article 6 or article 7, the party which makes the request shall send to the appointing authority a copy of the notice of arbitration, a copy of the contract out of or in relation to which the dispute has arisen and a copy of the arbitration agreement if it is not contained in the contract. The appointing authority may require from either party such information as it deems necessary to fulfil its function.

2. Where the names of one or more persons are proposed for appointment as arbitrators, their full names, addresses and nationalities shall be indicated, together with a description of their qualifications.

CHALLENGE OF ARBITRATORS (ARTICLES 9 TO 12)

Article 9

A prospective arbitrator shall disclose to those who approach him in connexion with his possible appointment any circumstances likely to give rise to justifiable doubts as to his impartiality or independence. An arbitrator, once appointed or chosen, shall disclose such circumstance to the parties unless they have already been informed by him of these circumstances.

Article 10

1. Any arbitrator may be challenged if circumstances exist that give rise to justifiable doubts as to the arbitrator's impartiality or independence.

2. A party may challenge the arbitrator appointed by him only for reasons of which he becomes aware after the appointment has been made.

Article 11

1. A party who intends to challenge an arbitrator shall send notice of his challenge within 15 days after the appointment of the challenged arbitrator has been notified to the challenging party or within 15 days after the circumstances mentioned in articles 9 and 10 became known to that party.

2. The challenge shall be notified to the other party, to the arbitrator who is challenged and to the other members of the arbitral tribunal. The notification shall be in writing and shall state the reason for the challenge.

3. When an arbitrator has been challenged by one party, the other party may agree to the challenge. The arbitrator may also, after the challenge, withdraw from his office. In neither case does this imply acceptance of the validity of the grounds for the challenge. In both cases the procedure provided in article 6 or 7 shall be used in full for the appointment of the substitute arbitrator, even if during the process of appointing the challenged arbitrator a party had failed to exercise his right to appoint or to participate in the appointment.

Article 12

1. If the other party does not agree to the challenge and the challenged arbitrator does not withdraw, the decision on the challenge will be made:

(a) When the initial appointment was made by an appointing authority, by that authority;

(b) When the initial appointment was not made by an appointing authority, but an appointing authority has been previously designated, by that authority;

(c) In all other cases, by the appointing authority to be designated in accordance with the procedure for designating an appointing authority as provided for in article 6.

140

2. If the appointing authority sustains the challenge, a substitute arbitrator shall be appointed or chosen pursuant to the procedure applicable to the appointment or choice of an arbitrator as provided in articles 6 to 9 except that, when this procedure would call for the designation of an appointing authority, the appointment of the arbitrator shall be made by the appointing authority which decided on the challenge.

Article 13

1. In the event of the death or resignation of an arbitrator during the course of the arbitral proceedings, a substitute arbitrator shall be appointed or chosen pursuant to the procedure provided for in articles 6 to 9 that was applicable to the appointment or choice of the arbitrator being replaced.

2. In the event that an arbitrator fails to act or in the event of the *de jure* or *de facto* impossibility of his performing his functions, the procedure in respect of the challenge and replacement of an arbitrator as provided in the preceding articles shall apply.

REPETITION OF HEARINGS IN THE EVENT OF THE REPLACEMENT OF AN ARBITRATOR

Article 14

If under articles 11 to 13 the sole or presiding arbitrator is replaced, any hearings held previously shall be repeated; if any other arbitrator is replaced, such prior hearings may be repeated at the discretion of the arbitral tribunal.

Section III. Arbitral proceedings

GENERAL PROVISIONS

Article 15

1. Subject to these Rules, the arbitral tribunal may conduct the arbitration in such manner as it considers appropriate, provided that the parties are treated with equality and that at any stage of the proceedings each party is given a full opportunity of presenting his case.

2. If either party so requests at any stage of the proceedings, the arbitral tribunal shall hold hearings for the presentation of evidence by witnesses, including expert witnesses, or for oral argument. In the absence of such a request, the arbitral tribunal shall decide whether to hold such hearings or whether the proceedings shall be conducted on the basis of documents and other materials.

3. All documents or information supplied to the arbitral tribunal by one party shall at the same time be communicated by that party to the other party.

PLACE OF ARBITRATION

Article 16

1. Unless the parties have agreed upon the place where the arbitration is to be held, such place shall be determined by the arbitral tribunal, having regard to the circumstances of the arbitration.

2.   The arbitral tribunal may determine the locale of the arbitration within the country agreed upon by the parties. It may hear witnesses and hold meetings for consultation among its members at any place it deems appropriate, having regard to the circumstances of the arbitration.

3.   The arbitral tribunal may meet at any place it deems appropriate for the inspection of goods, other property or documents. The parties shall be given sufficient notice to enable them to be present at such inspection.

LANGUAGE

Article 17

1.   Subject to an agreement by the parties, the arbitral tribunal shall, promptly after its appointment, determine the language or languages to be used in the proceedings. This determination shall apply to the statement of claim, the statement of defence, and any further written statements and, if oral hearings take place, to the language or languages to be used in such hearings.

2.   The arbitral tribunal may order that any documents annexed to the statement of claim or statement of defence, and any supplementary documents or exhibits submitted in the course of the proceedings, delivered in their original language, shall be accompanied by a translation into the language or languages agreed upon by the parties or determined by the arbitral tribunal.

STATEMENT OF CLAIM

Article 18

1.   Unless the statement of claim was contained in the notice of arbitration, within a period of time to be determined by the arbitral tribunal, the claimant shall communicate his statement of claim in writing to the respondent and to each of the arbitrators. A copy of the contract, and of the arbitration agreement if not contained in the contract, shall be annexed thereto.

2.   The statement of claim shall include the following particulars:
(a)   The names and addresses of the parties;
(b)   A statement of the facts supporting the claim;
(c)   The points at issue;
(d)   The relief or remedy sought.

The claimant may annex to his statement of claim all documents he deems relevant or may add a reference to the documents or other evidence he will submit.

STATEMENT OF DEFENCE

Article 19

1.   Within a period of time to be determined by the arbitral tribunal, the respondent shall communicate his statement of defence in writing to the claimant and to each of the arbitrators.

2.   The statement of defence shall reply to the particulars *(b)*, *(c)* and *(d)* of the statement of claim (article 18, para. 2). The respondent may annex to his statement the documents on which he relies for his defence or may add a reference to the documents or other evidence he will submit.

3. In his statement of defence, or at a later stage in the arbitral proceedings if the arbitral tribunal decides that the delay was justified under the circumstances, the respondent may make a counter-claim arising out of the same contract or rely on a claim arising out of the same contract for the purpose of a set-off.

4. The provisions of article 18, paragraph 2, shall apply to a counter-claim and a claim relied on for the purpose of a set-off.

AMENDMENTS TO THE CLAIM OR DEFENCE

Article 20

During the course of the arbitral proceedings either party may amend or supplement his claim or defence unless the arbitral tribunal considers it inappropriate to allow such amendment having regard to the delay in making it or prejudice to the other party or any other circumstances. However, a claim may not be amended in such a manner that the amended claim falls outside the scope of the arbitration clause or separate arbitration agreement.

PLEAS AS TO THE JURISDICTION OF THE ARBITRAL TRIBUNAL

Article 21

1. The arbitral tribunal shall have the power to rule on objections that it has no jurisdiction, including any objections with respect to the existence or validity of the arbitration clause or of the separate arbitration agreement.

2. The arbitral tribunal shall have the power to determine the existence or the validity of the contract of which an arbitration clause forms a part. For the purposes of article 21, an arbitration clause which forms part of a contract and which provides for arbitration under these Rules shall be treated as an agreement independent of the other terms of the contract. A decision by the arbitral tribunal that the contract is null and void shall not entail *ipso jure* the invalidity of the arbitration clause.

3. A plea that the arbitral tribunal does not have jurisdiction shall be raised not later than in the statement of defence or, with respect to a counter-claim, in the reply to the counter-claim.

4. In general, the arbitral tribunal should rule on a plea concerning its jurisdiction as a preliminary question. However, the arbitral tribunal may proceed with the arbitration and rule on such a plea in their final award.

FURTHER WRITTEN STATEMENTS

Article 22

The arbitral tribunal shall decide which further written statements, in addition to the statement of claim and the statement of defence, shall be required from the parties or may be presented by them and shall fix the periods of time for communicating such statements.

PERIODS OF TIME

Article 23

The periods of time fixed by the arbitral tribunal for the communication of written statements (including the statement of claim and statement of defence) should not exceed 45 days. However, the arbitral tribunal may extend the time-limits if it concludes that an extension is justified.

Article 24

1.   Each party shall have the burden of proving the facts relied on to support his claim or defence.

2.   The arbitral tribunal may, if it considers it appropriate, require a party to deliver to the tribunal and to the other party, within such a period of time as the arbitral tribunal shall decide, a summary of the documents and other evidence which that party intends to present in support of the facts in issue set out in his statement of claim or statement of defence.

3.   At any time during the arbitral proceedings the arbitral tribunal may require the parties to produce documents, exhibits or other evidence within such a period of time as the tribunal shall determine.

Article 25

1.   In the event of an oral hearing, the arbitral tribunal shall give the parties adequate advance notice of the date, time and place thereof.

2.   If witnesses are to be heard, at least 15 days before the hearing each party shall communicate to the arbitral tribunal and to the other party the names and addresses of the witnesses be intends to present, the subject upon and the languages in which such witnesses will give their testimony.

3.   The arbitral tribunal shall make arrangements for the translation of oral statements made at a hearing and for a record of the hearing if either is deemed necessary by the tribunal under the circumstances of the case, or if the parties have agreed thereto and have communicated such agreement to the tribunal at least 15 days before the hearing.

4.   Hearings shall be held *in camera* unless the parties agree otherwise. The arbitral tribunal may require the retirement of any witness or witnesses during the testimony of other witnesses. The arbitral tribunal is free to determine the manner in which witnesses are examined.

5.   Evidence of witnesses may also be presented in the form of written statements signed by them.

6.   The arbitral tribunal shall determine the admissibility, relevance, materiality and weight of the evidence offered.

INTERIM MEASURES OF PROTECTION

Article 26

1.   At the request of either party, the arbitral tribunal may take any interim measures it deems necessary in respect of the subject-matter of the dispute, including measures for the conservation of the goods forming the subject-matter in dispute, such as ordering their deposit with a third person or the sale of perishable goods.

2.   Such interim measures may be established in the form of an interim award. The arbitral tribunal shall be entitled to require security for the costs of such measures.

3.   A request for interim measures addressed by any party to a judicial authority shall not be deemed incompatible with the agreement to arbitrate, or as a waiver of that agreement.

EXPERTS

Article 27

1.   The arbitral tribunal may appoint one or more experts to report to it, in writing, on specific issues to be determined by the tribunal. A copy of the expert's terms of reference, established by the arbitral tribunal, shall be communicated to the parties.

2.   The parties shall give the expert any relevant information or produce for his inspection any relevant documents or goods that he may require of them. Any dispute between a party and such expert as to the relevance of the required information or production shall be referred to the arbitral tribunal for decision.

3.   Upon receipt of the expert's report, the arbitral tribunal shall communicate a copy of the report to the parties who shall be given the opportunity to express, in writing, their opinion on the report. A party shall be entitled to examine any document on which the expert has relied in his report.

4.   At the request of either party the expert, after delivery of the report, may be heard at a hearing where the parties shall have the opportunity to be present and to interrogate the expert. At this hearing either party may present expert witnesses in order to testify on the points at issue. The provisions of article 25 shall be applicable to such proceedings.

DEFAULT

Article 28

1.   If, within the period of time fixed by the arbitral tribunal, the claimant has failed to communicate his claim without showing sufficient cause for such failure, the arbitral tribunal shall issue an order for the termination of the arbitral proceedings. If, within the period of time fixed by the arbitral tribunal, the respondent has failed to communicate his statement of defence without showing sufficient cause for such failure, the arbitral tribunal shall order that the proceedings continue.

2.   If one of the parties, duly notified under these Rules, fails to appear at a hearing, without showing sufficient cause for such failure, the arbitral tribunal may proceed with the arbitration.

3.   If one of the parties, duly invited to produce documentary evidence, fails to do so within the established period of time, without showing sufficient cause for such failure, the arbitral tribunal may make the award on the evidence before it.

CLOSURE OF HEARINGS

Article 29

1.   The arbitral tribunal may inquire of the parties if they have any further proof to offer or witnesses to be heard or submissions to make and, if there are none, it may declare the hearings closed.

2.   The arbitral tribunal may, if it considers it necessary owing to exceptional circumstances, decide, on its own motion or upon application of a party, to reopen the hearings at any time before the award is made.

WAIVER OF RULES

Article 30

A party who knows that any provision of, or requirement under, these Rules has not been complied with and yet proceeds with the arbitration without promptly stating his objection to such non-compliance, shall be deemed to have waived his right to object.

Section IV.   The award

Article 31

1.   When there are three arbitrators, any award or other decision of the arbitral tribunal shall be made by a majority of the arbitrators.

2.   In the case of questions of procedure, when there is no majority or when the arbitral tribunal so authorizes, the presiding arbitrator may decide on his own, subject to revision, if any, by the arbitral tribunal.

FORM AND EFFECT OF THE AWARD

Article 32

1.   In addition to making a final award, the arbitral tribunal shall be entitled to make interim, interlocutory, or partial awards.

2.   The award shall be made in writing and shall be final and binding on the parties. The parties undertake to carry out the award without delay.

3.   The arbitral tribunal shall state the reasons upon which the award is based, unless the parties have agreed that no reasons are to be given.

4.   An award shall be signed by the arbitrators and it shall contain the date on which and the place where the award was made. Where there are three arbitrators and one of them fails to sign, the award shall state the reason for the absence of the signature.

5.   The award may be made public only with the consent of both parties.

6.   Copies of the award signed by the arbitrators shall be communicated to the parties by the arbitral tribunal.

7.   If the arbitration law of the country where the award is made requires that the award be filed or registered by the arbitral tribunal, the tribunal shall comply with this requirement within the period of time required by law.

APPLICABLE LAW, *amiable compositeur*

Article 33

1.   The arbitral tribunal shall apply the law designated by the parties as applicable to the substance of the dispute. Failing such designation by the parties, the arbitral tribunal shall apply the law determined by the conflict of laws rules which it considers applicable.

2.   The arbitral tribunal shall decide as *amiable compositeur* or *ex aequo et bono* only if the parties have expressly authorized the arbitral tribunal to do so and if the law applicable to the arbitral procedure permits such arbitration.

3.   In all cases, the arbitral tribunal shall decide in accordance with the terms of the contract and shall take into account the usages of the trade applicable to the transaction.

SETTLEMENT OR OTHER GROUNDS FOR TERMINATION

Article 34

1.   If, before the award is made, the parties agree on a settlement of the dispute, the arbitral tribunal shall either issue an order for the termination of the arbitral

proceedings or, if requested by both parties and accepted by the tribunal, record the settlement in the form of an arbitral award on agreed terms. The arbitral tribunal is not obliged to give reasons for such an award.

2.   If, before the award is made, the continuation of the arbitral proceedings becomes unnecessary or impossible for any reason not mentioned in paragraph 1, the arbitral tribunal shall inform the parties of its intention to issue an order for the termination of the proceedings. The arbitral tribunal shall have the power to issue such an order unless a party raises justifiable grounds for objection.

3.   Copies of the order for termination of the arbitral proceedings or of the arbitral award on agreed terms, signed by the arbitrators, shall be communicated by the arbitral tribunal to the parties. Where an arbitral award on agreed terms is made, the provisions of article 32, paragraphs 2 and 4 to 7, shall apply.

INTERPRETATION OF THE AWARD

Article 35

1.   Within 30 days after the receipt of the award, either party, with notice to the other party, may request that the arbitral tribunal give an interpretation of the award.

2.   The interpretation shall be given in writing within 45 days after the receipt of the request. The interpretation shall form part of the award and the provisions of article 32, paragraphs 2 to 7, shall apply.

CORRECTION OF THE AWARD

Article 36

1.   Within 30 days after the receipt of the award, either party, with notice to the other party, may request the arbitral tribunal to correct in the award any errors in computation, any clerical or typographical errors, or any errors of similar nature. The arbitral tribunal may within 30 days after the communication of the award make such corrections on its own initiative.

2.   Such corrections shall be in writing, and the provisions of article 32, paragraphs 2 to 7, shall apply.

ADDITIONAL AWARD

Article 37

1.   Within 30 days after the receipt of the award, either party, with notice to the other party, may request the arbitral tribunal to make an additional award as to claims presented in the arbitral proceedings but omitted from the award.

2.   If the arbitral tribunal considers the request for an additional award to be justified and considers that the omission can be rectified without any further hearings or evidence, it shall complete its award within 60 days after the receipt of the request.

3.   When an additional award is made, the provisions of article 32, paragraphs 2 to 7, shall apply.

Article 38

The arbitral tribunal shall fix the costs of arbitration in its award. The term "costs" includes only:

(a) The fees of the arbitral tribunal to be stated separately as to each arbitrator and to be fixed by the tribunal itself in accordance with article 39;

(b) The travel and other expenses incurred by the arbitrators;

(c) The costs of expert advice and of other assistance required by the arbitral tribunal;

(d) The travel and other expenses of witnesses to the extent such expenses are approved by the arbitral tribunal;

(e) The costs for legal representation and assistance of the successful party if such costs were claimed during the arbitral proceedings, and only to the extent that the arbitral tribunal determines that the amount of such costs in reasonable;

(f) Any fees and expenses of the appointing authority as well as the expenses of the Secretary-General of the Permanent Court of Arbitration at The Hague.

Article 39

1. The fees of the arbitral tribunal shall be reasonable in amount, taking into account the amount in dispute, the complexity of the subject-matter, the time spent by the arbitrators and any other relevant circumstances of the case.

2. If an appointing authority has been agreed upon by the parties or designated by the Secretary-General of the Permanent Court of Arbitration at The Hague, and if that authority has issued a schedule of fees for arbitrators in international cases which it administers, the arbitral tribunal in fixing its fees shall take that schedule of fees into account to the extent that it considers appropriate in the circumstances of the case.

3. If such appointing authority has not issued a schedule of fees for arbitrators in international cases, any party may at any time request the appointing authority to furnish a statement setting forth the basis for establishing fees which is customarily followed in international cases in which the authority appoints arbitrators. If the appointing authority consents to provide such a statement, the arbitral tribunal in fixing its fees shall take such information into account to the extent that it considers appropriate in the circumstances of the case.

4. In cases referred to in paragraphs 2 and 3, when a party so requests and the appointing authority consents to perform the function, the arbitral tribunal shall fix its fees only after consultation with the appointing authority, which may make any comment it deems appropriate to the arbitral tribunal concerning the fees.

Article 40

1. Except as provided in paragraph 2, the costs of arbitration shall in principle be borne by the unsuccessful party. However, the arbitral tribunal may apportion each of such costs between the parties if it determines that apportionment is reasonable, taking into account the circumstances of the case.

2. With respect to the costs of legal representation and assistance referred to in article 38, paragraph *(e)*, the arbitral tribunal, taking into account the circumstances of the case, shall be free to determine which party shall bear such costs or may apportion such costs between the parties if it determines that apportionment is reasonable.

3. When the arbitral tribunal issues an order for the termination of the arbitral proceedings or makes an award on agreed terms it shall fix the costs of arbitration referred to in article 38 and article 39, paragraph 1, in the text of that order or award.

4. No additional fees may be charged by an arbitral tribunal for interpretation or correction or completion of its award under articles 35 to 37.

Article 41

1.   The arbitral tribunal, on its establishment, may request each party to deposit an equal amount as an advance for the costs referred to in article 38, paragraphs *(a)*, *(b)* and *(c)*.

2.   During the course of the arbitral proceedings the arbitral tribunal may request supplementary deposits from the parties.

3.   If an appointing authority has been agreed upon by the parties or designated by the Secretary-General of the Permanent Court of Arbitration at The Hague, and when a party so requests and the appointing authority consents to perform the function, the arbitral tribunal shall fix the amount of any deposits or supplementary deposits only after consultation with the appointing authority which may make any comments to the arbitral tribunal which it deems appropriate concerning the amount of such deposits and supplementary deposits.

4.   If the required deposits are not paid in full within 30 days after the receipt of the request, the arbitral tribunal shall so inform the parties in order that one or another of them may make the required payment. If such payment is not made, the arbitral tribunal may order the suspension or termination of the arbitral proceedings.

5.   After the award has been made, the arbitral tribunal shall render an accounting to the parties of the deposits received and return any unexpended balance to the parties.

B.   General Assembly resolution 31/98 of 15 December 1976

31/98.   ARBITRATION RULES OF THE UNITED NATIONS COMMISSION ON INTERNATIONAL TRADE LAW

The General Assembly,

Recognizing the value of arbitration as a method of settling disputes arising in the context of international commercial relations,

Convinced that the establishment of rules for *ad hoc* arbitration that are acceptable in countries with different legal, social and economic systems would significantly contribute to the development of harmonious international economic relations,

Bearing in mind that the Arbitration Rules of the United Nations Commission on International Trade Law have been prepared after extensive consultation with arbitral institutions and centres of international commercial arbitration,

Noting that the Arbitration Rules were adopted by the United Nations Commission on International Trade Law at its ninth session[1] after due deliberation,

1.   *Recommends* the use of the Arbitration Rules of the United Nations Commission on International Trade Law in the settlement of disputes arising in the context of international commercial relations, particularly by reference to the Arbitration Rules in commercial contracts;

2.   *Requests* the Secretary-General to arrange for the widest possible distribution of the Arbitration Rules.

99th plenary meeting,
15 December 1976

---

[1] *Official Records of the General Assembly, Thirty-first Session, Supplement No. 17* (A/31/17), chap. V, sect. C.

C. Recommendations to assist arbitral institutions and other interested bodies with regard to arbitrations under the UNCITRAL Arbitration Rules (1982)

Introduction

1.   The UNCITRAL Arbitration Rules were adopted by the United Nations Commission on International Trade Law in 1976, after extensive consultations with arbitral institutions and arbitration experts. In the same year, the General Assembly of the United Nations, by its resolution 31/98, recommended the use of these Rules in the settlement of disputes arising in the context of international commercial relations. This recommendation was based on the conviction that the establishment of rules for *ad hoc* arbitration that were acceptable in countries with different legal, social and economic systems would significantly contribute to the development of harmonious international economic relations.

2.   Since then, the UNCITRAL Arbitration Rules have become well known and are widely used around the world, not only in *ad hoc* arbitrations. Contracting parties increasingly refer to these Rules in their arbitration clauses or agreements, and a subtantial number of arbitral institutions have, in a variety of ways, accepted or adopted these Rules.

3.   One way in which the UNCITRAL Arbitration Rules have been accepted is that arbitral bodies have drawn on them in preparing their own institutional arbitration rules. This has taken two different forms. One has been to use the UNCITRAL Arbitration Rules as a drafting model, either in full (e.g., the 1978 Rules of Procedure of the Inter-American Commercial Arbitration Commission) or in part (e.g., the 1980 Procedures for Arbitration and Additional Rules of the International Energy Agency Dispute Settlement Centre).

4.   The other form has been to adopt the UNCITRAL Arbitration Rules as such, maintaining their name, and to include in the statutes or administrative rules of an institution a provision that disputes referred to the institution shall be settled in accordance with the UNCITRAL Arbitration Rules, subject to any modifications set forth in those statutes or administrative rules. Prime examples of institutions adopting this approach are the two arbitration centres established under the auspices of the Asian-African Legal Consultative Committee (see Rule I of the Rules for Arbitration of the Kuala Lumpur Regional Arbitration Centre; arts. 4 and 11 of the Statutes of the Cairo Centre for International Commercial Arbitration). In addition, a provision similar to the one described above was included in the "Declaration of the Government of the Democratic and Popular Republic of Algeria concerning the settlement of claims by the Government of the United States of America and the Government of the Islamic Republic of Iran" of 19 January 1981 (art. III, para. 2).

5.   In addition to the above cases, which concern an arbitral body's own and only rules, a great number of institutions which have their own established arbitration rules have accepted, in a variety of ways, the use of the UNCITRAL Arbitration Rules if parties so wished. Some institutions have, for example, embodied that option into their established institutional rules (e.g. London Court of Arbitration, 1981 International Arbitration Rules; Foreign Trade Arbitration of the Economic Chamber of Yugoslavia, 1981 Rules). Another form of acceptance has been to offer the administrative facilities of an arbitral institution in co-operation agreements between arbitration associations or chambers of commerce and in recommendations or model clauses providing for the use of the UNCITRAL Arbitration Rules. The prime example, which was also the first international agreement to include the UNCITRAL Arbitration Rules, is the "Optional Arbitration Clause for use in contracts in the U.S.A.—U.S.S.R. Trade—1977 (prepared by American Arbitration Association and U.S.S.R. Chamber of Commerce and Industry)", with the Stockholm Chamber of Commerce acting as appointing authority.

6. Of the many other institutions that have declared their willingness to act as appointing authority and to provide administrative services in arbitration cases under the UNCITRAL Arbitration Rules only one should be mentioned here. The American Arbitration Association (AAA) has adopted a specific set of administrative "Procedures for Cases under the UNCITRAL Arbitration Rules" setting forth in detail how the AAA would perform the functions of an appointing authority and provide administrative services in conformity with the UNCITRAL Arbitration Rules.

7. In view of the promising trend in favour of the use of the UNCITRAL Arbitration Rules, these recommendations are intended to provide information and assistance to arbitral institutions and other relevant bodies, such as chambers of commerce. As the above examples indicate, there are a number of ways in which the UNCITRAL Arbitration Rules and their use in arbitration proceedings may be accepted.

A. Adoption of UNCITRAL Arbitration Rules as institutional rules of an arbitral body

8. Arbitral institutions, when preparing or revising their institutional rules, may wish to consider the advisability of adopting the UNCITRAL Arbitration Rules. While it would clearly be in the interest of the desired unification of the rules on arbitral procedure that arbitral institutions adopt these Rules in full, some institutions may have reasons for incorporating, at least for the time being, only some of the provisions of these Rules. Even such adoption in part would constitute a step towards the harmonization of the rules on arbitral procedure.

9. However, if an institution intends to adopt such provisions and to maintain the name UNCITRAL Arbitration Rules, special considerations come into play which relate to the interest and expectations of the parties to an arbitration agreement or to a contract including an arbitration clause. Parties, and their lawyers, who have gained familiarity with and confidence in the use of the UNCITRAL Arbitration Rules tend to rely on the uniform and full application of these Rules by any arbitral institution which in its rules provides for the application of the UNCITRAL Arbitration Rules.

10. Therefore, an arbitral institution which intends to refer in its institutional rules to the UNCITRAL Arbitration Rules should take into account this interest of the parties in having certainty about which procedures to expect. Accordingly, it is recommended that institutions, when adopting the UNCITRAL Aribtration Rules and maintaining their name, refrain from modifying them.

11. This appeal to leave the UNCITRAL Arbitration Rules unchanged does not mean, of course, that the particular organizational structure and needs of a given institution should be neglected. Such specific features normally relate to matters not regulated in the UNCITRAL Arbitration Rules. For example, there are no special provisions in these Rules concerning the various facilities and procedures relating to administrative services or on such particular matters as fee schedules. It should, therefore, be possible to adopt institutional rules consisting of the UNCITRAL Arbitration Rules and some administrative rules which are tailored to the particular organizational structure and needs of the institution and are in conformity with the UNCITRAL Arbitration Rules.

12. If, in exceptional circumstances, an institution deems it necessary, for administrative purposes, to adopt a rule which modifies the UNCITRAL Arbitration Rules, it is strongly recommended to clearly indicate that modification. An appropriate way of doing so is to specify the provision of the UNCITRAL Arbitration Rules involved, as done, for example, in the Rules for Arbitration of the Kuala Lumpur Regional Arbitration Centre (opening words of Rule 8: "In lieu of the provisions of article 41 of

the UNCITRAL Arbitration Rules the following provisions shall apply: . . ."). This indication would be of great help to the reader and potential user who would otherwise have to embark on a comparative analysis of the administrative procedures and all provisions of the UNCITRAL Arbitration Rules in order to discover any disparity between them.

B. Arbitral institution or other body acting as appointing authority or providing administrative services in *ad hoc* arbitration under the UNCITRAL Arbitration Rules

1. *Offer of services*

13.   *Ad hoc* arbitrations conducted under the UNCITRAL Arbitration Rules may be facilitated by a body acting as appointing authority or providing administrative services of a secretarial, technical nature. These kinds of assistance could be rendered not only by arbitral institutions but also by other bodies, in particular chambers of commerce or trade associations.

14.   Such institutions and bodies are invited to consider offering their services in this regard. If they decide to do so, they may wish to make that willingness known to the interested public. It is advisable that they describe in detail the services offered and the relevant administrative procedures.[a]

15.   In devising these administrative procedures or rules, the institutions should have due regard to the interests of the parties. Since the parties in these cases have agreed that the arbitration is to be conducted under the UNCITRAL Arbitration Rules, their expectations should not be frustrated by an administrative rule which is in conflict with the UNCITRAL Arbitration Rules. Thus, the considerations and the appeal expressed above in the context of adopting these Rules as institutional rules (see paras. 9-12) apply here with even greater force.

16.   The following remarks and suggestions are intended to assist any interested institution in taking the necessary organizational measures and in devising appropriate administrative procedures in conformity with the UNCITRAL Arbitration Rules.

17.   It is recommended that the administrative procedures of the institution distinguish clearly between the functions of an appointing authority as envisaged under the UNCITRAL Arbitration Rules and other administrative assistance of a technical, secretarial nature. The institution should declare whether it is offering both or only one of these types of service. When offering both types the institution may declare its willingness to provide only one of these services in a given case, if so requested.

18.   The distinction between these two types of services is also of relevance to the question of which party may request these services. On the one hand, an institution may act as appointing authority under the UNCITRAL Arbitration Rules only if it has been so designated by the parties, whether in the arbitral clause or in a separate agreement. An institution should so state in its administrative procedures, possibly with the

---

[a]In an introductory part, the institution may wish to provide, in addition to the customary description of its aims and traditional activities, some information regarding the UNCITRAL Arbitration Rules. In particular, it may state that these Rules were adopted in 1976, after extensive deliberations, by the United Nations Commission on International Trade Law, that this Commission consists of 36 member States representing the different legal, economic and social systems and geographic regions of the world; that in the preparation of these Rules, various interested international organizations and leading arbitration experts were consulted; that the General Assembly of the United Nations has recommended the use of these Rules for inclusion in international commercial contracts; and that these Rules have become widely known and been accepted around the world.

additional provision (as a rule of interpretation) that it would also act as appointing authority if the parties submit a dispute to it under the UNCITRAL Arbitration Rules without specifically designating it as the appointing authority. On the other hand, administrative services of a technical, secretarial nature might be requested not only by the parties, but also by the arbitral tribunal (cf. art. 15, para. (1) and art. 38, para. *(c)* of the UNCITRAL Arbitration Rules).

19. In order to assist parties, the institution may wish to set forth in its administrative procedures model arbitration clauses covering the above services. The first part of any such model clause should be identical with the model clause of the UNCITRAL Arbitration Rules:

"Any dispute, controversy or claim arising out of or relating to this contract, or the breach, termination or invalidity thereof, shall be settled by arbitration in accordance with the UNCITRAL Arbitration Rules as at present in force."

The agreement as to the services which are requested should follow. For example:

"The appointing authority shall be the XYZ-Institution."

or:

"The XYZ-Institution shall act as appointing authority and provide administrative services in accordance with its administrative procedures for cases under the UNCITRAL Arbitration Rules."

As suggested in the UNCITRAL Model Arbitration Clause, the following note may be added:

"Note—Parties may wish to consider adding:

(a) The number of arbitrators shall be . . . (one or three);

(b) The place of arbitration shall be . . . (town or country);

(c) The language(s) to be used in the arbitral proceedings shall be . . .".

20. In view of the considerations and concerns expressed above in paragraphs 12 and 15, if the administrative procedures of the institution are such as to lead to a modification in substance of the UNCITRAL Arbitration Rules, it may be advisable that this modification be reflected in the model clause.

2. *Functions as appointing authority*

21. An institution which is willing to act as appointing authority under the UNCITRAL Arbitration Rules should specify in its administrative procedures the various functions of an appointing authority envisaged by these Rules which it will perform. It might also describe the manner in which it intends to perform these functions.

(a) *Appointment of arbitrators*

22. The UNCITRAL Arbitration Rules envisage various possibilities concerning the appointment of an arbitrator by an appointing authority. Under article 6, paragraph 2, the appointing authority may be requested to appoint a sole arbitrator, in accordance with certain procedures and criteria set forth in article 6, paragraphs 3 and 4. Further, it may be requested, under article 7, paragraph 2, to appoint the second of three arbitrators. Finally, it may be called upon to appoint a substitute arbitrator under articles 11, 12 or 13 (successful challenge and other reasons for replacement).

23. For each of these cases, the institution may indicate details as to how it would select the arbitrator in accordance with the UNCITRAL Arbitration Rules. In particular, it may state whether it maintains a panel or list of arbitrators, from which it would select appropriate candidates, and may provide information on the composition of such panel. It may also specify which person or organ within the institution would in fact make the appointment (e.g. president, director, secretary or a committee).

(b) Decision on challenge of arbitrator

24. Under article 10 of the UNCITRAL Arbitration Rules, any arbitrator may be challenged if circumstances exist that give rise to justifiable doubts as to his impartiality or independence. When such a challenge is contested (e.g. if the other party does not agree to the challenge or the challenged arbitrator does not withdraw), the decision on the challenge is to be made by the appointing authority according to article 12, paragraph 1. If the appointing authority sustains the challenge, it may also be called upon to appoint the substitute arbitrator.

25. The institution may indicate details as to how it would make the decision on such a challenge in accordance with the UNCITRAL Arbitration Rules. In particular, it may state which person or organ within the institution would make the decision. The institution may also wish to identify any code of ethics or other written principles which it would apply in ascertaining the independence and impartiality of arbitrators.

(c) Replacement of arbitrator

26. In the event that an arbitrator fails to act or in the event of the *de jure* or *de facto* impossibility of his performing his functions, the appointing authority may, under article 13, paragraph 2, be called upon to decide on whether such a reason for replacement exists, and it may be involved in appointing a substitute arbitrator. What has been said above in regard to the challenge of an arbitrator applies also to such cases of replacement of an arbitrator.

27. The situation is different with regard to those cases of replacement covered by paragraph 1 of article 13. In the event of the death or resignation of an arbitrator during the course of the arbitral proceedings, the only task which may be entrusted to an appointing authority is to appoint a substitute arbitrator.

(d) Assistance in fixing fees of arbitrators

28. Under the UNCITRAL Arbitration Rules, the arbitral tribunal fixes its fees, which shall be reasonable in amount, taking into account the amount in dispute, the complexity of the subject-matter, the time spent by the arbitrators and any other relevant circumstances of the case. In this task, the arbitral tribunal may be assisted by an appointing authority in three different ways:

  (i) If the appointing authority has issued a schedule of fees for arbitrators in international cases which it administers, the arbitral tribunal in fixing its fees shall take that schedule of fees into account to the extent that it considers appropriate in the circumstances of the case (art. 39, para. 2);

  (ii) In the absence of such a schedule of fees, the appointing authority may provide, upon a party's request, a statement setting forth the basis for establishing fees which is customarily followed in international cases in which the authority appoints arbitrators (art. 39, para. 3);

  (iii) In cases referred to under (i) and (ii), when a party so requests and the appointing authority consents, the arbitral tribunal shall fix its fees only after consultation with the appointing authority, which may make any comment it deems appropriate to the arbitral tribunal concerning the fees (art. 39, para. 4).

29. An institution willing to act as appointing authority may indicate, in its administrative procedures any relevant details in respect of these three possible ways of assistance in fixing fees. In particular, it may state whether it has issued a schedule of fees as envisaged under (i). The institution might also declare its willingness to perform the function envisaged under (ii), if it has not issued a fee schedule, and to perform the function under (iii).

(e) *Advisory comments regarding desposits*

30.   Under article 41, paragraph 3, of the UNCITRAL Arbitration Rules, the arbitral tribunal shall fix the amounts of any initial or supplementary deposits only after consultation with the appointing authority, which may make any pertinent comment it deems appropriate, if a party so requests and the appointing authority consents to perform this function. The institution may wish to indicate in its administrative procedures its general willingness to do so.

31.   It should be noted that, under the UNCITRAL Arbitration Rules, this kind of advice is the only task relating to deposits which an appointing authority may be requested to fulfil. Thus, if an institution offers to perform any other function (e.g. to hold deposits, to render an accounting thereof), it should be pointed out that this is a modification of article 41 of the UNCITRAL Arbitration Rules.

3.   *Administrative services*

32.   An institution which is prepared to provide administrative services of a technical, secretarial nature may describe in its administrative procedures the various services offered. Such services may be rendered upon request of the parties or the arbitral tribunal.

33.   In describing the various services, the institution should specify those services which would not be covered by its general administrative fee and which, therefore, would be billed separately (e.g. interpretation services). The institution may also wish to indicate which of the services it can provide itself, with its own facilities, and which it might merely arrange to be rendered by others.

34.   The following list of possible administrative services, which is not intended to be exhaustive, may assist institutions in considering and publicizing which services it may offer:

(a)   Forwarding of written communications of a party or the arbitrators;

(b)   Assisting the arbitral tribunal in establishing the date, time and place of hearings, and giving advance notice to the parties (cf. art. 25, para. 1 of UNCITRAL Arbitration Rules);

(c)   Providing, or arranging for, meeting rooms for hearings or deliberations of the arbitral tribunal;

(d)   Arranging for stenographic transcripts of hearings;

(e)   Assisting in filing or registering arbitral awards in those countries where such filing or registration is required by law;

(f)   Providing secretarial or clerical assistance in other respects.

4.   *Administrative fee schedule*

35.   The institution may wish to state the fees which it charges for its services. It might reproduce its administrative fee schedule or, in the absence thereof, indicate the basis for calculating its administrative fees.

36.   In view of the two possible categories of services an institution may offer, it is recommended that the fee for each category be stated separately. Thus, if an institution offers both categories of service, it may indicate its fees for the following three functions:

(a)   Acting as appointing authority and providing administrative services;

(b)   Acting as appointing authority only;

(c)   Providing administrative services without acting as appointing authority.

(In addition to the information and suggestions set forth herein, assistance may be obtained from the secretariat of the Commission (International Trade Law Branch, Office of Legal Affairs, United Nations, Vienna International Centre, P.O. Box 500, A-1400 Vienna, Austria). The secretariat could, for example, provide any interested institution with copies of the institutional rules or administrative procedures of a given other institution. It may also, if so requested, assist in the drafting of an administrative provision or make suggestions in this regard.)

ANNEX V.   LAW ON INTERNATIONAL COMMERCIAL ARBITRATION

A.   UNCITRAL Model Law on International Commercial Arbitration

CHAPTER I.   GENERAL PROVISIONS

Article 1.   Scope of application*

(1) This Law applies to international commercial** arbitration, subject to any agreement in force between this State and any other State or States.

(2) The provisions of this Law, except articles 8, 9, 35 and 36, apply only if the place of arbitration is in the territory of this State.

(3) An arbitration is international if:

(a) the parties to an arbitration agreement have, at the time of the conclusion of that agreement, their places of business in different States; or

(b) one of the following places is situated outside the State in which the parties have their places of business:

(i) the place of arbitration if determined in, or pursuant to, the arbitration agreement;

(ii) any place where a substantial part of the obligations of the commercial relationship is to be performed or the place with which the subject-matter of the dispute is most closely connected; or

(c) the parties have expressly agreed that the subject-matter of the arbitration agreement relates to more than one country.

(4) For the purposes of paragraph (3) of this article:

(a) if a party has more than one place of business, the place of business is that which has the closest relationship to the arbitration agreement;

(b) if a party does not have a place of business, reference is to be made to his habitual residence.

(5) This Law shall not affect any other law of this State by virtue of which certain disputes may not be submitted to arbitration or may be submitted to arbitration only according to provisions other than those of this Law.

---

*Article headings are for reference purposes only and are not to be used for purposes of interpretation.

**The term "commercial" should be given a wide interpretation so as to cover matters arising from all relationships of a commercial nature, whether contractual or not. Relationships of a commercial nature include, but are not limited to, the following transactions: any trade transaction for the supply or exchange of goods or services; distribution agreement; commercial representation or agency; factoring; leasing; construction of works; consulting; engineering; licensing; investment; financing; banking; insurance; exploitation agreement or concession; joint venture and other forms of industrial or business co-operation; carriage of goods or passengers by air, sea, rail or road.

Article 2.   Definitions and rules of interpretation

For the purposes of this Law:

(a) "arbitration" means any arbitration whether or not administered by a permanent arbitral institution;

(b) "arbitral tribunal" means a sole arbitrator or a panel of arbitrators;

(c) "court" means a body or organ of the judicial system of a State;

(d) where a provision of this Law, except article 28, leaves the parties free to determine a certain issue, such freedom includes the right of the parties to authorize a third party, including an institution, to make that determination;

(e) where a provision of this Law refers to the fact that the parties have agreed or that they may agree or in any other way refers to an agreement of the parties, such agreement includes any arbitration rules referred to in that agreement;

(f) where a provision of this Law, other than in articles 25 *(a)* and 32 (2) *(a)*, refers to a claim, it also applies to a counter-claim, and where it refers to a defence, it also applies to a defence to such counter-claim.

Article 3.   Receipt of written communications

(1)   Unless otherwise agreed by the parties:

(a) any written communication is deemed to have been received if it is delivered to the addressee personally or if it is delivered at his place of business, habitual residence or mailing address; if none of these can be found after making a reasonable inquiry, a written communication is deemed to have been received if it is sent to the addressee's last-known place of business, habitual residence or mailing address by registered letter or any other means which provides a record of the attempt to deliver it;

(b) the communication is deemed to have been received on the day it is so delivered.

(2)   The provisions of this article do not apply to communications in court proceedings.

Article 4.   Waiver of right to object

A party who knows that any provision of this Law from which the parties may derogate or any requirement under the arbitration agreement has not been complied with and yet proceeds with the arbitration without stating his objection to such non-compliance without undue delay or, if a time-limit is provided therefor, within such period of time, shall be deemed to have waived his right to object.

Article 5.   Extent of court intervention

In matters governed by this Law, no court shall intervene except where so provided in this Law.

Article 6.   Court or other authority for certain functions of arbitration assistance and supervision

The functions referred to in articles 11 (3), 11 (4), 13 (3), 14, 16 (3) and 34 (2) shall be performed by . . . [Each State enacting this model law specifies the court, courts or, where referred to therein, other authority competent to perform these functions.]

CHAPTER II. ARBITRATION AGREEMENT

Article 7. *Definition and form of arbitration agreement*

(1) "Arbitration agreement" is an agreement by the parties to submit to arbitration all or certain disputes which have arisen or which may arise between them in respect of a defined legal relationship, whether contractual or not. An arbitration agreement may be in the form of an arbitration clause in a contract or in the form of a separate agreement.

(2) The arbitration agreement shall be in writing. An agreement is in writing if it is contained in a document signed by the parties or in an exchange of letters, telex, telegrams or other means of telecommunication which provide a record of the agreement, or in an exchange of statements of claim and defence in which the existence of an agreement is alleged by one party and not denied by another. The reference in a contract to a document containing an arbitration clause constitutes an arbitration agreement provided that the contract is in writing and the reference is such as to make that clause part of the contract.

Article 8. *Arbitration agreement and substantive claim before court*

(1) A court before which an action is brought in a matter which is the subject of an arbitration agreement shall, if a party so requests not later than when submitting his first statement on the substance of the dispute, refer the parties to arbitration unless it finds that the agreement is null and void, inoperative or incapable of being performed.

(2) Where an action referred to in paragraph (1) of this article has been brought, arbitral proceedings may nevertheless be commenced or continued, and an award may be made, while the issue is pending before the court.

Article 9. *Arbitration agreement and interim measures by court*

It is not incompatible with an arbitration agreement for a party to request, before or during arbitral proceedings, from a court an interim measure of protection and for a court to grant such measure.

CHAPTER III. COMPOSITION OF ARBITRAL TRIBUNAL

Article 10. *Number of arbitrators*

(1) The parties are free to determine the number of arbitrators.

(2) Failing such determination, the number of arbitrators shall be three.

Article 11. *Appointment of arbitrators*

(1) No person shall be precluded by reason of his nationality from acting as an arbitrator, unless otherwise agreed by the parties.

(2) The parties are free to agree on a procedure of appointing the arbitrator or arbitrators, subject to the provisions of paragraphs (4) and (5) of this article.

(3) Failing such agreement,

(a) in an arbitration with three arbitrators, each party shall appoint one arbitrator, and the two arbitrators thus appointed shall appoint the third arbitrator; if a party fails to appoint the arbitrator within thirty days of receipt of a request to do so from the other party, or if the two arbitrators fail to agree on the third arbitrator within thirty days of their appointment, the appointment shall be made, upon request of a party, by the court or other authority specified in article 6;

(b) in an arbitration with a sole arbitrator, if the parties are unable to agree on the arbitrator, he shall be appointed, upon request of a party, by the court or other authority specified in article 6.

(4) Where, under an appointment procedure agreed upon by the parties,

(a) a party fails to act as required under such procedure, or

(b) the parties, or two arbitrators, are unable to reach an agreement expected of them under such procedure, or

(c) a third party, including an institution, fails to perform any function entrusted to it under such procedure,

any party may request the court or other authority specified in article 6 to take the necessary measure, unless the agreement on the appointment procedure provides other means for securing the appointment.

(5) A decision on a matter entrusted by paragraph (3) or (4) of this article to the court or other authority specified in article 6 shall be subject to no appeal. The court or other authority, in appointing an arbitrator, shall have due regard to any qualifications required of the arbitrator by the agreement of the parties and to such considerations as are likely to secure the appointment of an independent and impartial arbitrator and, in the case of a sole or third arbitrator, shall take into account as well the advisability of appointing an arbitrator of a nationality other than those of the parties.

Article 12.   Grounds for challenge

(1) When a person is approached in connection with his possible appointment as an arbitrator, he shall disclose any circumstances likely to give rise to justifiable doubts as to his impartiality or independence. An arbitrator, from the time of his appointment and throughout the arbitral proceedings, shall without delay disclose any such circumstances to the parties unless they have already been informed of them by him.

(2) An arbitrator may be challenged only if circumstances exist that give rise to justifiable doubts as to his impartiality or independence, or if he does not possess qualifications agreed to by the parties. A party may challenge an arbitrator appointed by him, or in whose appointment he has participated, only for reasons of which he becomes aware after the appointment has been made.

Article 13.   Challenge procedure

(1) The parties are free to agree on a procedure for challenging an arbitrator, subject to the provisions of paragraph (3) of this article.

(2) Failing such agreement, a party who intends to challenge an arbitrator shall, within fifteen days after becoming aware of the constitution of the arbitral tribunal or after becoming aware of any circumstance referred to in article 12 (2), send a written statement of the reasons for the challenge to the arbitral tribunal. Unless the challenged arbitrator withdraws from his office or the other party agrees to the challenge, the arbitral tribunal shall decide on the challenge.

(3) If a challenge under any procedure agreed upon by the parties or under the procedure of paragraph (2) of this article is not successful, the challenging party may request, within thirty days after having received notice of the decision rejecting the

challenge, the court or other authority specified in article 6 to decide on the challenge, which decision shall be subject to no appeal; while such a request is pending, the arbitral tribunal, including the challenged arbitrator, may continue the arbitral proceedings and make an award.

Article 14.   Failure or impossibility to act

(1)   If an arbitrator becomes *de jure* or *de facto* unable to perform his functions or for other reasons fails to act without undue delay, his mandate terminates if he withdraws from his office or if the parties agree on the termination. Otherwise, if a controversy remains concerning any of these grounds, any party may request the court or other authority specified in article 6 to decide on the termination of the mandate, which decision shall be subject to no appeal.

(2)   If, under this article or article 13 (2), an arbitrator withdraws from his office or a party agrees to the termination of the mandate of an arbitrator, this does not imply acceptance of the validity of any ground referred to in this article or article 12 (2).

Article 15.   Appointment of substitute arbitrator

Where the mandate of an arbitrator terminates under article 13 or 14 or because of his withdrawal from office for any other reason or because of the revocation of his mandate by agreement of the parties or in any other case of termination of his mandate, a substitute arbitrator shall be appointed according to the rules that were applicable to the appointment of the arbitrator being replaced.

CHAPTER IV.   JURISDICTION OF ARBITRAL TRIBUNAL

Article 16.   Competence of arbitral tribunal to rule on its jurisdiction

(1)   The arbitral tribunal may rule on its own jurisdiction, including any objections with respect to the existence or validity of the arbitration agreement. For that purpose, an arbitration clause which forms part of a contract shall be treated as an agreement independent of the other terms of the contract. A decision by the arbitral tribunal that the contract is null and void shall not entail *ipso jure* the invalidity of the arbitration clause.

(2)   A plea that the arbitral tribunal does not have jurisdiction shall be raised not later than the submission of the statement of defence. A party is not precluded from raising such a plea by the fact that he has appointed, or participated in the appointment of, an arbitrator. A plea that the arbitral tribunal is exceeding the scope of its authority shall be raised as soon as the matter alleged to be beyond the scope of its authority is raised during the arbitral proceedings. The arbitral tribunal may, in either case, admit a later plea if it considers the delay justified.

(3)   The arbitral tribunal may rule on a plea referred to in paragraph (2) of this article either as a preliminary question or in an award on the merits. If the arbitral tribunal rules as a preliminary question that it has jurisdiction, any party may request, within thirty days after having received notice of that ruling, the court specified in article 6 to decide the matter, which decision shall be subject to no appeal; while such a request is pending, the arbitral tribunal may continue the arbitral proceedings and make an award.

Article 17. Power of arbitral tribunal to order interim measures

Unless otherwise agreed by the parties, the arbitral tribunal may, at the request of a party, order any party to take such interim measure of protection as the arbitral tribunal may consider necessary in respect of the subject-matter of the dispute. The arbitral tribunal may require any party to provide appropriate security in connection with such measure.

CHAPTER V.   CONDUCT OF ARBITRAL PROCEEDINGS

Article 18.   Equal treatment of parties

The parties shall be treated with equality and each party shall be given a full opportunity of presenting his case.

Article 19.   Determination of rules of procedure

(1)   Subject to the provisions of this Law, the parties are free to agree on the procedure to be followed by the arbitral tribunal in conducting the proceedings.

(2)   Failing such agreement, the arbitral tribunal may, subject to the provisions of this Law, conduct the arbitration in such manner as it considers appropriate. The power conferred upon the arbitral tribunal includes the power to determine the admissibility, relevance, materiality and weight of any evidence.

Article 20.   Place of arbitration

(1)   The parties are free to agree on the place of arbitration. Failing such agreement, the place of arbitration shall be determined by the arbitral tribunal having regard to the circumstances of the case, including the convenience of the parties.

(2)   Notwithstanding the provisions of paragraph (1) of this article, the arbitral tribunal may, unless otherwise agreed by the parties, meet at any place it considers appropriate for consultation among its members, for hearing witnesses, experts or the parties, or for inspection of goods, other property or documents.

Article 21.   Commencement of arbitral proceedings

Unless otherwise agreed by the parties, the arbitral proceedings in respect of a particular dispute commence on the date on which a request for that dispute to be referred to arbitration is received by the respondent.

Article 22.   Language

(1)   The parties are free to agree on the language or languages to be used in the arbitral proceedings. Failing such agreement, the arbitral tribunal shall determine the language or languages to be used in the proceedings. This agreement or determination, unless otherwise specified therein, shall apply to any written statement by a party, any hearing and any award, decision or other communication by the arbitral tribunal.

(2)   The arbitral tribunal may order that any documentary evidence shall be accompanied by a translation into the language or languages agreed upon by the parties or determined by the arbitral tribunal.

162

Article 23. Statements of claim and defence

(1) Within the period of time agreed by the parties or determined by the arbitral tribunal, the claimant shall state the facts supporting his claim, the points at issue and the relief or remedy sought, and the respondent shall state his defence in respect of these particulars, unless the parties have otherwise agreed as to the required elements of such statements. The parties may submit with their statements all documents they consider to be relevant or may add a reference to the documents or other evidence they will submit.

(2) Unless otherwise agreed by the parties, either party may amend or supplement his claim or defence during the course of the arbitral proceedings, unless the arbitral tribunal considers it inappropriate to allow such amendment having regard to the delay in making it.

Article 24. Hearings and written proceedings

(1) Subject to any contrary agreement by the parties, the arbitral tribunal shall decide whether to hold oral hearings for the presentation of evidence or for oral argument, or whether the proceedings shall be conducted on the basis of documents and other materials. However, unless the parties have agreed that no hearings shall be held, the arbitral tribunal shall hold such hearings at an appropriate stage of the proceedings, if so requested by a party.

(2) The parties shall be given sufficient advance notice of any hearing and of any meeting of the arbitral tribunal for the purposes of inspection of goods, other property or documents.

(3) All statements, documents or other information supplied to the arbitral tribunal by one party shall be communicated to the other party. Also any expert report or evidentiary document on which the arbitral tribunal may rely in making its decision shall be communicated to the parties.

Article 25. Default of a party

Unless otherwise agreed by the parties, if, without showing sufficient cause,

(a) the claimant fails to communicate his statement of claim in accordance with article 23 (1), the arbitral tribunal shall terminate the proceedings;

(b) the respondent fails to communicate his statement of defence in accordance with article 23 (1), the arbitral tribunal shall continue the proceedings without treating such failure in itself as an admission of the claimant's allegations;

(c) any party fails to appear at a hearing or to produce documentary evidence, the arbitral tribunal may continue the proceedings and make the award on the evidence before it.

Article 26. Expert appointed by arbitral tribunal

(1) Unless otherwise agreed by the parties, the arbitral tribunal

(a) may appoint one or more experts to report to it on specific issues to be determined by the arbitral tribunal;

(b) may require a party to give the expert any relevant information or to produce, or to provide access to, any relevant documents, goods or other property for his inspection.

(2) Unless otherwise agreed by the parties, if a party so requests or if the arbitral tribunal considers it necessary, the expert shall, after delivery of his written or oral report, participate in a hearing where the parties have the opportunity to put questions to him and to present expert witnesses in order to testify on the points at issue.

Article 27. Court assistance in taking evidence

The arbitral tribunal or a party with the approval of the arbitral tribunal may request from a competent court of this State assistance in taking evidence. The court may execute the request within its competence and according to its rules on taking evidence.

CHAPTER VI. MAKING OF AWARD AND TERMINATION OF PROCEEDINGS

Article 28. Rules applicable to substance of dispute

(1) The arbitral tribunal shall decide the dispute in accordance with such rules of law as are chosen by the parties as applicable to the substance of the dispute. Any designation of the law or legal system of a given State shall be construed, unless otherwise expressed, as directly referring to the substantive law of that State and not to its conflict of laws rules.

(2) Failing any designation by the parties, the arbitral tribunal shall apply the law determined by the conflict of laws rules which it considers applicable.

(3) The arbitral tribunal shall decide *ex aequo et bono* or as *amiable compositeur* only if the parties have expressly authorized it to do so.

(4) In all cases, the arbitral tribunal shall decide in accordance with the terms of the contract and shall take into account the usages of the trade applicable to the transaction.

Article 29. Decision making by panel of arbitrators

In arbitral proceedings with more than one arbitrator, any decision of the arbitral tribunal shall be made, unless otherwise agreed by the parties, by a majority of all its members. However, questions of procedure may be decided by a presiding arbitrator, if so authorized by the parties or all members of the arbitral tribunal.

Article 30. Settlement

(1) If, during arbitral proceedings, the parties settle the dispute, the arbitral tribunal shall terminate the proceedings and, if requested by the parties and not objected to by the arbitral tribunal, record the settlement in the form of an arbitral award on agreed terms.

(2) An award on agreed terms shall be made in accordance with the provisions of article 31 and shall state that it is an award. Such an award has the same status and effect as any other award on the merits of the case.

Article 31. Form and contents of award

(1) The award shall be made in writing and shall be signed by the arbitrator or arbitrators. In arbitral proceedings with more than one arbitrator, the signatures of the majority of all members of the arbitral tribunal shall suffice, provided that the reason for any omitted signature is stated.

(2) The award shall state the reasons upon which it is based, unless the parties have agreed that no reasons are to be given or the award is an award on agreed terms under article 30.

(3) The award shall state its date and the place of arbitration as determined in accordance with article 20 (1). The award shall be deemed to have been made at that place.

(4) After the award is made, a copy signed by the arbitrators in accordance with paragraph (1) of this article shall be delivered to each party.

Article 32. Termination of proceedings

(1) The arbitral proceedings are terminated by the final award or by an order of the arbitral tribunal in accordance with paragraph (2) of this article.

(2) The arbitral tribunal shall issue an order for the termination of the arbitral proceedings when:

(a) the claimant withdraws his claim, unless the respondent objects thereto and the arbitral tribunal recognizes a legitimate interest on his part in obtaining a final settlement of the dispute;

(b) the parties agree on the termination of the proceedings;

(c) the arbitral tribunal finds that the continuation of the proceedings has for any other reason become unnecessary or impossible.

(3) The mandate of the arbitral tribunal terminates with the termination of the arbitral proceedings, subject to the provisions of articles 33 and 34 (4).

Article 33. Correction and interpretation of award; additional award

(1) Within thirty days of receipt of the award, unless another period of time has been agreed upon by the parties:

(a) a party, with notice to the other party, may request the arbitral tribunal to correct in the award any errors in computation, any clerical or typographical errors or any errors of similar nature;

(b) if so agreed by the parties, a party, with notice to the other party, may request the arbitral tribunal to give an interpretation of a specific point or part of the award.

If the arbitral tribunal considers the request to be justified, it shall make the correction or give the interpretation within thirty days of receipt of the request. The interpretation shall form part of the award.

(2) The arbitral tribunal may correct any error of the type referred to in paragraph (1) *(a)* of this article on its own initiative within thirty days of the date of the award.

(3) Unless otherwise agreed by the parties, a party, with notice to the other party, may request, within thirty days of receipt of the award, the arbitral tribunal to make an additional award as to claims presented in the arbitral proceedings but omitted from the award. If the arbitral tribunal considers the request to be justified, it shall make the additional award within sixty days.

(4) The arbitral tribunal may extend, if necessary, the period of time within which it shall make a correction, interpretation or an additional award under paragraph (1) or (3) of this article.

(5) The provisions of article 31 shall apply to a correction or interpretation of the award or to an additional award.

Article 34. Application for setting aside as exclusive recourse against arbitral award

(1) Recourse to a court against an arbitral award may be made only by an application for setting aside in accordance with paragraphs (2) and (3) of this article.

(2) An arbitral award may be set aside by the court specified in article 6 only if:

(a) the party making the application furnishes proof that:

(i) a party to the arbitration agreement referred to in article 7 was under some incapacity; or the said agreement is not valid under the law to which the parties have subjected it or, failing any indication thereon, under the law of this State; or

(ii) the party making the application was not given proper notice of the appointment of an arbitrator or of the arbitral proceedings or was otherwise unable to present his case; or

(iii) the award deals with a dispute not contemplated by or not falling within the terms of the submission to arbitration, or contains decisions on matters beyond the scope of the submission to arbitration, provided that, if the decisions on matters submitted to arbitration can be separated from those not so submitted, only that part of the award which contains decisions on matters not submitted to arbitration may be set aside; or

(iv) the composition of the arbitral tribunal or the arbitral procedure was not in accordance with the agreement of the parties, unless such agreement was in conflict with a provision of this Law from which the parties cannot derogate, or, failing such agreement, was not in accordance with this Law; or

(b) the court finds that:

(i) the subject-matter of the dispute is not capable of settlement by arbitration under the law of this State; or

(ii) the award is in conflict with the public policy of this State.

(3) An application for setting aside may not be made after three months have elapsed from the date on which the party making that application had received the award or, if a request had been made under article 33, from the date on which that request had been disposed of by the arbitral tribunal.

(4) The court, when asked to set aside an award, may, where appropriate and so requested by a party, suspend the setting aside proceedings for a period of time determined by it in order to give the arbitral tribunal an opportunity to resume the arbitral proceedings or to take such other action as in the arbitral tribunal's opinion will eliminate the grounds for setting aside.

CHAPTER VIII. RECOGNITION AND ENFORCEMENT OF AWARDS

Article 35. Recognition and enforcement

(1) An arbitral award, irrespective of the country in which it was made, shall be recognized as binding and, upon application in writing to the competent court, shall be enforced subject to the provisions of this article and of article 36.

(2) The party relying on an award or applying for its enforcement shall supply the duly authenticated original award or a duly certified copy thereof, and the original arbitration agreement referred to in article 7 or a duly certified copy thereof. If the award or agreement is not made in an official language of this State, the party shall supply a duly certified translation thereof into such language.***

***The conditions set forth in this paragraph are intended to set maximum standards. It would, thus, not be contrary to the harmonization to be achieved by the model law if a State retained even less onerous conditions.

Article 36. Grounds for refusing recognition or enforcement

(1)   Recognition or enforcement of an arbitral award, irrespective of the country in which it was made, may be refused only:

(a)   at the request of the party against whom it is invoked, if that party furnishes to the competent court where recognition or enforcement is sought proof that:

  (i)   a party to the arbitration agreement referred to in article 7 was under some incapacity; or the said agreement is not valid under the law to which the parties have subjected it or, failing any indication thereon, under the law of the country where the award was made; or

  (ii)   the party against whom the award is invoked was not given proper notice of the appointment of an arbitrator or of the arbitral proceedings or was otherwise unable to present his case; or

  (iii)   the award deals with a dispute not contemplated by or not falling within the terms of the submission to arbitration, or it contains decisions on matters beyond the scope of the submission to arbitration, provided that, if the decisions on matters submitted to arbitration can be separated from those not so submitted, that part of the award which contains decisions on matters submitted to arbitration may be recognized and enforced; or

  (iv)   the composition of the arbitral tribunal or the arbitral procedure was not in accordance with the agreement of the parties or, failing such agreement, was not in accordance with the law of the country where the arbitration took place; or

  (v)   the award has not yet become binding on the parties or has been set aside or suspended by a court of the country in which, or under the law of which, that award was made; or

(b)   if the court finds that:

  (i)   the subject-matter of the dispute is not capable of settlement by arbitration under the law of this State; or

  (ii)   the recognition or enforcement of the award would be contrary to the public policy of this State.

(2)   If an application for setting aside or suspension of an award has been made to a court referred to in paragraph (1) *(a)* (v) of this article, the court where recognition or enforcement is sought may, if it considers it proper, adjourn its decision and may also, on the application of the party claiming recognition or enforcement of the award, order the other party to provide appropriate security.

B.   General Assembly resolution 40/72 of 11 December 1985

40/72.   MODEL LAW ON INTERNATIONAL COMMERCIAL ARBITRATION OF THE UNITED NATIONS COMMISSION ON INTERNATIONAL TRADE LAW

The General Assembly,

Recognizing the value of arbitration as a method of settling disputes arising in international commercial relations,

Being convinced that the establishment of a model law on arbitration that is acceptable to States with different legal, social and economic systems contributes to the development of harmonious international economic relations,

Noting that the Model Law on International Commercial Arbitration[1] was adopted by the United Nations Commission on International Trade Law at its eighteenth session, after due deliberation and extensive consultation with arbitral institutions and individual experts on international commercial arbitration,

Being convinced that the Model Law, together with the Convention on the Recognition and Enforcement of Foreign Arbitral Awards[2] and the Arbitration Rules of the United Nations Commission on International Trade Law,[3] recommended by the General Assembly in its resolution 31/98 of 15 December 1976, significantly contributes to the establishment of a unified legal framework for the fair and efficient settlement of disputes arising in international commercial relations,

1. *Requests* the Secretary-General to transmit the text of the Model Law on International Commercial Arbitration of the United Nations Commission on International Trade Law, together with the *travaux préparatoires* from the eighteenth session of the Commission, to Governments and to arbitral institutions and other interested bodies, such as chambers of commerce;

2. *Recommends* that all States give due consideration to the Model Law on International Commercial Arbitration, in view of the desirability of uniformity of the law of arbitral procedures and the specific needs of international commercial arbitration practice.

112th plenary meeting,
11 December 1985

---

[1]*Official Records of the General Assembly, Fortieth Session, Supplement No. 17* (A/40/17), annex I.
[2]United Nations, *Treaty Series,* vol. 330, No. 4739, p. 38.
[3]United Nations publication, Sales No. E.77.V.6.

ANNEX VI.   RULES OF CONCILIATION PROCEDURE

A.   UNCITRAL Conciliation Rules

APPLICATION OF THE RULES

Article 1

(1)   These Rules apply to conciliation of disputes arising out of or relating to a contractual or other legal relationship where the parties seeking an amicable settlement of their dispute have agreed that the UNCITRAL Conciliation Rules apply.

(2)   The parties may agree to exclude or vary any of these Rules at any time.

(3)   Where any of these Rules is in conflict with a provision of law from which the parties cannot derogate, that provision prevails.

COMMENCEMENT OF CONCILIATION PROCEEDINGS

Article 2

(1)   The party initiating conciliation sends to the other party a written invitation to conciliate under these Rules, briefly identifying the subject of the dispute.

(2)   Conciliation proceedings commence when the other party accepts the invitation to conciliate. If the acceptance is made orally, it is advisable that it be confirmed in writing.

(3)   If the other party rejects the invitation, there will be no conciliation proceedings.

(4)   If the party initiating conciliation does not receive a reply within thirty days from the date on which he sends the invitation, or within such other period of time as specified in the invitation, he may elect to treat this as a rejection of the invitation to conciliate. If he so elects, he informs the other party accordingly.

NUMBER OF CONCILIATORS

Article 3

There shall be one conciliator unless the parties agree that there shall be two or three conciliators. Where there is more than one conciliator, they ought, as a general rule, to act jointly.

APPOINTMENT OF CONCILIATORS

Article 4

(1)   *(a)*   In conciliation proceedings with one conciliator, the parties shall endeavour to reach agreement on the name of a sole conciliator;

(b)   In conciliation proceedings with two conciliators, each party appoints one conciliator;

(c) In conciliation proceedings with three conciliators, each party appoints one conciliator. The parties shall endeavour to reach agreement on the name of the third conciliator.

(2) Parties may enlist the assistance of an appropriate institution or person in connexion with the appointment of conciliators. In particular,

(a) A party may request such an institution or person to recommend the names of suitable individuals to act as conciliator; or

(b) The parties may agree that the appointment of one or more conciliators be made directly by such an institution or person.

In recommending or appointing individuals to act as conciliator, the institution or person shall have regard to such considerations as are likely to secure the appointment of an independent and impartial conciliator and, with respect to a sole or third conciliator, shall take into account the advisability of appointing a conciliator of a nationality other than the nationalities of the parties.

SUBMISSION OF STATEMENTS TO CONCILIATOR

Article 5

(1) The conciliator,* upon his appointment, requests each party to submit to him a brief written statement describing the general nature of the dispute and the points at issue. Each party sends a copy of his statement to the other party.

(2) The conciliator may request each party to submit to him a further written statement of his position and the facts and grounds in support thereof, supplemented by any documents and other evidence that such party deems appropriate. The party sends a copy of his statement to the other party.

(3) At any stage of the conciliation proceedings the conciliator may request a party to submit to him such additional information as he deems appropriate.

REPRESENTATION AND ASSISTANCE

Article 6

The parties may be represented or assisted by persons of their choice. The names and addresses of such persons are to be communicated in writing to the other party and to the conciliator; such communication is to specify whether the appointment is made for purposes of representation or of assistance.

ROLE OF CONCILIATOR

Article 7

(1) The conciliator assists the parties in an independent and impartial manner in their attempt to reach an amicable settlement of their dispute.

(2) The conciliator will be guided by principles of objectivity, fairness and justice, giving consideration to, among other things, the rights and obligations of the parties, the usages of the trade concerned and the circumstances surrounding the dispute, including any previous business practices between the parties.

---

*In this and all following articles, the term "conciliator" applies to a sole conciliator, two or three conciliators, as the case may be.

(3) The conciliator may conduct the conciliation proceedings in such a manner as he considers appropriate, taking into account the circumstances of the case, the wishes the parties may express, including any request by a party that the conciliator hear oral statements, and the need for a speedy settlement of the dispute.

(4) The conciliator may, at any stage of the conciliation proceedings, make proposals for a settlement of the dispute. Such proposals need not be in writing and need not be accompanied by a statement of the reasons therefor.

ADMINISTRATIVE ASSISTANCE

Article 8

In order to facilitate the conduct of the conciliation proceedings, the parties, or the conciliator with the consent of the parties, may arrange for administrative assistance by a suitable institution or person.

COMMUNICATION BETWEEN CONCILIATOR AND PARTIES

Article 9

(1) The conciliator may invite the parties to meet with him or may communicate with them orally or in writing. He may meet or communicate with the parties together or with each of them separately.

(2) Unless the parties have agreed upon the place where meetings with the conciliator are to be held, such place will be determined by the conciliator, after consultation with the parties, having regard to the circumstances of the conciliation proceedings.

DISCLOSURE OF INFORMATION

Article 10

When the conciliator receives factual information concerning the dispute from a party, he discloses the substance of that information to the other party in order that the other party may have the opportunity to present any explanation which he considers appropriate. However, when a party gives any information to the conciliator subject to a specific condition that it be kept confidential, the conciliator does not disclose that information to the other party.

CO-OPERATION OF PARTIES WITH CONCILIATOR

Article 11

The parties will in good faith co-operate with the conciliator and, in particular, will endeavour to comply with requests by the conciliator to submit written materials, provide evidence and attend meetings.

SUGGESTIONS BY PARTIES FOR SETTLEMENT OF DISPUTE

Article 12

Each party may, on his own initiative or at the invitation of the conciliator, submit to the conciliator suggestions for the settlement of the dispute.

SETTLEMENT AGREEMENT

Article 13

(1) When it appears to the conciliator that there exist elements of a settlement which would be acceptable to the parties, he formulates the terms of a possible settlement and submits them to the parties for their observations. After receiving the observations of the parties, the conciliator may reformulate the terms of a possible settlement in the light of such observations.

(2) If the parties reach agreement on a settlement of the dispute, they draw up and sign a written settlement agreement.* If requested by the parties, the conciliator draws up, or assists the parties in drawing up, the settlement agreement.

(3) The parties by signing the settlement agreement put an end to the dispute and are bound by the agreement.

CONFIDENTIALITY

Article 14

The conciliator and the parties must keep confidential all matters relating to the conciliation proceedings. Confidentiality extends also to the settlement agreement, except where its disclosure is necessary for purposes of implementation and enforcement.

TERMINATION OF CONCILIATION PROCEEDINGS

Article 15

The conciliation proceedings are terminated:

(a) By the signing of the settlement agreement by the parties, on the date of the agreement; or

(b) By a written declaration of the conciliator, after consultation with the parties, to the effect that further efforts at conciliation are no longer justified, on the date of the declaration; or

(c) By a written declaration of the parties addressed to the conciliator to the effect that the conciliation proceedings are terminated, on the date of the declaration; or

(d) By a written declaration of a party to the other party and the conciliator, if appointed, to the effect that the conciliation proceedings are terminated, on the date of the declaration.

RESORT TO ARBITRAL OR JUDICIAL PROCEEDINGS

Article 16

The parties undertake not to initiate, during the conciliation proceedings, any arbitral or judicial proceedings in respect of a dispute that is the subject of the conciliation proceedings, except that a party may initiate arbitral or judicial proceedings where, in his opinion, such proceedings are necessary for preserving his rights.

---

*The parties may wish to consider including in the settlement agreement a clause that any dispute arising out of or relating to the settlement agreement shall be submitted to arbitration.

COSTS

Article 17

(1)   Upon termination of the conciliation proceedings, the conciliator fixes the costs of the conciliation and gives written notice thereof to the parties. The term "costs" includes only:

  (a)   The fee of the conciliator which shall be reasonable in amount;

  (b)   The travel and other expenses of the conciliator;

  (c)   The travel and other expenses of witnesses requested by the conciliator with the consent of the parties;

  (d)   The cost of any assistance provided pursuant to articles 4, paragraph 2 *(b)*, and 8 of these Rules.

(2)   The costs, as defined above, are borne equally by the parties unless the settlement agreement provides for a different apportionment. All other expenses incurred by a party are borne by that party.

DEPOSITS

Article 18

(1)   The conciliator, upon his appointment, may request each party to deposit an equal amount as an advance for the costs referred to in article 17, paragraph (1) which he expects will be incurred.

(2)   During the course of the conciliation proceedings the conciliator may request supplementary deposits in an equal amount from each party.

(3)   If the required deposits under paragraphs (1) and (2) of this article are not paid in full by both parties within thirty days, the conciliator may suspend the proceedings or may make a written declaration of termination to the parties, effective on the date of that declaration.

(4)   Upon termination of the conciliation proceedings, the conciliator renders an accounting to the parties of the deposits received and returns any unexpended balance to the parties.

ROLE OF CONCILIATOR IN OTHER PROCEEDINGS

Article 19

The parties and the conciliator undertake that the conciliator will not act as an arbitrator or as a representative or counsel of a party in any arbitral or judicial proceedings in respect of a dispute that is the subject of the conciliation proceedings. The parties also undertake that they will not present the conciliator as a witness in any such proceedings.

ADMISSIBILITY OF EVIDENCE IN OTHER PROCEEDINGS

Article 20

The parties undertake not to rely on or introduce as evidence in arbitral or judicial proceedings, whether or not such proceedings relate to the dispute that is the subject of the conciliation proceedings:

  (a)   Views expressed or suggestions made by the other party in respect of a possible settlement of the dispute;

(b) Admissions made by the other party in the course of the conciliation proceedings;

(c) Proposals made by the conciliator;

(d) The fact that the other party had indicated his willingness to accept a proposal for settlement made by the conciliator.

MODEL CONCILIATON CLAUSE

Where, in the event of a dispute arising out of or relating to this contract, the parties wish to seek an amicable settlement of that dispute by conciliation, the conciliation shall take place in accordance with the UNCITRAL Conciliation Rules as at present in force.

(The parties may agree on other conciliation clauses.)

B. General Assembly resolution 35/52 of 4 December 1980

35/52. CONCILIATION RULES OF THE UNITED NATIONS COMMISSION ON INTERNATIONAL TRADE LAW

The General Assembly,

Recognizing the value of conciliation as a method of amicably settling disputes arising in the context of international commercial relations,

Convinced that the establishment of conciliation rules that are acceptable in countries with different legal, social and economic systems could significantly contribute to the development of harmonious international economic relations,

Noting that the Conciliation Rules of the United Nations Commission on International Trade Law were adopted by the Commission at its thirteenth session[1] after consideration of the observations of Governments and interested organizations,

1. *Recommends* the use of the Conciliation Rules of the United Nations Commission on International Trade Law in cases where a dispute arises in the context of international commercial relations and the parties seek an amicable settlement of that dispute by recourse to conciliation;

2. *Requests* the Secretary-General to arrange for the widest possible distribution of the Conciliation Rules.

81st plenary meeting,
4 December 1980

---

[1]*Official Records of the General Assembly, Thirty-fifth Session, Supplement No. 17* (A/35/17), paras. 105 and 106.

ANNEX VII.   CARRIAGE OF GOODS BY SEA

A.   United Nations Convention on the Carriage of Goods by Sea, 1978 (Hamburg)

Preamble

The States Parties to this Convention,

Having recognized the desirability of determining by agreement certain rules relating to the carriage of goods by sea,

Have decided to conclude a convention for this purpose and have thereto agreed as follows:

Part I.   General provisions

Article 1.   Definitions

In this Convention:

1.   "Carrier" means any person by whom or in whose name a contract of carriage of goods by sea has been concluded with a shipper.

2.   "Actual carrier" means any person to whom the performance of the carriage of the goods, or of part of the carriage, has been entrusted by the carrier, and includes any other person to whom such performance has been entrusted.

3.   "Shipper" means any person by whom or in whose name or on whose behalf a contract of carriage of goods by sea has been concluded with a carrier, or any person by whom or in whose name or on whose behalf the goods are actually delivered to the carrier in relation to the contract of carriage by sea.

4.   "Consignee" means the person entitled to take delivery of the goods.

5.   "Goods" includes live animals; where the goods are consolidated in a container, pallet or similar article of transport or where they are packed, "goods" includes such article of transport or packaging if supplied by the shipper.

6.   "Contract of carriage by sea" means any contract whereby the carrier undertakes against payment of freight to carry goods by sea from one port to another; however, a contract which involves carriage by sea and also carriage by some other means is deemed to be a contract of carriage by sea for the purposes of this Convention only in so far as it relates to the carriage by sea.

7.   "Bill of lading" means a document which evidences a contract of carriage by sea and the taking over or loading of the goods by the carrier, and by which the carrier undertakes to deliver the goods against surrender of the document. A provision in the document that the goods are to be delivered to the order of a named person, or to order, or to bearer, constitutes such an undertaking.

8.   "Writing" includes, *inter alia*, telegram and telex.

Article 2. Scope of application

1. The provisions of this Convention are applicable to all contracts of carriage by sea between two different States, if:

(a) the port of loading as provided for in the contract of carriage by sea is located in a Contracting State, or

(b) the port of discharge as provided for in the contract of carriage by sea is located in a Contracting State, or

(c) one of the optional ports of discharge provided for in the contract of carriage by sea is the actual port of discharge and such port is located in a Contracting State, or

(d) the bill of lading or other document evidencing the contract of carriage by sea is issued in a Contracting State, or

(e) the bill of lading or other document evidencing the contract of carriage by sea provides that the provisions of this Convention or the legislation of any State giving effect to them are to govern the contract.

2. The provisions of this Convention are applicable without regard to the nationality of the ship, the carrier, the actual carrier, the shipper, the consignee or any other interested person.

3. The provisions of this Convention are not applicable to charter-parties. However, where a bill of lading is issued pursuant to a charter-party, the provisions of the Convention apply to such a bill of lading if it governs the relation between the carrier and the holder of the bill of lading, not being the charterer.

4. If a contract provides for future carriage of goods in a series of shipments during an agreed period, the provisions of this Convention apply to each shipment. However, where a shipment is made under a charter-party, the provisions of paragraph 3 of this article apply.

Article 3. Interpretation of the Convention

In the interpretation and application of the provisions of this Convention regard shall be had to its international character and to the need to promote uniformity.

Part II. Liability of the carrier

Article 4. Period of responsibility

1. The responsibility of the carrier for the goods under this Convention covers the period during which the carrier is in charge of the goods at the port of loading, during the carriage and at the port of discharge.

2. For the purpose of paragraph 1 of this article, the carrier is deemed to be in charge of the goods

(a) from the time he has taken over the goods from:

(i) the shipper, or a person acting on his behalf; or

(ii) an authority or other third party to whom, pursuant to law or regulations applicable at the port of loading, the goods must be handed over for shipment;

(b) until the time he has delivered the goods:

(i) by handing over the goods to the consignee; or

(ii) in cases where the consignee does not receive the goods from the carrier, by placing them at the disposal of the consignee in accordance with the contract or with the law or with the usage of the particular trade, applicable at the port of discharge; or

(iii) by handing over the goods to an authority or other third party to whom, pursuant to law or regulations applicable at the port of discharge, the goods must be handed over.

3.   In paragraphs 1 and 2 of this article, reference to the carrier or to the consignee means, in addition to the carrier or the consignee, the servants or agents, respectively of the carrier or the consignee.

Article 5.   Basis of liability

1.   The carrier is liable for loss resulting from loss of or damage to the goods, as well as from delay in delivery, if the occurrence which caused the loss, damage or delay took place while the goods were in his charge as defined in article 4, unless the carrier proves that he, his servants or agents took all measures that could reasonably be required to avoid the occurrence and its consequences.

2.   Delay in delivery occurs when the goods have not been delivered at the port of discharge provided for in the contract of carriage by sea within the time expressly agreed upon or, in the absence of such agreement, within the time which it would be reasonable to require of a diligent carrier, having regard to the circumstances of the case.

3.   The person entitled to make a claim for the loss of goods may treat the goods as lost if they have not been delivered as required by article 4 within 60 consecutive days following the expiry of the time for delivery according to paragraph 2 of this article.

4.   (a)   The carrier is liable
 (i)   for loss of or damage to the goods or delay in delivery caused by fire, if the claimant proves that the fire arose from fault or neglect on the part of the carrier, his servants or agents;
(ii)   for such loss, damage or delay in delivery which is proved by the claimant to have resulted from the fault or neglect of the carrier, his servants or agents in taking all measures that could reasonably be required to put out the fire and avoid or mitigate its consequences.

(b)   In case of fire on board the ship affecting the goods, if the claimant or the carrier so desires, a survey in accordance with shipping practices must be held into the cause and circumstances of the fire, and a copy of the surveyor's report shall be made available on demand to the carrier and the claimant.

5.   With respect to live animals, the carrier is not liable for loss, damage or delay in delivery resulting from any special risks inherent in that kind of carriage. If the carrier proves that he has complied with any special instructions given to him by the shipper respecting the animals and that, in the circumstances of the case, the loss, damage or delay in delivery could be attributed to such risks, it is presumed that the loss, damage or delay in delivery was so caused, unless there is proof that all or a part of the loss, damage or delay in delivery resulted from fault or neglect on the part of the carrier, his servants or agents.

6.   The carrier is not liable, except in general average, where loss, damage or delay in delivery resulted from measures to save life or from reasonable measures to save property at sea.

7.   Where fault or neglect on the part of the carrier, his servants or agents combines with another cause to produce loss, damage or delay in delivery, the carrier is liable only to the extent that the loss, damage or delay in delivery is attributable to such fault or neglect, provided that the carrier proves the amount of the loss, damage or delay in delivery not attributable thereto.

Article 6. Limits of liability

1. *(a)* The liability of the carrier for loss resulting from loss of or damage to goods according to the provisions of article 5 is limited to an amount equivalent to 835 units of account per package or other shipping unit or 2.5 units of account per kilogram of gross weight of the goods lost or damaged, whichever is the higher.

(b) The liability of the carrier for delay in delivery according to the provisions of article 5 is limited to an amount equivalent to two and a half times the freight payable for the goods delayed, but not exceeding the total freight payable under the contract of carriage of goods by sea.

(c) In no case shall the aggregate liability of the carrier, under both subparagraphs *(a)* and *(b)* of this paragraph, exceed the limitation which would be established under subparagraph *(a)* of this paragraph for total loss of the goods with respect to which such liability was incurred.

2. For the purpose of calculating which amount is the higher in accordance with paragraph 1 *(a)* of this article, the following rules apply:

(a) Where a container, pallet or similar article of transport is used to consolidate goods, the package or other shipping units enumerated in the bill of lading, if issued, or otherwise in any other document evidencing the contract of carriage by sea, as packed in such article of transport are deemed packages or shipping units. Except as aforesaid the goods in such article of transport are deemed one shipping unit.

(b) In cases where the article of transport itself has been lost or damaged, that article of transport, if not owned or otherwise supplied by the carrier, is considered one separate shipping unit.

3. Unit of account means the unit of account mentioned in article 26.

4. By agreement between the carrier and the shipper, limits of liability exceeding those provided for in paragraph 1 may be fixed.

Article 7. Application to non-contractual claims

1. The defences and limits of liability provided for in this Convention apply in any action against the carrier in respect of loss of or damage to the goods covered by the contract of carriage by sea, as well as of delay in delivery whether the action is founded in contract, in tort or otherwise.

2. If such an action is brought against a servant or agent of the carrier, such servant or agent, if he proves that he acted within the scope of his employment, is entitled to avail himself of the defences and limits of liability which the carrier is entitled to invoke under this Convention.

3. Except as provided in article 8, the aggregate of the amounts recoverable from the carrier and from any persons referred to in paragraph 2 of this article shall not exceed the limits of liability provided for in this Convention.

Article 8. Loss of right to limit responsibility

1. The carrier is not entitled to the benefit of the limitation of liability provided for in article 6 if it is proved that the loss, damage or delay in delivery resulted from an act or omission of the carrier done with the intent to cause such loss, damage or delay, or recklessly and with knowledge that such loss, damage or delay would probably result.

2. Notwithstanding the provisions of paragraph 2 of article 7, a servant or agent of the carrier is not entitled to the benefit of the limitation of liability provided for in

article 6 if it is proved that the loss, damage or delay in delivery resulted from an act or omission of such servant or agent, done with the intent to cause such loss, damage or delay, or recklessly and with knowledge that such loss, damage or delay would probably result.

Article 9. Deck cargo

1. The carrier is entitled to carry the goods on deck only if such carriage is in accordance with an agreement with the shipper or with the usage of the particular trade or is required by statutory rules or regulations.

2. If the carrier and the shipper have agreed that the goods shall or may be carried on deck, the carrier must insert in the bill of lading or other document evidencing the contract of carriage by sea a statement to that effect. In the absence of such a statement the carrier has the burden of proving that an agreement for carriage on deck has been entered into; however, the carrier is not entitled to invoke such an agreement against a third party, including a consignee, who has acquired the bill of lading in good faith.

3. Where the goods have been carried on deck contrary to the provisions of paragraph 1 of this article or where the carrier may not under paragraph 2 of this article invoke an agreement for carriage on deck, the carrier, notwithstanding the provisions of paragraph 1 of article 5, is liable for loss of or damage to the goods, as well as for delay in delivery, resulting solely from the carriage on deck, and the extent of his liability is to be determined in accordance with the provisions of article 6 or article 8 of this Convention, as the case may be.

4. Carriage of goods on deck contrary to express agreement for carriage under deck is deemed to be an act or omission of the carrier within the meaning of article 8.

Article 10. Liability of the carrier and actual carrier

1. Where the performance of the carriage or part thereof has been entrusted to an actual carrier, whether or not in pusuance of a liberty under the contract of carriage by sea to do so, the carrier nevertheless remains responsible for the entire carriage according to the provisions of this Convention. The carrier is responsible, in relation to the carriage performed by the actual carrier, for the acts and omissions of the actual carrier and of his servants and agents acting within the scope of their employment.

2. All the provisions of this Convention governing the responsibility of the carrier also apply to the responsibility of the actual carrier for the carriage performed by him. The provisions of paragraphs 2 and 3 of article 7 and of paragraph 2 of article 8 apply if an action is brought against a servant or agent of the actual carrier.

3. Any special agreement under which the carrier assumes obligations not imposed by this Convention or waives rights conferred by this Convention affects the actual carrier only if agreed to by him expressly and in writing. Whether or not the actual carrier has so agreed, the carrier nevertheless remains bound by the obligations or waivers resulting from such special agreement.

4. Where and to the extent that both the carrier and the actual carrier are liable, their liability is joint and several.

5. The aggregate of the amounts recoverable from the carrier, the actual carrier and their servants and agents shall not exceed the limits of liability provided for in this Convention.

6. Nothing in this article shall prejudice any right of recourse as between the carrier and the actual carrier.

Article 11.   Through carriage

1.   Notwithstanding the provisions of paragraph 1 of article 10, where a contract of carriage by sea provides explicitly that a specified part of the carriage covered by the said contract is to be performed by a named person other than the carrier, the contract may also provide that the carrier is not liable for loss, damage or delay in delivery caused by an occurrence which takes place while the goods are in the charge of the actual carrier during such part of the carriage. Nevertheless, any stipulation limiting or excluding such liability is without effect if no judicial proceedings can be instituted against the actual carrier in a court competent under paragraph 1 or 2 of article 21. The burden of proving that any loss, damage or delay in delivery has been caused by such an occurrence rests upon the carrier.

2.   The actual carrier is responsible in accordance with the provisions of paragraph 2 of article 10 for loss, damage or delay in delivery caused by an occurrence which takes place while the goods are in his charge.

Part III.   Liability of the shippers

Article 12.   General rule

The shipper is not liable for loss sustained by the carrier or actual carrier, or for damage sustained by the ship, unless such loss or damage was caused by the fault or neglect of the shipper, his servants or agents. Nor is any servant or agent of the shipper liable for such loss or damage unless the loss or damage was caused by fault or neglect on his part.

Article 13.   Special rules on dangerous goods

1.   The shipper must mark or label in a suitable manner dangerous goods as dangerous.

2.   Where the shipper hands over dangerous goods to the carrier or an actual carrier, as the case may be, the shipper must inform him of the dangerous character of the goods and, if necessary, of the precautions to be taken. If the shipper fails to do so and such carrier or actual carrier does not otherwise have knowledge of their dangerous character:

(a)   the shipper is liable to the carrier and any actual carrier for the loss resulting from the shipment of such goods, and

(b)   the goods may at any time be unloaded, destroyed or rendered innocuous, as the circumstances may require, without payment of compensation.

3.   The provisions of paragraph 2 of this article may not be invoked by any person if during the carriage he has taken the goods in his charge with knowledge of their dangerous character.

4.   If, in cases where the provisions of paragraph 2, subparagraph *(b)*, of this article do not apply or may not be invoked, dangerous goods become an actual danger to life or property, they may be unloaded, destroyed or rendered innocuous, as the circumstances may require, without payment of compensation except where there is an obligation to contribute in general average or where the carrier is liable in accordance with the provisions of article 5.

Part IV. Transport documents

Article 14. Issue of bill of lading

1. When the carrier or the actual carrier takes the goods in his charge, the carrier must, on demand of the shipper, issue to the shipper a bill of lading.

2. The bill of lading may be signed by a person having authority from the carrier. A bill of lading signed by the master of the ship carrying the goods is deemed to have been signed on behalf of the carrier.

3. The signature on the bill of lading may be in handwriting, printed in facsimile, perforated, stamped, in symbols, or made by any other mechanical or electronic means, if not inconsistent with the law of the country where the bill of lading is issued.

Article 15. Contents of bill of lading

1. The bill of lading must include, *inter alia*, the following particulars:

(a)   the general nature of the goods, the leading marks necessary for identification of the goods, an express statement, if applicable, as to the dangerous character of the goods, the number of packages or pieces, and the weight of the goods or their quantity otherwise expressed, all such particulars as furnished by the shipper;

(b)   the apparent condition of the goods;

(c)   the name and principal place of business of the carrier;

(d)   the name of the shipper;

(e)   the consignee if named by the shipper;

(f)   the port of loading under the contract of carriage by sea and the date on which the goods were taken over by the carrier at the port of loading;

(g)   the port of discharge under the contract of carriage by sea;

(h)   the number of originals of the bill of lading, if more than one;

(i)   the place of issuance of the bill of lading;

(j)   the signature of the carrier or a person acting on his behalf;

(k)   the freight to the extent payable by the consignee or other indication that freight is payable by him;

(l)   the statement referred to in paragraph 3 of article 23;

(m)   the statement, if applicable, that the goods shall or may be carried on deck;

(n)   the date or the period of delivery of the goods at the port of discharge if expressly agreed upon between the parties; and

(o)   any increased limit or limits of liability where agreed in accordance with paragraph 4 of article 6.

2. After the goods have been loaded on board, if the shipper so demands, the carrier must issue to the shipper a "shipped" bill of lading which, in addition to the particulars required under paragraph 1 of this article, must state that the goods are on board a named ship or ships, and the date or dates of loading. If the carrier has previously issued to the shipper a bill of lading or other document of title with respect to any of such goods, on request of the carrier the shipper must surrender such document in exchange for a "shipped" bill of lading. The carrier may amend any previously issued document in order to meet the shipper's demand for a "shipped" bill of lading if, as amended, such document includes all the information required to be contained in a "shipped" bill of lading.

3. The absence in the bill of lading of one or more particulars referred to in this article does not affect the legal character of the document as a bill of lading provided that it nevertheless meets the requirements set out in paragraph 7 of article 1.

Article 16. Bills of lading: reservations and evidentiary effect

1. If the bill of lading contains particulars concerning the general nature, leading marks, number of packages of pieces, weight or quantity of the goods which the carrier or other person issuing the bill of lading on his behalf knows or has reasonable grounds to suspect do not accurately represent the goods actually taken over or, where a "shipped" bill of lading is issued, loaded, or if he had no reasonable means of checking such particulars, the carrier or such other person must insert in the bill of lading a reservation specifying these inaccuracies, grounds of suspicion or the absence of reasonable means of checking.

2. If the carrier or other person issuing the bill of lading on his behalf fails to note on the bill of lading the apparent condition of the goods, he is deemed to have noted on the bill of lading that the goods were in apparent good condition.

3. Except for particulars in respect of which and to the extent to which a reservation permitted under paragraph 1 of this article has been entered:

(a) the bill of lading is *prima facie* evidence of the taking over or, where a "shipped" bill of lading is issued, loading, by the carrier of the goods as described in the bill of lading; and

(b) proof to the contrary by the carrier is not admissible if the bill of lading has been transferred to a third party, including a consignee, who in good faith has acted in reliance on the description of the goods therein.

4. A bill of lading which does not, as provided in paragraph 1, subparagraph *(k)*, of article 15, set forth the freight or otherwise indicate that freight is payable by the consignee or does not set forth demurrage incurred at the port of loading payable by the consignee, is *prima facie* evidence that no freight or such demurrage is payable by him. However, proof to the contrary by the carrier is not admissible when the bill of lading has been transferred to a third party, including a consignee, who in good faith has acted in reliance on the absence in the bill of lading of any such indication.

Article 17. Guarantees by the shipper

1. The shipper is deemed to have guaranteed to the carrier the accuracy of particulars relating to the general nature of the goods, their marks, number, weight and quantity as furnished by him for insertion in the bill of lading. The shipper must indemnify the carrier against the loss resulting from inaccuracies in such particulars. The shipper remains liable even if the bill of lading has been transferred by him. The right of the carrier to such indemnity in no way limits his liability under the contract of carriage by sea to any person other than the shipper.

2. Any letter of guarantee or agreement by which the shipper undertakes to indemnify the carrier against loss resulting from the issuance of the bill of lading by the carrier, or by a person acting on his behalf, without entering a reservation relating to particulars furnished by the shipper for insertion in the bill of lading, or to the apparent condition of the goods, is void and of no effect as against any third party, including a consignee, to whom the bill of lading has been transferred.

3. Such a letter of guarantee or agreement is valid as against the shipper unless the carrier or the person acting on his behalf, by omitting the reservation referred to in paragraph 2 of this article, intends to defraud a third party, including a consignee, who acts in reliance on the description of the goods in the bill of lading. In the latter case, if the reservation omitted relates to particulars furnished by the shipper for insertion in the bill of lading, the carrier has no right of indemnity from the shipper pursuant to paragraph 1 of this article.

4. In the case of intended fraud referred to in paragraph 3 of this article, the carrier is liable, without the benefit of the limitation of liability provided for in this Convention, for the loss incurred by a third party, including a consignee, because he has acted in reliance on the description of the goods in the bill of lading.

Article 18. Documents other than bills of lading

Where a carrier issues a document other than a bill of lading to evidence the receipt of the goods to be carried, such a document is *prima facie* evidence of the conclusion of the contract of carriage by sea and the taking over by the carrier of the goods as therein described.

Part V.   Claims and actions

Article 19.   Notice of loss, damage or delay

1. Unless notice of loss or damage, specifying the general nature of such loss or damage, is given in writing by the consignee to the carrier not later than the working day after the day when the goods were handed over to the consignee, such handing over is *prima facie* evidence of the delivery by the carrier of the goods as described in the document of transport or, if no such document has been issued, in good condition.

2. Where the loss or damage is not apparent, the provisions of paragraph 1 of this article apply correspondingly if notice in writing is not given within 15 consecutive days after the day when the goods were handed over to the consignee.

3. If the state of the goods at the time they were handed over to the consignee has been the subject of a joint survey or inspection by the parties, notice in writing need not be given of loss or damage ascertained during such survey or inspection.

4. In the case of any actual or apprehended loss or damage, the carrier and the consignee must give all reasonable facilities to each other for inspecting and tallying the goods.

5. No compensation shall be payable for loss resulting from delay in delivery unless a notice has been given in writing to the carrier within 60 consecutive days after the day when the goods were handed over to the consignee.

6. If the goods have been delivered by an actual carrier, any notice given under this article to him shall have the same effect as if it had ben given to the carrier; and any notice given to the carrier shall have effect as if given to such actual carrier.

7. Unless notice of loss or damage, specifying the general nature of the loss or damage, is given in writing by the carrier or actual carrier to the shipper not later than 90 consecutive days after the occurrence of such loss or damage or after the delivery of the goods in accordance with paragraph 2 of article 4, whichever is later, the failure to give such notice is *prima facie* evidence that the carrier or the actual carrier has sustained no loss or damage due to the fault or neglect of the shipper, his servants or agents.

8. For the purpose of this article, notice given to a person acting on the carrier's or the actual carrier's behalf, including the master or the officer in charge of the ship, or to a person acting on the shipper's behalf is deemed to have been given to the carrier, to the actual carrier or to the shipper, respectively.

Article 20.   Limitation of actions

1.   Any action relating to carriage of goods under this Convention is time-barred if judicial or arbitral proceedings have not been instituted within a period of two years.

2.   The limitation period commences on the day on which the carrier has delivered the goods or part thereof or, in cases where no goods have been delivered, on the last day on which the goods should have been delivered.

3.   The day on which the limitation period commences is not included in the period.

4.   The person against whom a claim is made may at any time during the running of the limitation period extend that period by a declaration in writing to the claimant. This period may be further extended by another declaration or declarations.

5.   An action for indemnity by a person held liable may be instituted even after the expiration of the limitation period provided for in the preceding paragraphs if instituted within the time allowed by the law of the State where proceedings are instituted. However, the time allowed shall not be less than 90 days commencing from the day when the person instituting such action for indemnity has settled the claim or has been served with process in the action against himself.

Article 21.   Jurisdiction

1.   In judicial proceedings relating to carriage of goods under this Convention the plaintiff, at his option, may institute an action in a court which according to the law of the State where the court is situated, is competent and within the jurisdiction of which is situated one of the following places:

(a)   the principal place of business or, in the absence thereof, the habitual residence of the defendant; or

(b)   the place where the contract was made, provided that the defendant has there a place of business, branch or agency through which the contract was made; or

(c)   the port of loading or the port of discharge; or

(d)   any additional place designated for that purpose in the contract of carriage by sea.

2.   (a)   Notwithstanding the preceding provisions of this article, an action may be instituted in the courts of any port or place in a Contracting State at which the carrying vessel or any other vessel of the same ownership may have been arrested in accordance with applicable rules of the law of that State and of international law. However, in such a case, at the petition of the defendant, the claimant must remove the action, at his choice, to one of the jurisdictions referred to in paragraph 1 of this article for the determination of the claim, but before such removal the defendant must furnish security sufficient to ensure payment of any judgement that may subsequently be awarded to the claimant in the action.

(b)   All questions relating to the sufficiency or otherwise of the security shall be determined by the court of the port or place of the arrest.

3.   No judicial proceedings relating to carriage of goods under this Convention may be instituted in a place not specified in paragraph 1 or 2 of this article. The provisions of this paragraph do not constitute an obstacle to the jurisdiction of the Contracting States for provisional or protective measures.

4.   (a)   Where an action has been instituted in a court competent under paragraph 1 and 2 of this article or where judgement has been delivered by such a court, no new action may be started between the same parties on the same grounds unless the judgement of the court before which the first action was instituted is not enforceable in the country in which the new proceedings are instituted;

(b) For the purpose of this article, the institution of measures with a view to obtaining enforcement of a judgement is not to be considered as the starting of a new action;

(c) For the purpose of this article, the removal of an action to a different court within the same country, or to a court in another country, in accordance with paragraph 2 *(a)* of this article, is not to be considered as the starting of a new action.

5. Notwithstanding the provisions of the preceding paragraphs, an agreement made by the parties, after a claim under the contract of carriage by sea has arisen, which designates the place where the claimant may institute an actions, is effective.

Article 22. Arbitration

1. Subject to the provisions of this article, parties may provide by agreement evidenced in writing that any dispute that may arise relating to carriage of goods under this Convention shall be referred to arbitration.

2. Where a charter-party contains a provision that disputes arising thereunder shall be referred to arbitration and a bill of lading issued pursuant to the charter-party does not contain a special annotation providing that such provision shall be binding upon the holder of the bill of lading, the carrier may not invoke such provision as against a holder having acquired the bill of lading in good faith.

3. The arbitration proceedings shall, at the option of the claimant, be instituted at one of the following places:

(a) a place in a State within whose territory is situated:

  (i) the principal place of business of the defendant or, in the absence thereof, the habitual residence of the defendant; or

  (ii) the place where the contract was made, provided that the defendant has there a place of business, branch or agency through which the contract was made; or

  (iii) the port of loading or the port of discharge; or

(b) any place designated for that purpose in the arbitration clause or agreement.

4. The arbitrator or arbitration tribunal shall apply the rules of this Convention.

5. The provisions of paragraphs 2 and 4 of this article are deemed to be part of every arbitration clause or agreement, and any term of such clause or agreement which is inconsistent therewith is null and void.

6. Nothing in this article affects the validity of an agreement relating to arbitration made by the parties after the claim under the contract of carriage by sea has arisen.

Part IV. Supplementary provisions

Article 23. Contractual stipulations

1. Any stipulation in a contract of carriage by sea, in a bill of lading, or in any other document evidencing the contract of carriage by sea is null and void to the extent that it derogates, directly or indirectly, from the provisions of this Convention. The nullity of such a stipulation does not affect the validity of the other provisions of the contract or document of which it forms a part. A clause assigning benefit of insurance of goods in favour of the carrier, or any similar clause, is null and void.

2. Notwithstanding the provisions of paragraph 1 of this article, a carrier may increase his responsibilities and obligations under this Convention.

3. Where a bill of lading or any other document evidencing the contract of carriage by sea is issued, it must contain a statement that the carriage is subject to the provisions of this Convention which nullify any stipulation derogating therefrom to the detriment of the shipper or the consignee.

4. Where the claimant in respect of the goods has incurred loss as a result of a stipulation which is null and void by virtue of the present article, or as a result of the omission of the statement referred to in paragraph 3 of this article, the carrier must pay compensation to the extent required in order to give the claimant compensation in accordance with the provisions of this Convention for any loss of or damage to the goods as well as for delay in delivery. The carrier must, in addition, pay compensation for costs incurred by the claimant for the purpose of exercising his right, provided that costs incurred in the action where the foregoing provision is invoked are to be determined in accordance with the law of the State where proceedings are instituted.

Article 24.   General average

1. Nothing in this Convention shall prevent the application of provisions in the contract of carriage by sea or national law regarding the adjustment of general average.

2. With the exception of article 20, the provisions of this Convention relating to the liability of the carrier for loss of or damage to the goods also determine whether the consignee may refuse contribution in general average and the liability of the carrier to indemnify the consignee in respect of any such contribution made or any salvage paid.

Article 25.   Other conventions

1. This Convention does not modify the rights or duties of the carrier, the actual carrier and their servants and agents provided for in international conventions or national law relating to the limitation of liability of owners of seagoing ships.

2. The provisions of articles 21 and 22 of this Convention do not prevent the application of the mandatory provisions of any other multilateral convention already in force at the date of this Convention relating to matters dealt with in the said articles, provided that the dispute arises exclusively between parties having their principal place of business in States members of such other convention. However, this paragraph does not affect the application of paragraph 4 of article 22 of this Convention.

3. No liability shall arise under the provisions of this Convention for damage caused by a nuclear incident if the operator of a nuclear installation is liable for such damage:

(a)   under either the Paris Convention of 29 July 1960 on Third Party Liability in the Field of Nuclear Energy as amended by the Additional Protocol of 28 January 1964, or the Vienna Convention of 21 May 1963 on Civil Liability for Nuclear Damage, or

(b)   by virtue of national law governing the liability for such damage, provided that such law is in all respects as favourable to persons who may suffer damage as is either the Paris Convention or the Vienna Convention.

4. No liability shall arise under the provisions of this Convention for any loss of or damage to or delay in delivery of luggage for which the carrier is responsible under any international convention or national law relating to the carriage of passengers and their luggage by sea.

5. Nothing contained in this Convention prevents a Contracting State from applying any other international convention which is already in force at the date of this Convention and which applies mandatorily to contracts of carriage of goods primarily by a mode of transport other than transport by sea. This provision also applies to any subsequent revision or amendment of such international convention.

Article 26. Unit of account

1.   The unit of account referred to in article 6 of this Convention is the special drawing right as defined by the International Monetary Fund. The amounts mentioned in article 6 are to be converted into the national currency of a State according to the value of such currency at the date of judgement or the date agreed upon by the parties. The value of a national currency, in terms of the special drawing right, of a Contracting State which is a member of the International Monetary Fund is to be calculated in accordance with the method of valuation applied by the International Monetary Fund in effect at the date in question for its operations and transactions. The value of a national currency, in terms of the special drawing right, of a Contracting State which is not a member of the International Monetary Fund is to be calculated in a manner determined by that State.

2.   Nevertheless, those States which are not members of the International Monetary Fund and whose law does not permit the application of the provisions of paragraph 1 of this article may, at the time of signature, or at the time of ratification, acceptance, approval or accession or at any time thereafter, declare that the limits of liability provided for in this Convention to be applied in their territories shall be fixed as 12,500 monetary units per package or other shipping unit or 37.5 monetary units per kilogram of gross weight of the goods.

3.   The monetary unit referred to in paragraph 2 of this article corresponds to sixty-five and a half milligrams of gold of millesimal fineness nine hundred. The conversion of the amounts referred to in paragraph 2 into the national currency is to be made according to the law of the State concerned.

4.   The calculation mentioned in the last sentence of paragraph 1 and the conversion mentioned in paragraph 3 of this article is to be made in such a manner as to express in the national currency of the Contracting State as far as possible the same real value for the amounts in article 6 as is expressed there in units of account. Contracting States must communicate to the depositary the manner of calculation pursuant to paragraph 1 of this article, or the result of the conversion mentioned in paragraph 3 of this article, as the case may be, at the time of signature or when depositing their instruments of ratification, acceptance, approval or accession, or when availing themselves of the option provided for in paragraph 2 of this article and whenever there is a change in the manner of such calculation or in the result of such conversion.

Part VII.   Final clauses

Article 27.   Depositary

The Secretary-General of the United Nations is hereby designated as the depositary of this Convention.

Article 28.   Signature, Ratification, Acceptance, Approval, Accession

1.   This Convention is open for signature by all States until 30 April 1979 at the Headquarters of the United Nations, New York.

2.   This Convention is subject to ratification, acceptance or approval by the signatory States.

3.   After 30 April 1979, this Convention will be open for accession by all States which are not signatory States.

4.   Instruments of ratification, acceptance, approval and accession are to be deposited with the Secretary-General of the United Nations.

187

Article 29. Reservations

No reservations may be made to this Convention.

Article 30. Entry into force

1. This Convention enters into force on the first day of the month following the expiration of one year from the date of deposit of the twentieth instrument of ratification, acceptance, approval or accession.

2. For each State which becomes a Contracting State to this Convention after the date of the deposit of the twentieth instrument of ratification, acceptance, approval or accession, this Convention enters into force on the first day of the month following the expiration of one year after the deposit of the appropriate instrument on behalf of that State.

3. Each Contracting State shall apply the provisions of this Convention to contracts of carriage by sea concluded on or after the date of the entry into force of this Convention in respect of that State.

Article 31. Denunciation of other conventions

1. Upon becoming a Contracting State to this Convention, any State Party to the International Convention for the Unification of certain Rules relating to Bills of Lading signed at Brussels on 25 August 1924 (1924 Convention) must notify the Government of Belgium as the depositary of the 1924 Convention of its denunciation of the said Convention with a declaration that the denunciation is to take effect as from the date when this Convention enters into force in respect of that State.

2. Upon the entry into force of this Convention under paragraph 1 of article 30, the depositary of this Convention must notify the Government of Belgium as the depositary of the 1924 Convention of the date of such entry into force, and of the names of the Contracting States in respect of which the Convention has entered into force.

3. The provisions of paragraphs 1 and 2 of this article apply correspondingly in respect of States Parties to the Protocol signed on 23 February 1968 to amend the International Convention for the Unification of certain Rules relating to Bills of Lading signed at Brussels on 25 August 1924.

4. Notwithstanding article 2 of this Convention, for the purposes of paragraph 1 of this article, a Contracting State may, if it deems it desirable, defer the denunciation of the 1924 Convention and of the 1924 Convention as modified by the 1968 Protocol for a maximum period of five years from the entry into force of this Convention. It will then notify the Government of Belgium of its intention. During this transitory period, it must apply to the Contracting States this Convention to the exclusion of any other one.

Article 32. Revision and amendment

1. At the request of not less than one third of the Contracting States to this Convention, the depositary shall convene a conference of the Contracting States for revising or amending it.

2. Any instrument of ratification, acceptance, approval or accession deposited after the entry into force of an amendment to this Convention is deemed to apply to the Convention as amended.

Article 33.   Revision of the limitation amounts and unit of account or monetary unit

1.   Notwithstanding the provisions of article 32, a conference only for the purpose of altering the amount specified in article 6 and paragraph 2 of article 26, or of substituting either or both of the units defined in paragraphs 1 and 3 of article 26 by other units is to be convened by the depositary in accordance with paragraph 2 of this article. An alteration of the amounts shall be made only because of a significant change in their real value.

2.   A revision conference is to be convened by the depositary when not less than one fourth of the Contracting States so request.

3.   Any decision by the conference must be taken by a two-thirds majority of the participating States. The amendment is communicated by the depositary to all the Contracting States for acceptance and to all the States signatories of the Convention for information.

4.   Any amendment adopted enters into force on the first day of the month following one year after its acceptance by two thirds of the Contracting States. Acceptance is to be effected by the deposit of a formal instrument to that effect with the depositary.

5.   After entry into force of an amendment a Contracting State which has accepted the amendment is entitled to apply the Convention as amended in its relations with Contracting States which have not within six months after the adoption of the amendment notified the depositary that they are not bound by the amendment.

6.   Any instrument of ratification, acceptance, approval or accession deposited after the entry into force of an amendment to this Convention is deemed to apply to the Convention as amended.

Article 34.   Denunciation

1.   A Contracting State may denounce this Convention at any time by means of a notification in writing addressed to the depositary.

2.   The denunciation takes effect on the first day of the month following the expiration of one year after the notification is received by the depositary. Where a longer period is specified in the notification, the denunciation takes effect upon the expiration of such longer period after the notification is received by the depositary.

DONE at Hamburg, this thirty-first day of March one thousand nine hundred and seventy-eight, in a single original, of which the Arabic, Chinese, English, French, Russian and Spanish texts are equally authentic.

IN WITNESS WHEREOF the undersigned plenipotentiaries, being duly authorized by their respective Governments, have signed the present Convention.

B.   Common understanding adopted by the United Nations Conference on the Carriage of Goods by Sea

It is the common understanding that the liability of the carrier under this Convention is based on the principle of presumed fault or neglect. This means that, as a rule, the burden of proof rests on the carrier but, with respect to certain cases, the provisions of the Convention modify this rule.

ANNEX VIII. LIQUIDATED DAMAGES AND PENALTY CLAUSES

A. Uniform Rules on Contract Clauses for an Agreed Sum due upon Failure of Performance

Part one. Scope of application

Article 1

These Rules apply to international contracts in which the parties have agreed that, upon a failure of performance by one party (the obligor) the other party (the obligee) is entitled to an agreed sum from the obligor, whether as a penalty or as compensation.

Article 2

For the purpose of these Rules:

(a) A contract shall be considered international if, at the time of the conclusion of the contract, the parties have their places of business in different States;

(b) The fact that the parties have their places of business in different States is to be disregarded whenever this fact does not appear either from the contract or from any dealings between, or from information disclosed by, the parties at any time before or at the conclusion of the contract;

(c) Neither the nationality of the parties nor the civil or commercial character of the parties or of the contract is to be taken into consideration in determining the application of these Rules.

Article 3

For the purposes of these Rules:

(a) If a party has more than one place of business, his place of business is that which has the closest relationship to the contract and its performance, having regard to the circumstances known to or contemplated by the parties at any time before or at the conclusion of the contract;

(b) If a party does not have a place of business, reference is to be made to his habitual residence.

Article 4

These Rules do not apply to contracts concerning goods, other property or services which are to be supplied for the personal, family or household purposes of a party, unless the other party, at any time before or at the conclusion of the contract, neither knew nor ought to have known that the contract was concluded for such purposes.

Part two. Substantive provisions

Article 5

The obligee is not entitled to the agreed sum if the obligor is not liable for the failure of performance.

Article 6

(1) If the contract provides that the obligee is entitled to the agreed sum upon delay in performance, he is entitled to both performance of the obligation and the agreed sum.

(2) If the contract provides that the obligee is entitled to the agreed sum upon a failure of performance other than delay, he is entitled either to performance or to the agreed sum. If, however, the agreed sum cannot reasonably be regarded as compensation for that failure of performance, the obligee is entitled to both performance of the obligation and the agreed sum.

Article 7

If the obligee is entitled to the agreed sum, he may not claim damages to the extent of the loss covered by the agreed sum. Nevertheless, he may claim damages to the extent of the loss not covered by the agreed sum if the loss substantially exceeds the agreed sum.

Article 8

The agreed sum shall not be reduced by a court or arbitral tribunal unless the agreed sum is substantially disproportionate in relation to the loss that has been suffered by the obligee.

Article 9

The parties may derogate from or vary the effect of articles 5, 6 and 7 of these Rules.

B.   General Assembly resolution 38/135 of 19 December 1983

38/135.   UNIFORM RULES ON CONTRACT CLAUSES FOR AN AGREED SUM DUE UPON FAILURE OF PERFORMANCE ADOPTED BY THE UNITED NATIONS COMMISSION ON INTERNATIONAL TRADE LAW

The General Assembly,

Recognizing that a wide range of international trade contracts contain clauses obligating a party that fails to perform an obligation under the contract to pay an agreed sum to the other party,

Noting that the effect and validity of such clauses are often uncertain owing to disparities in the treatment of such clauses in various legal systems,

Believing that these uncertainties constitute an obstacle to the flow of international trade,

Being of the opinion that it would be desirable for the legal rules applicable to such clauses to be harmonized so as to reduce or eliminate the uncertainties concerning such clauses and remove these uncertainties as a barrier to the flow of international trade,

Noting that the United Nations Commission on International Trade Law has adopted Uniform Rules on Contract Clauses for an Agreed Sum Due upon Failure of Performance,[1]

Recognizing that there are various ways in which the Uniform Rules on Contract Clauses for an Agreed Sum Due upon Failure of Performance could be implemented by States, and being of the opinion that a recommendation by the General Assembly to States that they should implement the Uniform Rules in an appropriate manner would not prejudice the Assembly from making a further recommendation or taking further action with respect to the Uniform Rules if circumstances so warrant,

Recommends that States should give serious consideration to the Uniform Rules on Contract Clauses for an Agreed Sum Due upon Failure of Performance adopted by the United Nations Commission on International Trade Law and, where appropriate, implement them in the form of either a model law or a convention.

101st plenary meeting,
19 December 1983

---

[1]See *Official Records of the General Assembly, Thirty-eighth Session, Supplement No. 17* (A/38/17), paras. 11-78 and annex I.

ANNEX IX. PROVISIONS ON UNIT OF ACCOUNT AND ADJUSTMENT OF LIMIT OF LIABILITY IN INTERNATIONAL TRANSPORT AND LIABILITY CONVENTIONS

A. Provisions on universal unit of account

1. The unit of account referred to in article [ ] of this Convention is the Special Drawing Right as defined by the International Monetary Fund. The amounts mentioned in article [ ] are to be expressed in the national currency of a State according to the value of such currency at the date of judgment or the date agreed upon by the parties. The equivalence between the national currency of a Contracting State which is a member of the International Monetary Fund and the Special Drawing Right is to be calculated in accordance with the method of valuation applied by the International Monetary Fund in effect at the date in question for its operations and transactions. The equivalence between the national currency of a Contracting State which is not a member of the International Monetary Fund and the Special Drawing Right is to be calculated in a manner determined by that State.

2. The calculation mentioned in the last sentence of paragraph 1 is to be made in such a manner as to express in the national currency of the Contracting State as far as possible the same real value for amounts in article [ ] as is expressed there in units of account. Contracting States must communicate to the Depositary the manner of calculation at the time of signature or when depositing their instrument of ratification, acceptance, approval or accession and whenever there is a change in the manner of such calculation.

B. Alternative provisions for adjustment of limit of liability

1. SAMPLE PRICE INDEX

1. The amounts set forth in article [ ] shall be linked to [a specific price index which might be considered appropriate for a particular convention]. On coming into force of this [Protocol-Convention], the amounts set forth in article [ ] shall be adjusted by an amount, rounded to the nearest whole number, corresponding in percentage to the increase or decrease in the index for the year ending on the last day of December prior to which this [Protocol-Convention] came into force over its level for the year ending on the last day of December [of the year in which the Protocol or Convention was opened for signature]. Thereafter, they shall be adjusted on the first day of July of each year by an amount, rounded to the nearest whole number, corresponding in percentage to the increase or decrease in the level in the index for the year ending on the last day of the previous December over its level for the prior year.

2. The amounts set forth in article [ ] shall not, however, be increased or decreased if the increase or decrease in the index does not exceed [ ] per cent. Where no adjustment was made in the previous year because the change was less than [ ] per cent, the comparison shall be made with the level for the last year on the basis of which an adjustment was made.

3. By the first day of April of each year the Depositary shall notify each Contracting State and each State which has signed the [Protocol-Convention] of the amounts to be in force as of the first day of July following. Changes in the amounts shall be registered with the Secretariat of the United Nations in accordance with General Assembly regulations to give effect to Article 102 of the Charter of the United Nations.

2. SAMPLE AMENDMENT PROCEDURE FOR LIMIT OF LIABILITY

1. The Depositary shall convene a meeting of a Committee composed of a representative from each Contracting State to consider increasing or decreasing the amounts in article [ ]:

(a) Upon the request of at least [ ] Contracting States, or

(b) When five years have passed since the [Protocol-Convention] was opened for signature or since the Committee last met.

2. If the present [Protocol-Convention] comes into force more than five years after it was opened for signature, the Depositary shall convene a meeting of the Committee within the first year after it comes into force.

3. Amendments shall be adopted by the Committee by a [ ] majority of its members present and voting.[a]

4. Any amendment adopted in accordance with paragraph 3 of this article shall be notified by the Depositary to all Contracting States. The amendment shall be deemed to have been accepted at the end of a period of [6] months after it has been notified, unless within that period not less than [one-third] of the States that were Contracting States at the time of the adoption of the amendment by the Committee have communicated to the Depositary that they do not accept the amendment. An amendment deemed to have been accepted in accordance with this paragraph shall enter into force for all Contracting States [12] months after its acceptance.

5. A Contracting State which has not accepted an amendment shall nevertheless be bound by it, unless such State denounces the present Convention at least one month before the amendment has entered into force. Such denunciation shall take effect when the amendment enters into force.

6. When an amendment has been adopted by the Committee but the [6] month period for its acceptance has not yet expired, a State which becomes a Contracting State to this Convention during that period shall be bound by the amendment if it comes into force. A State which becomes a Contracting State to this Convention after that period shall be bound by any amendment which has been accepted in accordance with paragraph 4.

---

[a]The Conference of Plenipotentiaries may wish to insert a list of criteria to be taken into account by the Committee.

194

C. General Assembly resolution 37/107 of 16 December 1982

37/107. PROVISIONS FOR A UNIT OF ACCOUNT AND ADJUSTMENT
OF LIMITATIONS OF LIABILITY ADOPTED BY
THE UNITED NATIONS COMMISSION
ON INTERNATIONAL TRADE LAW

The General Assembly,

Recognizing that many international transport and liability conventions of both a global and a regional character contain limitation of liability provisions, wherein the limitation of liability is expressed in a unit of account,

Noting that the amount fixed in such a convention as the limitation of liability may become seriously affected over time by changes in monetary values, thereby destroying the intended balance of the convention as adopted,

Believing that a preferred unit of account for many conventions, particularly for those of global application, should be the special drawing right as determined by the International Monetary Fund,

Being of the opinion that the conventions should, in any event, contain a provision which would facilitate adjustment of the limit of liability to changes in monetary values,

Taking into consideration any preferential agreements between the States concerned,

Noting that the United Nations Commission on International Trade Law has adopted a provision for a universal unit of account for expressing monetary amounts in international transport and liability conventions and two alternative provisions for adjustment of the limits of liability in such conventions,[1]

1. *Recommends* that, in the preparation of future international conventions containing limitation of liability provisions or in the revision of existing conventions, the unit of account provision adopted by the United Nations Commission on International Trade Law should be used;

2. *Recommends further* that in such conventions one of the two alternative provisions for adjustment of the limitation of liability adopted by the United Nations Commission on International Trade Law should be used.

107th plenary meeting,
16 December 1982

---

[1] *Official Records of the General Assembly, Thirty-seventh Session, Supplement No. 17* (A/37/17 and Corr.1), para. 63.

ANNEX X.   AUTOMATIC DATA PROCESSING

Recommendation adopted by UNCITRAL on the legal value
of computer records

The United Nations Commission on International Trade Law,

Noting that the use of automatic data processing (ADP) is about to become firmly established throughout the world in many phases of domestic and international trade as well as in administrative services,

Noting also that legal rules based upon pre-ADP paper-based means of documenting international trade may create an obstacle to such use of ADP in that they lead to legal insecurity or impede the efficient use of ADP where its use is otherwise justified,

Noting further with appreciation the efforts of the Council of Europe, the Customs Co-operation Council and the United Nations Economic Commission for Europe to overcome obstacles to the use of ADP in international trade arising out of these legal rules,

Considering at the same time that there is no need for a unification of the rules of evidence regarding the use of computer records in international trade, in view of the experience showing that substantial differences in the rules of evidence as they apply to the paper-based system of documentation have caused so far no noticeable harm to the development of international trade,

Considering also that the developments in the use of ADP are creating a desirability in a number of legal systems for an adaptation of existing legal rules to these developments, having due regard, however, to the need to encourage the employment of such ADP means that would provide the same or greater reliability as paper-based documentation,

1.   *Recommends* to Governments:

(a)   to review the legal rules affecting the use of computer records as evidence in litigation in order to eliminate unnecessary obstacles to their admission, to be assured that the rules are consistent with developments in technology, and to provide appropriate means for a court to evaluate the credibility of the data contained in those records;

(b)   to review legal requirements that certain trade transactions or trade related documents be in writing, whether the written form is a condition to the enforceability or to the validity of the transaction or document, with a view to permitting, where appropriate, the transaction or document to be recorded and transmitted in computer-readable form;

(c)   to review legal requirements of a handwritten signature or other paper-based method of authentication on trade related documents with a view to permitting, where appropriate, the use of electronic means of authentication;

(d)   to review legal requirements that documents for submission to governments be in writing and manually signed with a view to permitting, where appropriate, such documents to be submitted in computer-readable form to those administrative services which have acquired the necessary equipment and established the necessary procedures;

2.   *Recommends* to international organizations elaborating legal texts related to trade to take account of the present Recommendation in adopting such texts and, where appropriate, to consider modifying existing legal texts in line with the present Recommendation.

APPENDIX I

Chairmen of UNCITRAL

First session (1968):	Mr. Emmanual Kodjoe Dadzie (Ghana)
Second session (1969):	Mr. Lászlo Réczei (Hungary)
Third session (1970):	Mr. Albert Lilar (Belgium)
Fourth session (1971):	Mr. Nagendra Singh (India)
Fifth session (1972):	Mr. Jorge Barrera-Graf (Mexico)
Sixth session (1973):	Mr. Mohsen Chafik (Egypt)
Seventh session (1974):	Mr. Jerzy Jakubowski (Poland)
Eighth session (1975):	Mr. R. Loewe (Austria)
Ninth session (1976):	Mr. L. H. Khoo (Singapore)
Tenth session (1977):	Mr. N. Gueiros (Brazil)
Eleventh session (1978):	Mr. S. K. Date-Bah (Ghana)
Twelfth session (1979):	Mr. L. Kopac (Czechoslovakia)
Thirteenth session (1980):	Mr. R. Herber (Federal Republic of Germany)
Fourteenth session (1981):	Mr. L. H. Khoo (Singapore)
Fifteenth session (1982):	Mr. Rafael Eyzaguirre (Chile)
Sixteenth session (1983):	Mr. Mohsen Chafik (Egypt)
Seventeenth session (1984):	Mr. I. Szász (Hungary)
Eighteenth session (1985):	Mr. R. Loewe (Austria)

APPENDIX II

Chairmen of UNCITRAL working groups

Working Group on Time-limits and Limitation (Prescription)

First session (1969):	Mr. Stein Rognlien (Norway)
Second session (1970):	Mr. Stein Rognlien (Norway)
Third session (1971):	Mr. Stein Rognlien (Norway)

Working Group on International Legislation on Shipping

First session (1971):	Mr. Nagendra Singh (India)
Second session (1971):	Mr. Rafael Lasalvia (Chile)
Third session (1972):	Mr. Nagendra Singh (India)
Fourth session (1972):	Mr. José Domingo Ray (Argentina)
Fifth session (1973):	Mr. José Domingo Ray (Argentina)
Sixth session (1974):	Mr. Mohsen Chafik (Egypt)
Seventh session (1974):	Mr. Mohsen Chafik (Egypt)
Eighth session (1975):	Mr. Mohsen Chafik (Egypt)

Working Group on the International Sale of Goods

First session (1970):	Mr. Jorge Barrera-Graf (Mexico)
Second session (1970):	Mr. Jorge Barrera-Graf (Mexico)
Third session (1972):	Mr. Jorge Barrera-Graf (Mexico)
Fourth session (1973):	Mr. Jorge Barrera-Graf (Mexico)
Fifth session (1974):	Mr. Jorge Barrera-Graf (Mexico)
Sixth session (1975):	Mr. Gyula Eörsi (Hungary)
Seventh session (1976):	Mr. Jorge Barrera-Graf (Mexico)
Eighth session (1977):	Mr. Jorge Barrera-Graf (Mexico)
Ninth session (1977):	Mr. Jorge Barrera-Graf (Mexico)
Tenth session (1980):	Mr. Gyola Eörsi (Hungary)

Working Group on International Negotiable Instruments

First session (1973):	Mr. Mohsen Chafik (Egypt)
Second session (1974):	Mr. René Roblot (France)
Third session (1975):	Mr. René Roblot (France)
Fourth session (1976):	Mr. René Roblot (France)
Fifth session (1977):	Mr. René Roblot (France)
Sixth session (1978):	Mr. René Roblot (France)
Seventh session (1979):	Mr. René Roblot (France)
Eighth session (1979):	Mr. René Roblot (France)
Ninth session (1980):	Mr. René Roblot (France)
Tenth session (1981):	Mr. René Roblot (France)
Eleventh session (1981):	Mr. René Roblot (France)
Twelfth session (1982):	Mr. Joë Galby (France)
Thirteenth session (1985):	Mr. Willem Vis (Netherlands)

Working Group on the New International Economic Order

First session (1980):	Mr. Kazuaki Sono (Japan)
Second session (1981):	Mr. Leif Sevon (Finland)
Third session (1982):	Mr. Leif Sevon (Finland)
Fourth session (1983):	Mr. Leif Sevon (Finland)
Fifth session (1984):	Mr. Leif Sevon (elected in his personal capacity)
Sixth session (1984):	Mr. Leif Sevon (elected in his personal capacity)
Seventh session (1985):	Mr. Leif Sevon (elected in his personal capacity)

Working Group on International Contract Practices

First session (1979):	Mr. José Barrera-Graf (Mexico)
Second session (1981):	Mr. I. Tarko (Austria)
Third session (1982):	Mr. I. Szász (Hungary)
Fourth session (1982):	Mr. I. Szász (Hungary)
Fifth session (1983):	Mr. I. Szász (Hungary)
Sixth session (1983):	Mr. I. Szász (Hungary)
Seventh session (1984):	Mr. I. Szász (Hungary)
Eighth session (1984):	Mr. Michael Joachim Bonell (Italy)

APPENDIX III

Secretaries of UNCITRAL and periods of service

Mr. Paolo CONTINI: 1968-1969

Mr. John HONNOLD: 1969-1974

Mr. Willem VIS: 1974-1980

Mr. Kazuaki SONO: 1980-1985

Mr. Eric BERGSTEN: 1985-